DANIELLE DE PICCIOTTO

The Beauty of Transgression

A BERLIN MEMOIR

gestalten

Contents

FOREWORD

While experiencing the great upheavals after Germany's reunification I witnessed a lot of events that would affect not only my life but also Berlin and international events in the long run. After about a decade I realized that many of these occasions were being forgotten and with them the understanding of how things developed and changed over the years. So to remember and honor them I started writing them down.

This book is about remembering some of the secret, magical moments of history, which are not planned or manipulated commercially. They prove that with the decisions we make, each step we take, we forge our world and demonstrate, once again, the unique importance of the individual.

1987–1990

The air smelled sweet, stale, and worn. Sensing an empty space in the bed, her swollen eyes sluggishly unlocked, confronting the bright midday sunshine.

Simon was standing in front of the tall mirror teasing his dyed black hair into spiky thorns, slapping wax into the roots and mumbling under his breath. His nose dripped, showing specks of speed he had probably just taken or consumed all night, and he snorted every so often, trying pull the gooey liquid back into his sinuses.

Slowly sitting up, she observed his movements, remembering that she had chosen to go home with him rather than the handsome ballet dancer who had courted her all night, shyly buying her pretzels and gin and tonics while speaking of his work with Pina Bausch.

"D'you think I look like Blixa Bargeld?"

"I don't know what he looks like."

Grunting with exasperation, Simon yanked a wax-smeared hand into his skin-tight, black leather pants and pulled out a newspaper clipping. Without turning from the mirror he leaned over and tossed the paper into her lap.

She took the worn document and studied the smudged picture of a man dressed in black with huge eyes and bristly hair.

"Why would you want to look like somebody else?" she asked, gazing past his thorny silhouette through the window into the clear blue sky of an early October day.

"Blixa is god."

Something inside her exploded. Pure exasperation boiled into her veins and culminated in an eruption of rage, filling her mouth with the taste of rancid disappointment.

"Fuck you," she hissed, climbing out of bed and reaching for her bathrobe. "When I saw you last night you were the only person in the room that didn't fit in, didn't make the effort to adapt, oblivious to what people were thinking or expecting, stubbornly ignoring convention or small talk. I was intrigued by your stance and now you turn out to be nothing more than yet another brainless moth circling bright lights."

She kicked open the bathroom door, hissing over her shoulder, "Show yourself out before I'm done with my shower."

The reflection in the bathroom mirror caught her by surprise, and she stared for a moment at her pallid face, disheveled hair, and clouded, disenchanted eyes. Wearily she inspected her skin, which was still bearing yesterday's make-up, as she reached for the soap.

"Oh, by the way," Simon's silhouette popped up in the small, square looking glass, his pupils dilated, "a girl I fucked two days ago called to tell me she might have AIDS."

Turning slowly, her grimace impelled him toward the apartment door: "Well then, I guess I'm lucky you were too out of it to have sex."

Laughing in his face, the door slammed shut.

Introduction

I decided to move to Berlin the day I was kicked out of a bakery in Cologne, Germany. I had been living in Europe for a couple of months, yielding to the moods of fate and taking pleasure in the experience of being on my own in a strange city far from home.

The rude awakening occurred on a Sunday morning in late fall. The sun had just risen and the deserted boulevards echoed, unusually, with the sounds of birds singing. Experiencing a newborn day, air hovering cool and clear, shiny office buildings looking freshly cleansed and more innocent than the evening before, their windows mirroring fallen leaves, has forever been one of my favorite sensations. I feel comfortable amid vacant parking places and shut-up shops in comparison to midday's bright merry-go-round. Walking through silent morning streets, sniffing the yeasty smell of fresh buns, or hearing my steps resonate on forlorn cobblestones has always allowed me a rare moment of peace.

Cologne isn't exceptionally large, but it is very old, with streets constructed spaciously in half circles around its center, at which resides the magnificent cathedral, Kölner Dom. Surrounded by busy flower shops, boutiques, jewelry stores, and banks, the third highest church structure in the world shoots into the sky with dark precision, dwarfing modern commerce and short-lived fashion trends, proudly advocating endurance and perseverance. Standing beneath its immense wings and staring up at the seemingly endless pinnacles, I spent countless afternoons imagining its history, the thick, cool stone walls reassuringly secure, reducing the clamor of Top Ten hits and news reports to tiny, crackling whispers. It was my secret haven to snuggle into and daydream.

Cologne today is a pleasant, bustling town with countless avant-garde galleries, experimental designers, and a large underground music scene; the Kölner inhabitant tends to be a cheerfully hedonistic character who loves dressing up for carnival, wearing the fool's caps proudly while drinking endless amounts of Kölsch. Nonetheless, the gothic images hovering beneath the cathedral's towers hark back to dark and hidden stories dealing with mystery and magic: the largest reliquary in the Western world supposedly holding the remains of the Three Wise Men, whose bones and 2,000-year-old clothes were discovered at the opening of the shrine in 1864. These were the stories I found interesting, and I was always on the lookout for unusual details, spending hours wandering slowly from the sacristy to the Gero Cross, which is believed to have been commissioned around 960 for Archbishop Gero and is not only the oldest large crucifix north of the Alps but also the earliest known significant free-standing Northern sculpture of the medieval period. Inspecting the wooden carving over and over again, I pondered how history influences our everyday lives.

The bakery was situated around the corner from my studio apartment, on Luxemburger Strasse, a busy avenue best known for its wild, alternative clubs and smoldering bars. From beneath the roof of the five-floor building I had an angled view of flickering signposts and bright green advertisements. The glitter of light was tempting, assuring nonstop music and pleasure. I passed the venues regularly after my late-night shifts, greeting the managers and bouncers lounging outside, smoking cigars and keeping an eye on business.

The Blue Shell, a legendary venue for New Wave, was one of my favorite places; it was painted a phosphoric aquamarine and filled with leather-clad Sex Pistol and Fad Gadget fans. The club liked to serve light blue drinks with pink cherries to the club-goers wearing tigerstripe-patterned pants, fluorescent T-shirts, heavy studded belts, bright pink rubber jackets, and junk jewelry. It was always a fun place to meet friends and good for hearing news about what bands were coming to town.

But it was the Rose Club, an important meeting place for experimental music lovers appreciating Clock DVA or Psychic TV where I felt most at home. This crowd was usually dressed in dark colors and consisted of intellectual music critics, anarchists, punks, New Wave fans, and artists, all of whom spent hours listening to the formidable bands, discussing their music enthusiastically, and buying their self-produced tapes as often as possible. Dietrich Dietrichsen, the former editor-in-chief of Germany's most intellectual music magazine, *Spex,* would come by frequently. He would curtly order a drink and then stand in a dark corner, hidden from the crowd, judging the quality of the music for his next cutting review.

This venue was my introduction to the underground music world, something I had only known about peripherally before, since I mainly paid attention to visual art while I lived in New York. I had been raised with classical music, playing Bach and Vivaldi when I was seven years old and singing the main soprano voice in a children's choir, but had always felt restricted by this structured world. Veering off into the direction of art and color I enjoyed the freedom of expressionism and Toulouse Lautrec boudoirs until the Rose Club introduced me to the uninhabited, discordant world of experimental music, which would exhilarate me for the rest of my life. The settings of my intermediate work, intermingling acoustic and visual details, had been with me from the very start but in Cologne I found the sound I had unconsciously been looking for.

The eclectic mix of characters coloring the city's nightlife were part of a group that could always be found in the blue-and-white checkered interior of a Greek restaurant that served fresh bread and creamed eggplant throughout the night. It was my last stop before going to bed.

This twenty-four-hour restaurant was the hot spot for prostitutes, musicians, artists, writers, late night dancers, drug dealers, addicts, and waitresses heading home—in other words, the usual restless twilight assembly, looking for inspiration or jobs. The owner, a charismatic, good-looking man with pitch-black, curly hair and sparkling white teeth was a regular fixture on the "Kölner" nightlife scene until he suddenly went bankrupt due to his cocaine addiction, and left town in a hurry, scared of large, angry beer companies and imaginary space-ships pursuing him.

I was working for an advertising agency that had contacted me in New York, explaining that they needed somebody to design costumes for them. After having studied painting and costume design, racing through the courses in a madcap manner, wanting to leave the cumbersome, claustrophobic air of home and school as quickly as possible, it seemed like a good deal. Today the agency advertises large shoe and restaurant chains in Germany. In the mid-1980s they were officially poor and could only pay tiny salaries, especially to visual artists like me. Young and naïve, I believed them when they told me that was all they could afford, ignoring the fact that even back then they were driving Porsches, wearing expensive designer suits, and ordering chrome refrigerators from Hawaii. I was too happy to be in the "real world" and didn't mind doing additional jobs on the side to pay my rent, greeting guests at wedding parties in penguin suits on roller skates, or serving cocktails at Café Central to Martin Kippenberger, a genial German artist who drank himself to death in the 1990s and who would sometimes invite me over to his apartment for food after work. Selling self-produced tapes of Die Tödliche Doris and Mania D. in punk stores, or go-go dancing to their music in bars, were a couple of other occupations easing my financial state.

Eventually I settled for serving drinks in the Rose Club while designing costumes in the form of seafood, or cubic ballet uniforms (worn by robot models), during the day. The contrast of moving between these two universes, each convinced of its own irrefutable importance, quenched my thirst for outrageous clashes, relying on the noise and garbage of Luxemburger Strasse to camouflage the rest of my fundamentally restless nature.

The night shift was my favorite. Christa and Dietz, a friendly couple consistently dressed in black leather, who carried whips to most events, invited underground heroes from all over the world to play at their venue. It was there, working at the Rose Club, that I witnessed a lineup of celebrated outlaws that would change my life forever. Snakefinger, the former front man of the famed Residents, a band known for appearing on stage masked and unrecognizable, proudly explained and showed me his legendary, self-made guitar in loving detail one week before he died of heart failure; Laibach, the Slovenian avant-garde industrial band, raising the roof with heavy Eastern choruses and bold symbolism; the Celibate Rifles, who were Australian and claimed to be the only band to have been kicked out of CBGBs in New York for being too loud; and many others, including Psychic TV, Blur, Crime and the City Solution, and Nikki Sudden. Several of these musicians became my friends, and their unconventional lifestyle and roaming natures struck a chord with me, an outcast. What I felt when I met them was comparable to when

I saw *The Good, the Bad and the Ugly* as a small, unhappy girl living on US army bases. Being an outcast and living life by one's own rules, succeeding in keeping up integrity inspite of injustice was a lifestyle I admired and had decided to follow.

Heiner Ebber, lanky drummer of The Waltons, a German rock-and-roll band, was the first of these musicians whom I spoke to in depth. After having excessively drunk, wildly danced, and unreservedly spoken to me throughout the night after his performance, he invited me to come and pay him a visit, pulling out photos, describing Kreuzberg, a beautiful drum set, and his girlfriend. Heiner had the edgy, driving passion typical of Berliners in the 1980s. He ignored convention and experimented with music, initiating numerous bands ranging from easy listening to hard core, organizing ludicrous Adriano Celentano theme parties in tiny nightclubs, appearing as his second personal, Palminger, wearing colossal tinted sunglasses, reading surreal lyrics written the night before, DJing unknown singles or exhibiting his black-and-white prints reminiscent of early George Grosz.

His sense of humor, paired with compassion for others and an intense longing for the exceptional, impressed me deeply.

It was after one of these nights at the Rose Club, around eight in the morning, that I was kicked out of the bakery by the buxom, blond, red-cheeked baker lady, who, after taking one look at my tired face, tartan skirt, and heavy black boots, immediately came around the counter hissing, "We do not serve people like you here, I will call the police if you do not leave immediately," pushing her fat face into mine.

She strongly smelled of detergent and onions. I stared at her cold, red eyes, square cut fingernails, the tiny beads of sweat on the blond mustache of her upper lip and envisioned the parade of air-headed models I would have to dress up as asparagus in the morning, my arrogant bosses in the background, smoking Cuban cigars with bored business associates. Although I had been treated rudely in boutiques and department stores before, due to my colorful, homemade outfits and odd accessories, unable to afford the luxury goods they were offering, this was the first time I had actually been threatened with the police for having entered a place only wanting to buy bread.

I decided it was time to abandon Cologne.

Leaving the high-pitched salesperson behind slamming glass doors, I continued down the street, contemplating my possibilities. Manhattan was not an alternative; it was too soon to go back. Remembering Heiner's invitation and a fascinating movie I had seen the day before, *Wings of Desire* by the German film director Wim Wenders, which depicted Berlin drenched in the golden glow of timelessness, I made up my mind. I decided to visit the infamous city of the 1920s for at least three weeks before deciding what to do with my future. Arriving home I packed my two suitcases, filling them with a collection of paintbrushes and books, slept a couple of hours, dropped my letter of resignation in the local mailbox and hitchhiked, not knowing what to expect, to the magical destination of Berlin.

Fall 1987

They had driven all night, the air in the truck thick with cigarette smoke and cheap wine. Before their eyes the industrial backdrops circling Cologne had quietly transformed into snow-covered, East German landscapes, barren and depressing, with relentless transitory roads piercing mud-covered pastures and shadowy forests, the unkept highway adorned with senselessly alternating speed limit signs and police cars hiding behind bushes or bridges, hoping to confront inexperienced "Wessi" drivers with overpriced speeding tickets. Villages were nowhere to be seen, an occasional colorless gas station offered appallingly sweet champagne and gray dishes of food they decided not to try. The border check had been slow, surly, but efficient, with GDR soldiers examining every tape or magazine for capitalistic propaganda, squeezing their sandwiches and poking at her suitcase.

Most of the time she sat with her legs pulled up against the dashboard, munching food and listening to the driver's tapes, watching him smoke one joint after another and trying to imagine what it would be like to live in the bleak region they were driving through.

"Is it ok if we go to my place first, somebody's waiting to give me the key?"

"Sure, I'm in no rush."

"I'll help you carry up your stuff afterwards."

"Cool."

After challenging their endurance to the utmost, the road finally succumbed to the city, a dark mirage of lights twinkling in the distance, smugly greeting the tired visitor with yet another set of tollbooths and unfriendly body checks, ensuring that nobody entered the metropolis with merely a superficial smile or shallow handshake. This gateway was not to be taken lightly; it was the first of many rituals in a sober society of strict rules and regulations, not to be ignored, nor to be accepted.

The streets shone unfavorably with dirty snow swept aside into murky puddles. Wraithlike shadows of subways rushed from one overpass to the next, breaking the silence in regular intervals, veins of blood pouring life into ruins of rust, a maze of brown and red graffiti, color boldly defying the menacing gray monolith of the Berlin Wall.

"I think this is it, wanna come inside?"

"Ok."

The flight of stairs was irregular, making them stumble awkwardly from one wooden step to the next, sliding their hands against the crumbling wall for stability.

"Boy, something smells terrible."

"Maybe a dead rat."

"This is your new apartment?"

"Yeah, it's really cheap and I can rent it for a couple of months until P. gets back."

The dim light went out while they were fumbling for the doorbell, groping in the darkness.

"What the fuck?"

The door opened, revealing the dark silhouette of a leather-clad man with long hair and a helmet in his hands.

"Hey, I was just leaving, thought you weren't gonna make it after all."

"Sorry M., we took longer than I thought."

"Here's your key, wanna come to a party? There's one in a squat around the corner."

Her driver turned to her, eyes gleaming with anticipation:

"We could check it out before bringing you home?"

"Well, if we don't stay too long. I wouldn't feel like carrying the stuff up if I'm really tired."

"No prob, just tell me when you're ready to go."

Stumbling down the creaking stairs, M. told them about the place, describing the cool people they would meet. Noticing his brown, rotting teeth, torn sweater, and nicotine-stained fingers nervously picking the leather jacket's zipper, she wondered if they had the same taste.

Squeezing into their truck once more, they drove for a couple of minutes, ending up in the dark alley of a former factory compound. Hurrying to keep from getting wet, they jumped from puddle to puddle and managed to enter the ruins with dry feet, the reception area so cold and damp it sent shivers up her spine. Hoping to find a warm room in the maze of empty, destroyed office spaces the group silently moved forward, their steps echoing loudly in the vast hallway, simulating an army of partygoers.

"Ah, here we are." M. knocked on a metal door with peeling green paint. "Who's there?" A muffled voice floated by vaguely.

Knocking once more their new companion replied:

"It's me, M."

Silently the door swung open, introducing a small space with low ceilings, dimly lit by melting candles, filled with empty bottles and countless cigarette butts.

Shabbily dressed, an unassuming group of inmates huddled around a tarnished kerosene lamp, holding slight squares of aluminum foil in their hands, ignoring the arrival of new guests. With shadows flickering on their dark *features, they nervously poured brown powder onto the foil, lighting it from underneath and inhaling the pungent fumes with a small glass pipe.*

"Hey!" M. took her hand, walking to a low table in the corner of the room. On its surface he distributed three piles of fine particles, two white, one brown, carelessly making lines on obviously new record covers depicting David Bowie.

"You can choose anything you like, be my guest, it's your welcome-to-Berlin present."

She hesitated. This city had bred well-known celebrities who were also heroin addicts, but she had never felt attracted to the painkiller.

"New to this stuff?"

"I've seen it around."

"Well, you'll see a lot of it around here."

"That's not what I came for."

"What did you come for?"

She paused, looking at the smudged scenario of slack faces and relaxed bodies. "I'm not sure."

BERLIN

In the 1980s a cement wall circled Berlin. The general atmosphere of Cold War paranoia and communistic suppression surrounded the isolated city, turning it into an icon, a glowing fortress for many, the German statue of liberty welcoming fugitives escaping from East Berlin politics or West Germany's army, harboring extraordinary lifestyles and famous rebels.

For me it was love at first sight.

The crumbling façades dyed black by the pollution of cars and coal stoves, the massive avenues lined with old-fashioned parks, chestnut trees, and twinkling weeping willows, monumental buildings constructed in gray ivory, decorated with turn-of-the-century symbols and plaques, remembrances of historic happenings and characters long gone but nearby nonetheless, the many backyards or "Hinterhöfe" in which one could easily get lost looking for friends, calling out to a Berlin Hausfrau hanging her laundry in the cool shade of the adjoining corridor, receiving no answer and delving even deeper into the abyss, plunged into murky depths of backyard alleyways, inhabited by rats, stray cats, old bicycle wheels and lost baby carriages, these were pictures comparable to my favorite childhood storybooks. The lumpy cobblestone streets leading to large, empty squares had generally been cleared of World War II rubble but not restored to beauty, leaving weeds and playing children to do the decorating, swimming in the gray smoke wafting in from the East, interlacing neighborhoods with its soft mesh, harboring an atmosphere of destitution and neglect, reminiscent of *Oliver Twist* or whispered film noir scenes.

The eccentric unconformity of its inhabitants, known for their rudeness to tourists and dry sense of humor, felt appropriate in the end-of-cycle atmosphere. It was comparable to the legendary 1920s, with people celebrating the challenge of their unconventional lives in an unconstrained uproar, flirtatiously tounting conformity, intolerance, death, and insanity, rejecting serious 9-5 day jobs, preferring eccentric scenarios enhanced by dropping temperatures and falling snow outside. Berlin winters were very cold, the temperature dropping to minus 30 degrees Celsius and snow lasting from November to May. Around March suicide rates would rise alarmingly, sensitive souls not being able to stand the heavy, gray sky any longer, unlike myself standing transfixed in front of the dreamlike quality of oppressive clouds and everlasting rain or snow.

Summer, in comparison, was gay, a flaunting transvestite with flapping skirts, baring torn, lacy underwear. The black-and-white city would transform into a Technicolor landscape overnight, with temperatures rising rapidly, tempting pale, left-over nightclub "snippets" to drape themselves on the River Spree's cement banks or in the cool shadows of the huge Tiergarten park in which hundreds of Turkish families quickly resurrected their grills, greeting the first rays of sun with singing, dancing, and delicious lamb chops.

Kreuzberg, one of Berlin's best-known districts, was sometimes refered to as "the third-largest Turkish city in the world." With meandering streets and large, old-fashioned apartments adorned with intricate stucco, parquetry, and huge kitchen pantries, the neighborhood was a maze filled with kebab restaurants, belly-dancing costume stores, Turkish travel agencies, banks, and cafés accommodating serious, black-suited men drinking tea and eating sweet cookies from the overflowing bakeries next door. Many of the disintegrating buildings, especially the ones close to educational centers, were covered by massive graffiti paintings, furtively sprayed at night by young Turkish artists or hip-hop musicians, clad in baggy pants and even wider T-shirts, tired of representing the outcast in Germany's cultural setup, demanding respect and consideration.

In the 1980s, Turks were generally considered dangerous and aggressive, turning Kreuzberg into a ghetto of low rents and colorful surroundings, an atmosphere of danger and excitement reigning wildly. Riots were popular, the customary First of May demonstration legendary, and encounters with the police, mainly protected by shields and clubs, regular occurrences. These attributes had transformed Kreuzberg into a haven for outsiders and adventurers, giving refuge to second-hand clothing stores, punk accessories, galleries, underground book stores, tattoo parlors, smoke shops, avant-garde cafés, punks, left-wing activists, hippie flower-power intellectuals, and artist communes.

In general it was difficult to enter or leave the city. Watchtowers and machine-gunned toll stations controlled every part of the Wall. The four allies had separate outlets with the Checkpoint Charlie for Americans down the street from my loft on Ritterstrasse 10 in Kreuzberg. Allies could visit the East for one day only and had to stand in line for hours to be able to pass the Iron Curtain. After making it through the long interrogations, unfriendly jibes, and rude baggage searches one would be pushed out from what was colloquialy known as the "Tränenpalast" (the Palace of Tears) into the narrow, winding back streets of East Berlin. Upon arriving on the other side of the Wall there were very few inhabitants to be seen among the gray Russian buildings and colorful Easter egg cars called "Trabi" scurrying along huge parade avenues. The scant stores were quiet and dark, their shelves displaying old-fashioned laces, sewing kits, faded knitting magazines, and lumpy bags of bread. Fruit was almost impossible to buy; in fact anything remotely healthy was very rare. The East Germans used black coal briquettes to heat their apartments, as did many of their western counterparts, covering Berlin with a thick cloud of ash throughout the winter, the smell of which still lingers in my nose.

Most people hated the soot, as much as the hundreds of pigeons they would shoot down with BB guns.

I loved it. I would walk down the snow-covered cobblestone boulevards lined with proud, long-standing Prussian stone buildings sniffing the musty air in freezing temperatures, buy some warm, sweet cookies in the local Turkish bakery, drink a hot chocolate on Oranienstrasse, the official riot street of Berlin, and watch people stroll by. The Berliners wore Russian rabbit-fur hats, old-fashioned, double-buttoned, black woolen coats and heavy army boots to keep warm, and listened to the wildest underground music I'd ever heard. They celebrated stormy parties in dark, muddy basement rooms, buried within catacombs of torn down buildings where drinks in plastic cups were served for a couple of pfennigs. People never smiled and you had to drink a bottle of vodka and not faint to impress them.

Small talk was nonexistent and if you said something, anything, it had to be on point and deeply anarchic to be even remotely listened to.

I was profoundly impressed.

In spite of my spontaneous arrival and the fact that apartments were difficult to find in the enclosed city, I was offered a room in a 300 square foot factory loft on Ritterstrasse in Kreuzberg. These huge, empty spaces have become extinct or very expensive, but back then they were quite common and astonishingly cheap. The heating in fact was free but turned off on weekends, while the factory below was closed. This resulted in roommates disappearing on frosty weekends, keeping warm in clubs or bars, turning them into their living rooms, and coming home on Monday morning.

My bedroom was the former broom and suitcase storage space over the bathroom cabinet and was as large as my mattress with enough space to hoard a couple books on the side.

A small, round window overhead allowed daring sunrays to enter in the early morning but otherwise my view consisted of pigeons roosting on the ledge. The hall in front of the alcove was transformed into a working area with just enough space for my valuables and, after squeezing in an antique desk, which a former subtenant had left behind, the room was filled to the brim. It was now the authentic underground studio I had always dreamed of, with my sketches and fabric displayed on the walls, next to my easel and sewing machine.

In comparison, the rest of the huge loft was a maze of generous rooms, spacious windows, and countless nooks and corners. In addition to four bedrooms, the inhabitants shared a 40 square meter telephone room, neatly furnished with one green telephone lying on the floor, as well as fifteen guitars standing upright, one next to the other; a 40 square meter TV room in which we would lounge around on the only piece of furniture, a soft, red sofa; and a spacious kitchen with generously proportioned windows and a massive wooden table, our late-night dinner hang out, with a large clothes-hanger looming above from the ceiling which could be lowered with a thick metal chain. We had two refrigerators to store enough food for months and never went out for dinner, which was just too expensive and, moreover, considered bourgeois.

Everybody was poor back then so if we met with friends it was either in the bars we were working at, at parties where we could drink for free, or at home, spending the evening together cooking, dyeing each other's hair, taking pictures, watching movies, or just sitting around and telling stories. The view from our roof was magnificent; in the summer we would sunbathe on the hot tar and gaze over the chimneys, into the far horizon of East Berlin's hazy rooftops, gossiping about the political state of things or newcomers that had just come to town. Living together with such a large group of people was a new experience for me. I had never been part of an apartment-sharing community before and I enjoyed the easy interaction, almost as if we were a family. Together we did the house chores, shopping, and interior decoration, deciding if we could afford having a new TV, should continue using the rattling washing machine, chasing away the few, confused rats that tried moving in, watering our plants, and doing laundry; everything always accompanied by an endless flow of laughing conversation.

DE PICCIOTTO

Before continuing further I would like to introduce myself: my name is Danielle. Danielle de Picciotto. When I went to Sicily for the first time I noticed the inhabitants looking at me in a strange manner whenever I was introduced. Later on I was told that a mafioso called Picciotto had been killed on a square around the corner from where I was staying in Palermo.

My parents never let on what my family name signifies: picciotto means "little killer," the one responsible for the everyday disappearances of Mafia nuisances. The first time I read a book on Sicily I was surprised to find our last name mentioned in almost every chapter and called my father in New York to ask him whether there was any association. He started whispering immediately, "Not now Danielle, not on the phone," and quickly hung up. A friend of mine, Max Dax, the publisher of *Alert,* an interview magazine in Hamburg, who years later was to become editor-in-chief of *Spex,* had produced a record of his favorite traditional Mafia songs called *Male Vita* and called me, laughingly commenting that my name is referred to in almost every song.

My father was born on a ship. A ship on its way to Egypt with full-blown sails just like those depicted on our family crest. My father's father was Sicilian, my grandmother Georgian, although our ancestors originate from Portugal and Syria. We have a long history of de Picciottos traveling the world. My grandfather had thirteen brothers and sisters that immigrated to Switzerland, Jerusalem, Paris, Palermo and, of course, the USA. When I give my name in Italy I get surprised looks in return; in Switzerland I am told legends of enormously rich bankers; in New York it led to a jeweler on 5th Avenue, who turned out to be a distant cousin of my father, selling me a watch; and in Germany everybody thinks it is the perfect artist's name that I must have invented.

During their exodus from Sicily to Cairo my grandfather made the acquaintance of the Prince of Egypt, a friendly, fun-loving guy, and they quickly became friends, gambling and drinking together. When the prince became king he asked my grandfather to become the land's caretaker and I suppose he was good at what he did because after a couple of years, the bankrupt prince had become incredibly wealthy.

From the stories my father told, Carlos de Picciotto was a strapping man of extreme habits, working for weeks without a break only to then jubilantly fall into a gambling spree, losing and winning huge amounts of money, buying hundreds of ties and expensive presents for his wife. He was one of the first car owners in Cairo, continuously crashing into something, driving my grandmother mad with worry. The legend goes that he met her when he fell off his horse in front of her house in Sicily, breaking a leg. Naturally she fell in love, saved him, and nursed him back to health.

My father grew up with cooks, housemaids, nannies, and gardeners, wonderful ingredients for thrilling bedtime stories. He admired and respected his father all of his life and spoke of his mother only in the most loving terms. One of his favorite remembrances was that she had the smooth skin of a peach and although being uneducated, such style and class that women from all over came to visit and ask her for advice on fashion, cooking, and cosmetics. The impressive mansion they lived in is now the Swiss consulate, my many relatives in Paris shyly disclosing an ancient, yellow-stained catalogue of the furniture auction which was held when the family left Cairo, faintly similar to Buckingham Palace furniture documentaries.

I was raised with stories of gambling in velvet-and-diamond encrusted casino halls where one rubbed shoulders with sheiks and belly dancers; racing camels in the desert; being bitten by a scorpion; mysterious mix-ups with spies; and chilling glimpses of concentration camps in China and Italy. My family has a long history of exodus and adventure throughout the Orient and Europe, the wooden ship on the middle of our family crest looms large, and I suppose that restlessness and pursuit of the unusual are in my blood. I am happiest while traveling; I love touring, taking a bus, or a train, enjoying the feeling of immobility while speeding ahead. Leading a creative, nomadic life had always been my dream and I couldn't imagine staying in one city for long. I was born in Tacoma, Washington, on a cold and snowy 19th of February at the hour zero, the end of one astrological sign and the beginning of the next, a transitory moment, as many an esoteric hippie has told me while pretentiously patting my hand. So officially I am an Aquarius, Pisces, and with two unknown ascendants. I am also left-handed, have a garlic allergy, was raised trilingual, moved fifteen times before I was twelve years old, grew up in American army barracks surrounded by drunkards beating their wives, cross-eyed boys torturing monkeys, flashers lifting their coats in front of the elementary schools, gang wars in second grade, racist stabbings among school children, and Halloween apartment decorations burning down complete military stations.

My father had joined the army after seeking refuge from the Italian fascists and I was condemned to the exodus he and his family had long become accustomed to. My mother, on the other hand, was born in Solingen, infusing German blood into my already mixed-up veins.

She considered me adorable in traditional dirndls from Bavaria, making baseball clad teenagers in Washington DC's suburbia gawk at my pink floral attire with white aprons silhouetted by drug infested playgrounds and back street swimming pools.

I became extremely short-sighted within a week by the age of nine, had to wear thick, heavy glasses that made smiling difficult, learned to play piano at the age of four, violin by ten, and was not allowed to watch TV, making normal interaction with people my age impossible. After my parents' violent separation I experienced the French *savoir vivre* in Paris with nine cousins and two enigmatic aunts that would cook ten-course meals while arguing about Kant's theory of knowledge with philosophy professors, or explain the family business in great detail, including little anecdotes of millionaire ship owners sailing past Crete or the latest gossip from the Bois de Bologne. I enjoyed seeing erotic movies in Montparnasse at three in the morning with one aunt who guiltily held my hand, telling me to keep it a secret, and drinking hot chocolate amid designer stores with the other, or watching the artists in the hills paint silly American tourists until my mother decided to put me into an esoteric Steiner school in the Black Forest in Germany. There I learned to spin wool and hammer metallic fruit bowls, was taught how to use guache paints and only allowed to wear woolen sweaters that made me itch and squirm. This was the beginning of a journey that continues to be, to put it mildly, challenging.

During a very difficult point in my life in 1995 I went to an astrologist hoping she would promise relief by telling me that peace was soon to come, but after one glimpse at my horoscope she cried out, "Oh my, it's surprising you haven't committed suicide, how on earth are you going to face what is yet to come?" Not mentioning the fact that I had hoped for something quite different I paid the three hundred bucks and left.

Until moving to Berlin, I had been convinced that my habit of moving restlessly from one city or continent to the next, on my quest for unusual encounters and adventures, would continue for the rest of my life, following our family tradition. I don't like repetition, stale customs, conservative lifestyles, or embarrassed lies, and many places become transparent and predictable after a couple of months. Little did I know that the city I was moving to would be so complex and sovereign that I would never even have the chance to think about leaving, since I would be so busy dealing with the day-to-day experiences for years to come.

The Berlin Vamp

I shared my new habitat with four flatmates: Gaby, a hairdresser, Claudia, an aspiring filmmaker, Markus, an archaeologist, and Roland Wolf, a talented musician who was playing piano for Nick Cave and the Bad Seeds.

Markus the archaeologist was seldom to be seen, he was usually busy studying. When I moved in, Roland was on a Brazilian tour with Nick, so I didn't catch sight of him for quite some time. But with Claudia and Gaby's help I discovered interesting clubs, bars, and cafés, and was thus introduced to the essential meeting places for finding jobs, collaborations, and contacts in general.

A couple of weeks after arriving I was hired as a chef in a local diner called Café Moskau. Needless to say I had never cooked in my life, usually subsisting on a diet of French fries and cheese, but as the owner's main interest was based on having young, pretty girls work for him, I was given the chance of proving my hidden skills. Solyanka, salad niçoise, and four different styles of eggs quickly became my specialty, and I practiced for hours in the small, stifling kitchen.

Everybody waited tables in Berlin, cafés being the essential meeting places, and instead of spending money on food and drinks most would prefer earning money by serving them to their friends. The gorgeous, attention-grabbing women working at the Café Moskau filled it with an audience of nonchalant, tattooed musicians lounging next to their carefully placed guitar or bass cases, paint-covered artists showing off small booklets filled with sketches and color dabblings, fashion designers offering modeling jobs for upcoming avant-garde fashion shows, and café owners trying to bribe the girls to come work at their newest business enterprises.

Berlin was then known for its strong and impressive women. The common mood was support, ingenuity and sticking together, not a common attitude among women in general. There was no competition for men or jobs. As soon as a new woman appeared on the horizon she would be taken possession of by the female community, curiously interrogated, examined, and then proudly presented to the world as a Berlin Vamp. To be considered a Berlin Vamp was considered a great achievement, it was the recognition of being individual, tough, and avant-garde, not so much a sex bomb. The goal was to be original and experimental and not bow to predictable standards of beauty or other female attributes. It was considered cool to be as resilient as any man, not permitting cattiness or pettiness to tarnish associations. Women protected and respected each other, working together to initiate projects, record labels, publishing companies, spoken-word festivals, in the process becoming internationally acclaimed DJs, musicians, or artists.

Claudia Skoda, Gudrun Gut, Bettina Köster, Françoise Cactus, Heike Mühlhaus, Beate Bartel, Ellen El Malki, Inga and Annette Humpe are but a few examples. I was exhilarated by this girls' world, and made fashion and music and painted with them for years to come. I came to understand the meaning of a muse. In my eyes it has nothing to do with external attributes such as fame or wealth as suggested in gossip columns today, it is actually the very opposite, finding somebody that inspires you, arousing a sentiment of unlimited creativity and freedom, and turning the world into a immeasurable playground of ingenuity.

If it is reciprocal you are very lucky.

Gudrun Gut

One of the most impressive women I met in Berlin was Gudrun Gut. We were introduced early on by Johnny Klimek, an Australian musician and her then-boyfriend.

Johnny had been member of the band The Other Ones, a family project with his brother Alf and twin sister Jayney that had landed a Top Ten hit, "Holiday," and catapulted them into worldwide recognition and international touring. Originally they had been brought to Berlin by Alf, who had joined the ex-Nina Hagen Band. That band then renamed themselves Spliff, and Alf was the front man and co-writer for the record *Spliff Radio Show*. Johnny quickly felt comfortable in the Prussian metropolis, renting a studio apartment and investing money earned by his success into keyboards and mixing desks to build a recording studio.

The first time we spoke at length he confessed a five-year plan of becoming a mogul, inviting me to design a logo and prepare the merchandise, making it sound like a joke, but actually taking it very seriously. After meeting the rough, underground musicians of the Geniale Dilletanten scene, the outgoing Australian veered towards the techno-oriented dance crowd, preferring the new electronic music to analogue sound. He began writing music with Paul van Dyk, Thomas Fehlmann (Palais Schaumburg), Dr. Motte, and Paul Browse (Clock DVA), and producing the first records of an upcoming electronic Berlin sound. The "Klimek Enterprise" studio quickly became popular because of his professional attitude, decent prices, and cozy atmosphere. Working within my commissioned velvet curtains and fluorescent 1970s design details (simulating a mad Mike Myers interior), Johnny was often booked out for long periods of time. As his success grew he rented one room after another in the Monumentenstrasse, calling his nephews to come from Australia and assist him with the productions. Then unexpectedly, after years of effort, his income started to drop with the demise of the techno mania, and tired of DJs having tantrums in his living room he decided to shift his working field. By chance an old friend, Reinhold Heil, Alf's former *Spliff Radio Show* partner, asked him to help compose music for a film by Tom Tykwer, then a young, unknown movie director. Reinhold, Tom, and Johnny clicked perfectly, sharing the same sense of humor and music taste.

After completing the movie *Wintersleepers* in 1996, they continued collaborating and achieved worldwide success in 1998 with the movie *Run Lola Run*, catapulting Johnny into the world of fame and success once more and bringing him to Hollywood.

Back in the 1980s Johnny asked me to sew curtains for him. We had met in a bar I was working at and he needed to soundproof his walls because of annoyed neighbors. Broke as usual and happy to receive a paid commission, I went to see him a couple of days later. When I arrived, the door was opened by a woman I hadn't met before who told me in a thick German accent where the studio was. Johnny introduced us later as "Gudrun, Danielle, Gudrun."

Gudrun was known as the toughest chick in town, cutting her way through the jungle of a male-dominated international music industry, determined to achieve as much success as any man. Her unusual beauty, slanted eyes, dark straight hair, and flared nostrils, reminiscent of an enchanting Eskimo woman, fascinated me, and her hands, which were strong, large, and beautifully formed, were continuously stroking keyboards, fabrics, food, or wine in a light but confident manner; she was never insecure, always very conscious of what profit she could achieve by participating. Though on first encounter she might initially seem wary, resembling a wild animal ready to take flight, she would then set about fulfilling the mission efficiently, driven by the force of her vision. Gudrun was singleminded about her art, ready to invest anything to make it happen in spite of living in dire poverty for a long time; anything, that is, except her meticulous taste or giving up on her dreams. Thanks to her talent and powerful erotic allure both men and women were seduced into supporting her, helping her to become an underground icon, achieving success in the business world. Obviously her ruthless ambition led to backlashes. While working with her I was often furious at the blunt comments she made, but in the long run her commitment and support of artistic capacity in the music industry have proven her integrity and she deserves all the admiration she has ever received and more.

After moving to Berlin in the 1980s, originally from West Germany, Gudrun quickly became part of the Geniale Dilletanten, the avant-garde music scene in Berlin, and together with Beate Bartel and Blixa Bargeld one of the original band members of Einstürzende Neubauten. Successively she founded the band Malaria (together with Bettina Köster), Matador, Mania D., and Madame Bovary. These female bands became renowned for their avant-garde music experimentation. Gudrun combined soft, harmonious eroticism with dry, abstract rhythms and unusual live sounds, creating a fascinating and complex world of her own and gaining recognition in the international music world with Nick Cave, Steven Severin (Siouxsie and the Banshees), and Martin Gore (Depeche Mode) becoming good friends. She continued working consistently throughout the years in spite of chauvinism and poverty, writing music, composing radio plays, representing artists, producing bands, founding her record label, Monika Enterprise, the radio show the *Ocean Club,* and paving the way for countless female musicians and producers worldwide.

After being introduced by Johnny we spent a couple of months eyeing each other carefully and admiring each other from afar. One evening, having met by chance at the launching of a new club, we simultaneously started provoking each other with outrageous stories and huge glasses of Fernet Branca. After a couple of hours, around four in the morning, I fainted after being sick in the public bathroom and Gudrun, too drunk to wait for me, fell off her bicycle on the way home. It was the prelude to a wonderful friendship.

We met frequently, Gudrun inviting me to sing for her planned *Ocean Club* project and me requesting her to come and listen to my Space Cowboy recording sessions, a band I had become part of, to my surprise. After aggressive female performers had become popular in the early 1980s, yelling and screaming on stage to make themselves heard, Gudrun's style of maintaining a very feminine touch (in spite of being bluntly honest) inspired me tremendously. Her femme fatale style of black leather jackets, blood-red lips, and heavy, metal jewelry was always contrasted with something surprisingly soft and elegant, a pink garter belt, a transparent silk blouse with polka dots, a flowing summer dress lined with lace, or soft bow ties accentuating neckline and breasts. This combination of tough Amazonian war stance and seductive female allure could be traced throughout her music, art, and film work. She was a major influence on the performance world of Berlin, adding a distinct female touch to many of the male-dominated underground events that took place during those years.

Miasma, one of Gudrun's long-term projects, initiated jointly with the Canadian spoken-word artist Myra Davies, was a good example of this complex female aura. Combining flowing sound structures with visually opulent film loops, they created an atmosphere that was compelling in its beauty and aesthetic. Only when the crowd had relaxed and let go of their inhibitions were they then excruciatingly cut apart by Myra's pointed texts and essays commenting on human shortcomings and excuses, arrows shot directly into the heart. Accustomed to visiting Gudrun on a daily basis, I watched their rehearsals enthusiastically until they asked me to participate, inviting me to do push-ups on stage in a wedding gown, sing back round arias, run in circles, or lift weights while teasing my hair.

This was the first exclusively female lineup I experienced and after performing, I stood and watched the other women speaking, singing, and dancing, discovering a universe of strong and beautiful allies, voicing opinions very differently to the clichéd picture of so-called feminists. These women were erotic and stylish, neither bitter nor prim, people that expected intelligence and respect, reacting lethally to belligerence and I stayed late into the night listening in wonder to Priscilla B., Margita Haberland, Lydia Lunch, Shawna Dempsey, the Voodoo Queens, the Cookie Crew and Cora E.

I had also been invited to do an art installation for a festival in one of the smaller tents of the Tempodrom, a commission inviting me to delve more deeply into the history of female achievement and so I decided to put together a large collage of feminine icons. While doing the research I was faced with the humiliating fact of how little I actually knew about my gender and began hunting the city for history books that not only spoke of male protagonists, but also of their female counterparts. I was shocked to discover that these books were almost impossible to find, and not wanting to believe that discrimination still prevailed to such a degree, I pursued an in-depth search for information and research, that would last for years to come.

After months of work finishing the large pieces and losing a contact lens in the process of hanging them from the high circus tent, I walked around blindly, relying on my ears, interviewing the many girls sitting beneath my colorful portraits about their knowledge of female artists and learned that although it was a festival of and by women very few had any specific knowledge on the women I had portrayed. Mentioning this to Gudrun she laughed in her dusky, somber manner and curtly said, "Yes, we have a lot of work to do."

In addition to motivating each other musically, I was delighted in Gudrun's minimal visual taste, watching her turn a stark, dark room into a feminine salon by simply placing a single flower or silk shawl in perfect symmetry. My tendency of creating intricate, intertwined installations of kitsch was influenced by her style of contrasting one strong element with another, and it encouraged me to focus on essential basics. Gudrun, on the other hand, was introduced to a supplementary playful world of pop influences due to our collaboration. As an American I was more outgoing, lightheartedly collaborating with different artistic styles, not as worried about white trash or bad taste, frequently shocking her serious attitude into giggles, leading her to shake her head in amusement at my antics.

Around 1994, a major music company offered Gudrun a record deal, the result of her music composition and our dedicated commitment to creating a world of our own, consistently writing down ideas on how to instigate and hype the music we had composed, making slim, elegant press releases, initiating intimate performance evenings to earn money, inviting acquaintances we thought would be interesting to collaborate with. We were jubilant that our unpaid work had resulted in this professional recognition and went about creating a concept of how to promote the ensuing compilation the *Ocean Club*.

Gudrun had recorded songs with many of her favorite musicians including Inga Humpe, Anita Lane, Blixa Bargeld, and myself. She continued recording songs with Jayney Klimek and Jovannka Wilsdorf (Quarks) while I composed a model of how the Ocean Club would actually look, creating a tangible space for the virtual concept, a home to invite journalists, friends, and fans, drink cocktails, present videos, CDs, and singles, have record release parties and create a general meeting place. Collecting demo tapes and photos, I put together a portfolio of visions, asking a loyal supporter of my work, Dimitri Hegeman, the owner of various clubs and bars, to rent us a room in his techno club Tresor. After listening to the idea of placing a melting pot of creativity into his club he decided to give us a small room in the basement for free, always happy to have unconventional projects popping up in his environment and I started decorating the damp concrete walls.

For weeks the basement was my home, and I dragged wood, fabric, and wire through its echoing staircase, painting, hammering, sewing, and gluing for nights on end, turning the gray bulwark into an underwater world of fish lamps, buying fabric from the flea market to create glittering curtains, bargaining with the tough-faced vendor of a fish store to part with last year's plastic decoration so I could stick the greasy lobster on the frame of a video screen, redesigning old chairs into golden thrones, and finding wooden planks on a deserted building site to construct a radiating bar in Yves Klein blue. Besides crashing a truck filled with seashells in the entrance of the club's driveway, everything went smoothly and the opening party was packed with friends and curious onlookers.

Berlin was visibly interested in seeing our videos, tasting the cocktails, and listening to the newest singles Gudrun had released. During the following months we presented all of our previously prepared projects, and organized panels, press conferences, screenings, parties, and events, becoming an institution people recognized. Eventually the Ocean Club was offered a regular radio show and Gudrun's dream of becoming a platform for interesting music had become true.

It was the most inspiring friendship I ever experienced with a woman, each continuously offering the other a new and fascinating universe not only within our art but every sphere imaginable. Gudrun familiarized me with an international crowd of artists, introducing me to Anita Lane, the bewitching Australian chanteuse, whose incredible imagination enthralled me instantly and has remained a unvarying inspiration until today; to Peaches who had just moved to Berlin, a wonderfully easy going, friendly, and incredibly talented woman; to Mick Harvey, a true gentleman, always ready for a good time in spite of working incessantly; to Nice Cave, listening politely to his huge group of eager fans after a two-hour-long show during which he jumped in the air, fell on his knees, and danced to his wild lyrics; and to Martin Gore from Depeche Mode while giving him a tour of Berlin's hottest clubs.

In turn I familiarized Gudrun with techno avant-garde club artists and DJs I had met during my collaboration with Motte, introducing her to the up-and-coming electronic music and art style of the 1990s. Our mutual bond was so conspicuous that we were often taken for sisters, interviewed or hyped as the Berlin "it" girls. During an interview we jokingly did for the TV station Viva, tired of the repetitive and boring questions on underground club life, we proclaimed that "we don't have sex and don't take drugs." The TV station enthusiastically put the comment on endless rotation with our pale faces, black eyes, and red lips repeating this sentence every hour for months to come, causing a ruckus among our friends, especially our boyfriends and male admirers, leading to hilarious conversations and questions, and people realizing that controversy and scandal were part of the fun. There was not much that wasn't included in our realm of experimentation, Gudrun's inclination towards dark and shadowy spheres, joyously including blood and bizarre earthy elements in our lyrics and visuals, gave my airy, dreamy inclination of broken hearts and ghosts firm ground to stand on. We were perfect opposites completing each other's visions and needs, a friendship not easily found among eccentric artists, the majority of whom were preoccupied with personal expressions of emotion and not necessarily interested in hearing about another's dreams. Her matter-of-fact attitude kept me on my feet while I experienced heart-wrenching incidents yet to come, insisting that I stay in her apartment for months, keeping an eye on me while I slept on her sofa, cooking elaborate dinners with good bottles of red wine and saying "it is good for you—it will thicken your blood," helping to redirect me through uplifting projects and interesting distractions, proving how vital friendship is in times of need.

Nonetheless both of us were striving to develop our capacities to the utmost and by 1995 Gudrun's music style and taste had changed and developed, leaving the rough analogue tunes of the 1980s behind, immersing herself in projects based more on digital electronic output. During the preparation for the Ocean Club, I realized that our tastes were shifting, both simultaneously moving into the direction the other had left; I was craving live music after experiencing the electronic upheaval of techno, interested in field recordings, searching the streets for unusual creaking or chirpings as back up for live slide guitars and percussion rhythms. Gudrun instead preferred to work with a sampler, fiddling with knobs and buttons, no longer interested in looking for rehearsal rooms or having endless band runthroughs, having done it for years. With our music taste going in different directions, new friendships were formed in unrelated crowds, and almost unnoticeably we slowly lost touch. Surprising as it might sound, within the continuously shifting maze of Berlin's creative scene, one could lose sight of each other for years; the constant interaction happening in clubs, galleries, and bars with a huge crowd of people was relentless, very unlike a life of coming home after work and deciding what to do. Our profession was entertainment, which meant preparing things during the day and performing or earning money at night and the best way to stay in touch was by collaborating constantly with new projects and people.

Years later in 1999 I was invited by the Goethe Institute to organize a cultural event in Milan presenting Berlin artists I had worked together with over the years. While deciding which artists to show I discovered an interview with

Gudrun about her newest release in a newspaper and immediately invited her to participate. After flying in from different cities, both of us having been on tour, we met up at the loud airport surrounded by Italian children screaming for attention. Seeing her in a pale beige silk scarf, wearing an elegant dark blue skirt, carrying a black computer bag, with her eyes still black and lips brilliantly red, it felt as if we'd never lost touch. I was as enthralled with her then as I had been years before.

We spent the weekend performing and working together, catching up on past experiences, telling each other about new music, men, and art, then separating again after but knowing our paths would continue crossing, the mutual pursuit of realizing unusual dreams entwining our souls forever and the encounter as magical and permanent as the initial introduction in Johnny's apartment.

The restaurant was very elegant, the kind she could usually not afford to go to, the waiters making more in a week than she would in months. Covertly admiring the gleaming wooden tabletops arranged in front of the shining glass wall filled with green corks, the large round slabs of Parmesan lying behind the counter beneath the powdered salamis hanging from the ceiling, to be cut into slices by starched white aprons and beaming cooks, she felt as if she were partaking in an dreamlike escapade.

She refocused on the group sitting at her table: two musicians and an actress. The musician was wearing a Spanish hat.

Pulling the empty bottle close he checked the label.

"So let's have more of that wine."

Murmuring assent she waved to the waiter, knowing food was out of the question, the bottles he was ordering cost more than her monthly rent.

Everybody was very drunk, the closed windows keeping out the cool evening breeze with cigarette smoke everywhere.

"Ahh yes," sighing with pleasure the bottle was inspected and opened. The waiter sniffed, poured, and smiled. The wine was good.

Conversation continued in small lightning bolts, intricately spun as fine cashmere, shooting from theme to theme, capturing a word, a comment, or a picture, fondling it, quickly placing it next to a contradiction, explaining the question, erasing the answer to replace it with a comparison. Remembrances were described in precise, instructive words, presenting worlds within philosophy, literature and music, baring hidden resemblances, illuminating veiled secrets.

The actress had dark brown hair cut short in a French bob and drank a glass of water between each glass of wine.

"If I don't drink water I'll embarrass you very quickly," she would murmur at regular intervals. The others drank the blood-red liquid. Another bottle was ordered. An Indian rose vendor came by, presenting a bouquet of lovely colors. Three were politely obtained and bestowed upon the three graces.

"Ah the rose!" Carefully taking the red blossom out of the elegant vase which the waiter had immediately brought, her neighbor at the table slowly dipped the plant into his wine glass.

"Aesthetic perfection with perfume and taste, the manifestation of eroticism." Hypnotized, she watched the dripping flower enter his wet lips. His tongue delicately wiped pearls of wine off of the petals, sucking the heart, then turning, his half-shut eyes gleaming, he held the shimmering object out to her.

Timidly she accepted, not knowing what to expect, sinking the glistening petals into her wine glass and slowly releasing the flower into her mouth.

The taste and texture was sweet and soft, caressing her tongue gently, yielding and smooth as the fruit of passion.

The urge to drink again was irrepressible.

"Stop—it's my turn."

Reluctantly she gave up the grail.

"Mmmmmhhhh—delicious," her neighbor sighed, her lips curling sensually with pleasure.

They each drunk from the roses, buying more as the hours slipped by, not perceiving that they were the last guests, that the waiters had taken off their white vests and were sniffing huge lines of cocaine at the neighboring table, that the owner had dimmed the lights and lowered the curtains.

Sensing each other's enchantment, they savored the taste of seduction and silently let their souls unite until they were politely asked to pay, which they did, before swaying off together into the perfumed darkness.

BERLIN FASHION

Berlin's slogan during the 1980s was "initiate and create." No one sat around waiting for offers or ideas.

Interaction consisted of friendly competition between those who wanted to break new artistic boundaries. Beautiful women pounded away on drums and spiky-haired, ashen-faced men screamed intricate, intellectual lyrics to metallic-sounding accompaniment. At wild festivals, experimental bands and performance artists outdid each other in excessive provocation, hazardously performing with fire, hanging precariously by their feet, initiating spiritual rituals, and defying gender roles. Living in Berlin meant always doing the opposite of what would normally be expected of you. Besides being provocative, dangerous, and positively destructive, this atmosphere was rich in magic and humor, meaning that it was easy to savor the surreal aspects of the most insignificant, routine events.

The day after I arrived in Berlin I called Heiner, who was on his way to what he mysteriously called a "second-hand party." He told me to meet him in Wiener Strasse; a street in Kreuzberg known for its many rock cafes—the Madonna, Wiener Blut, or Wild at Heart, all of them usually filled with rock musicians and exhilarating fans. I set out curious to see what kind of event awaited me. We met at a storefront overflowing with colorful 1970s fashion victims adorned in flared pants, short straight dresses, platform shoes, oddly colored patterned shirts, floral ties, and fake eyelashes. Inside the stucco-ceilinged room, a band was playing violently in the middle of hundreds of second-hand articles decorating the vicinity. A tiny, rough wooden board placed over two chairs served as the bar, which sold vodka or beer in chipped porcelain cups. The basement, accessible by a steep, narrow ladder, consisted of the same mixture of clothes and people, the sole variation being a toilet standing in the middle of the room. A continuous flow of people would nonchalantly sit and pee whenever necessary. Heiner introduced me to his friends: chatty bass players, giggly percussionists, and randy drummers, and he got a beer for me while commenting on different sock-and-tie combinations. The party stretched into the early morning hours with riotous dancing sprees, drunken guitar solos, séances, and impromptu fashion shows held on the toilet.

Everybody was very friendly. I soon realized that in Berlin everyone knew each another because of the Wall, which made getting in or out difficult and tedious. It was a situation comparable to a nightliner, filled to the brim with musicians who have to get along for months, ultimately developing a very courteous manner of approaching one another. People preferred fun parties and creating the legend of Berlin's insanity together.

A new acquaintance who was also an expat, Donna, took me to a similar get-together in East Berlin a couple of weeks later. She had been offered 10,000 DM to marry an East Berlin resident to help him escape the GDR, a common proposition that usually didn't pan out. She was supposed to meet him at a party that Udo Lindenberg, a German rock musician, was hosting, and had invited me to come along. We arrived later than expected because of being held up at Checkpoint Charlie, and the party was at its peak. After being handed two straight vodkas in the narrow hallway of the entrance, we were invited into the living room, which was bursting with singing, laughing, and crying people. It was almost impossible to hear the music coming from an old tape recorder in the corner, especially as two men started fighting in the back room, which was filled with bunk beds.

Donna was interested in fashion, which is how I came to be introduced to Sabine von Öttingen, member of an underground East Berlin fashion group called Allerleirau. After telling her about designing costumes in New York and Cologne she described GDR fashion shows in detail, describing abandoned swimming pools, coats made of leather that looked like trees, the difficulties of finding good materials in the East, and the band Rammstein, who were good friends of hers, and usually played music at the fashion events.

We became friends, meeting as often as possible, exchanging stories and gossip about life on opposite sides of the Wall. Hanging out in her apartment was a precious introduction into how people survived under the strict regime. They were constantly helping each other out, thinking not only of their own but five other families, always on the lookout for nice buttons, good shoes, unusual makeup, good bread, foreign newspapers, and so on. They met each other excitedly to distribute the loot, smelling the different perfumes brought over by friends from the West or recounting stories of relatives escaping. It was a closeknit society with enviable friendships. Sabine and her friends were like sisters, each more beautiful and creative than the other, and they turned the sad, drab, gray East into a colorful installation of imaginative objects.

In general I was fascinated by the discipline, which combined the different art scenes on both sides of the Wall, and in spite of long drinking sprees and excessive parties the creative output was constant. These eccentrics not only wrote music, lyrics, manifestos, and books, many of them designed their clothes, and jewelry, organizing concerts, readings, or fashion happenings to go along.

Nothing was left to chance—a consumer mentality was non-existent. This was an atmosphere I felt comfortable in. I had been doing music and art for as long as I could remember, combining them with fashion after studying costume design in New York, and it quickly became apparent that creating apparel in Berlin was quite different from the commercial guidelines I had been taught to follow in my classes.

My initial fashion experience came from being very poor. After having divorced my father, my mother moved from Washington DC to Germany, accepting a teaching position in an expensive, private Rudolf Steiner school.

My father, furious, refused to support her departure and closed her bank account, forcing us to move into an empty apartment without furniture or clothes. Part of the deal of my mother's contract was that her children were allowed to take classes for free, so I was given my grandmother's sweaters, my cousin's jeans, and my aunt's old sneakers and was thus attired when I went to meet my new classmates. Besides sporting heavy glasses and not being able to speak German, I was the incarnation of a painted bird, thrust into the life of the very rich without a cent of my own to speak of. My classmates lived in huge mansions and were surrounded by expensive fashion items. They were each given BMWs on their 18th birthday so they could drive out on their own to holiday villas.

I read books.

Having to be the geek and wear hand-me-downs impelled me to learn how to sew and become an expert on style and fashion. I went to exclusive designer boutiques, studied the fabrics, patterns, and designs and copied them at home on my sewing machine, adding new details I had seen in magazines or art books, thereby making the current fashion my own creation. I have always loved transforming materials into different shapes, putting colors together, and breaking rules. In this way I was able to fit in at school and quickly understood that, thanks to my creativity, I could become a contributing member of society.

To improve my talents I moved back to New York after graduation. My father paid my tuition, happy to have one of his children returning. He had become highly paranoid, the result of his concentration-camp experiences and living alone in one of the toughest and least hospitable American metropolises of the 1980s, where he was scared of getting mugged, raped, or murdered because of his accent. In spite of being highly educated and having lectured all over the world, he worked in a state hospital, earning a pittance in comparison to other oral surgeons that had moved into private practice while he was enrolled in the army to get American citizenship. Thus he would sit alone in the evenings, muttering along with the television, trusting nobody, experiencing imaginary spies or attacks on his life, suspecting each postal worker or gasman of being a traitor.

In spite or because of these bitter reminiscences and daily tragedies he was delighted to support me in every way, making my dream come true and hoping to give his daughter a better chance of leading a fulfilled life. I was accepted at Parsons, where I studied fashion illustration for a year and then transferred to the Fashion Institute of Technology on Seventh Avenue, wanting to learn more about practical, basic technologies. I enjoyed university life immeasurably, taking as many courses as possible, learning about oil painting, illustration, nude drawing, fabric sciences, art history, sociology, fashion and costume history, and jewelry design. Besides participating in the mandatory courses I also signed up for evening classes, where I enjoyed mingling with the older pupils and experienced teachers, participated in summer and winter school, made use of the added space in classrooms to spread out my fabric and paper work, always doing extra jobs on the side to earn some cash and take pressure off of my father's wallet. Experiencing New York in the 1980s was exhilarating. I caught a last glimpse of Andy Warhol, partied at Save the Robots, was tutored by Marc Jacobs, met Diane Brill, modeled on countless fashion shows and celebrated at Area. All the same, living together with my father was strenuous, even scary at times. Whenever his bouts of madness occurred I was in danger of being mistaken as one of his "enemies" and being attacked, so after receiving my cum laude degree I decided to visit Europe to escape the fearful atmosphere in which I lived.

This was when I discovered Berlin.

Having decided to stay I set out to discover the newest apparel trends in Germany. Being used to the seasonal designer collections presented in Bloomingdales or Sax 5th Ave, I was surprised and exhilarated by the fact that fashion in Berlin had a completely different goal. It was considered a means of expressing uniqueness and individuality, not mass consumption. It wasn't meant to be practical, sellable, or even necessarily wearable. Instead it was an illustration of dreams, turning the harsh Cold War reality into an enchanted world of beautiful colors, fabrics, and feathers.

I was introduced to many performing artists that quickly became loyal clients of my costume and fashion designs. To my surprise, my favorite, most original models sold best.

I had snake women requesting bead-encrusted, stretchable costumes covered with feathers, musicians calling for appliquéd leather jackets with personal logos and initials of their bands stitched on the back, actresses asking for elaborate evening gowns covered with flowers and silk, anything to make them stand out in the crowd, theater companies commissioning medieval costumes. My enormous hats made out of plastic blow-up animals became fashion-show favorites, while skintight, brightly colored jumpsuits covered with golden appliqués were de rigueur for press photos.

Berlin fashion in general was often described as unwearable, turning the model into a surreal action figure wearing asymmetrical hats, bulky shoes, and homemade fabrics. Whenever this style was presented in other cities it was smiled upon as eccentric and not really taken seriously by the industry. That is, until the designers stole the ideas for their next collections. Due to this disturbing trend most Berlin fashion designers went bankrupt after a few years, being unable to compete with the low prices of the international mass market.

Summer 1988

She had never liked him.
It wasn't the pockmarks on his white face, the greasy hair, or his bad way of dressing.
"So are you coming by today?"
It was the ingratiating smile pushed into her face, the bad posture twisting his back into a servile stoop, and the look in his eyes that made her feel uncomfortable. He had been sitting on the same chair for weeks ordering gallons of coffee and staring at her serving breakfast, flashing his teeth whenever their glance met.
"I guess so."
"Ring the bell at the blue door—there's no name tag."
Slowly walking towards the address he had written on the small piece of paper, a page torn out of the menu, she passed the familiar Turkish grocery stores adorned with bright pictures and blinking fountains. Pausing to inspect the mint-colored polyester bed sheets and lacy pillowcases, touching the glossy fibers carefully, following the interlacing golden threads with her fingers, treasuring the vibrant colors, religious paraphernalia, Mosque alarm clocks, and golden picture frames, she remembered detailed 1001 bedtime stories from long ago appreciatively.
Noticing her interest, a Turkish saleswomen shyly came out of a glittering cave, smiling cautiously, concealed beneath floral scarves and a warm overcoat, politely waiting for her to decide what to buy. Shaking her head slightly she continued down the road.
The air was cool for October, the shadows of Kreuzberg making her shiver slightly and wonder how the heating situation was at home.
Hesitating in front of the small brass bell on the blue door she put an arrogant expression on her face and added white powder to her already ashen features as supplementary protection.
The door opened.
"Hey! Great, come in, would you like some tea?
"No thanks, I'm fine."
"Oh well, welcome to my humble home, not many have crossed this threshold, but believe me, many have wanted to." A quick look of nastiness swept the flabby features. "But I haven't collected my treasures to show them off to just anybody, well, at least not for free."
The beady eyes noticed her look of disdain.
"Oh, don't worry, if you see something you like we can surely find easy terms of agreement."

The shiver was stronger this time.

"Hey, I really don't have much time, could I just see what you've got cause I have to get back home, the models are coming at six o'clock for their costume fitting."

The hideous smile was erased for a couple of heavenly moments, then replaced by an especially repulsive expression of regret.

"That's a pity, I thought we would have a little more time ... to show you everything in detail ..."

"Look, just show me the stuff you said you have and let me see if I can use it."

Impatiently she squirmed in her shiny, black rubber coat, turning to inspect the bare cement room, a light bulb screaming through its brilliant glare.

"By all means, I'm sure we'll get along just fine."

Letting the words echo soullessly behind his back the man opened a low metal door and disappeared.

Hesitantly she followed his shadow.

The space was huge. It was so large the back wall could not be seen from where she was standing. The low ceiling and dark lighting enhanced the dusty, untidy atmosphere of hundreds of wooden tables and shelves spread out unevenly throughout the room, each and every one covered with countless objects.

"Where on earth did you get all this stuff?" Slowly she walked from one table to the next opening boxes of intricate laces, suitcases with bolts of untouched gold brocade, tiny jars filled with buttons, books stacked precariously over, under, and in between cupboards, T-shirts with unusual logos intermingling with pin-striped men's suits and vests, shiny leather shoes, brilliantly colored sneakers, knitted woolen sweaters, chandeliers, brass instruments, glittering rhinestone jewelry, velvet sofas, leather armchairs, and old-fashioned umbrellas.

"Oh, this is only one room in my Ali Baba's cave."

The repulsive smile was back, looming closer and closer.

"I told you I had something special, choose whatever you want and we'll talk about expenses later."

Lovingly she stroked a dark red stretch of velvet embroidered with traditional patterns while letting soft pink lace flow through her other hand.

"But how? I mean where did you get all of these things, are they stolen?"

"Oh no."

A look of contemptuous disdain spread over the smirking face.

"You don't have to steal things, that's too risky, there's enough people around that have no idea of what wealth they own, that are willing to trade beautiful, valuable objects for lousy, fashionable junk, you just have to figure out what they want and how far they'll go to get it; just read the ads, people are so dumb, they come from all over trying to get rich fast. The East in general is

really easy, they consider all of this old-fashioned and worthless, it's so simple it's ridiculous—and everything's perfectly legal."

She stared at his silhouette dimly flickering in front of an Aladdin's lamp covered with delicate metal flowers.

"Look, you like this fabric, here take this too, take as much as you like, this is the deal, I need an assistant to clean up and categorize everything, I want to make a catalogue of the whole lot and you would be perfect. I've been watching you work and you're efficient, talented, and sexy, there's a small room in back that could be turned into a great office and don't worry about the money, I'll pay you well. I'm usually out and about meeting clients so you'd be on your own pretty much and when everything's cleaned up you can receive my guests and entertain them while I talk business."

She took another glance at the room, its stories staring back at her and started moving towards the door.

"Hey, wait, what's wrong? I told you it's ok, you can't get into trouble, honest." Grabbing he tried pulling her towards him.

"Don't be ridiculous, everybody is doing it, don't you ever go to the flea market and buy something really cheap, what's the difference? Those people travel for days to stand in the freezing cold and sell all they have for pennies, you go there and buy their stuff don't you? I just do it in another fashion, in fact I'm doing them a favor, they don't have to stand in the cold, I take everything for a fixed price before they go to the markets and they can easily live off of it for a month."

Stumbling, she pushed away his hand and opened the door, feeling the cold sunrays touch her sweat-covered brow, away from the stench of lost dreams, desperation, and tears.

Ignoring his fading shouts she swayed dizzily down the now darkened streets towards home, saddened and repulsed.

Berlin Designers

Thanks to my consistent clientele of performers I was able to finance one-of-a-kind street wear and stage collections that were hand-sewn and not very profitable, taking time to add countless, tiny details, incorporating beads, feathers, expensive golden leather and other luxury items. Organizing regular fashion shows in underground clubs, I asked my clients to model, not being able to hire expensive models, and resulting with spectacular evenings during which Marusha, DJ Clé (Martini Brös), or Dr. Motte (Love Parade) jauntily walked down the runway, fading in and out of pink smoke machine clouds, wearing heavy gold chains and appliquéd sweat suits, contortionists displaying stretchable evening wear and ballet dancers floating through complicated choreographies to heavy rock music.

Enjoying the interaction with other stylists I invited them to participate in the whirlwind of performance and we initiated colorful fashion events, presenting our designs happily, with hundreds of spectators lining up in front of the guarded club doors, hoping for a chance to get in. It was easy to receive press reviews in the closed-off city and my life turned into an exiting adventure of TV interviews, radio shows, and newspaper articles, everybody eager to be part of the fashion events put together by designers as unconventional and outrageous as the punk bands they listened to.

Claudia Skoda, the most legendary, and a good friend of Gudrun Gut and Martin Kippenberger, had started her knitting collection in the mid 1970s, designing striking patterns and unusual shapes, creating unique, internationally acclaimed organic designs. Her fashion shows were sought after for huge social gatherings so popular that trend agents would fly in, avidly watch her choreography, check the stage design and accompanying music, in order to be in the know about future designs. She was an icon by the time I moved to Berlin, undisputedly motivating and choreographing the city's style, one that I could not afford but admired from afar, shyly peeking through her large shop windows and interrogating friends that had gone to her sale parties.

Another interesting group, which impressed me profoundly, was called Scheederbauer. Their boutique was filled with small chestnut necklaces, berry earrings, fairy and elf-like costumes, self-made music tapes, and red velvet chairs covered with strange, unidentifiable objects. I was fascinated by their correlation with theatre performances, art exhibitions, and music enterprises, adoring the fantasy aspect of their items. Besides coming up with quaint details and one-of-a-kind objects, they launched unusual exhibitions at the "Bethanien," a former hospital, presenting new collections and friends such as Marc Brandenburg, an extremely gifted artist exhibiting unforgettable "Ausländerpullover," sweaters with knitted heads and hands in different shades meant to represent different skin colors for people of every nationality to try on.

This humorous and cocky approach to mixing art, politics, and fashion left me speechless, standing in the showroom for hours, thrust into a paradise in which anything was possible, the secret attribute of this encircled city. How often had I been weighed down by the constricting notion that, as a serious artist, one has to stick to one art form, one style, and one blueprint, unless willing to risk being called superficial and unprofessional if expressing oneself through other media. Here I could finally come alive, presenting my fashion before concerts, during art openings, theatre pieces, and of course on the newly founded off-fashion fairs. These had been brought to life especially for the underground and young designers, attracting an audience that wasn't interested in expensive or elegant prêt a porter but instead wanted to look like rock stars. "The Offline" was a three-day event filled with booths from which spilled out out pink wigs, hair extensions, pointed shoes, tight Boy George inspired leggings, asymmetrical skirts made from fake fur, metal jewellery, plastic tops, transparent trousers, tartan leggings, fishnet stockings of all colors, lace gloves, stud covered leatherjackets or hand sewn, pinstriped suits. Everything had a baroque, decadent feel to it, the morbid, forlorn breath of Berlin's wastelands and underground caverns quietly nestling within the colorful threads of the avant-garde. I was usually invited to participate by the fair itself, sharing the costs with fashion designer friends and I enjoyed watching the colourful crowd hanging out in our booth. Another difference from most other fairs was that it was more about having fun and exchanging ideas than actually selling, most of the audience being friends and acquaintances, just as poor as the designers. There were hardly any large, commercial labels participating and as our prices were very low we would usually make a little bit of money by selling one or two designs and covering the costs of the enterprise in the end. Not surprisingly the fair didn't last very long but the idea of representing young artists with a space of their own had been good and has been copied by many similar ventures.

Participating had also increased my reputation as an exceptionally outrageous designer and my French revolution balloon skirts adorned with Lotte Lenya's "Mack the Knife" look became a particular attraction. As with most of my designs, they were very intricate, with layers and layers of hand-stitched undergarments, carefully attached flowers and leather appliqués and it took weeks to finish an elaborate ballgown or exquisite hat, so I couldn't survive financially on fashion alone in order to pay my bills and continue buying fabric. Thus I continued waiting tables in cafés, bars, and clubs seven days a week. Working during the day was healthier because of the fresh air and lower alcohol consumption, but it was longer hours for less money, and I was cooking, serving food, and cleaning up, which left no time or strength for my studio afterwards.

Nightshifts at bars by comparison only required me to pour drinks, flirt with customers, and collect the glasses for much more money per hour but usually ended with my drinking too many shots with friends and coming home at ten in the morning, so I tried combining both which resulted in my working around the clock nonstop.

FALL 1988

The space was small, heavily heated, and filled with feathers. Languid, brilliantly made up women and men, softly stroking each other in slow movements, were draped lazily on cracked velvet chairs and sofas. Klaus Nomi filled the air with high-pitched tales accompanying a slow parade of bearded models, gliding in and out of the randomly placed furniture.
"Would you like some wine?"
She turned, looking toward the voice that had spoken, trying not to catch her lace on the broken armrest of a chair.
A small, sleek man with greased black hair and a razor thin mustache stood offering a golden goblet of red merlot.
"Would you like to have some wine?" he repeated with a thick Italian accent.
Accepting the glass was not an easy task, the tight Titian corset she was wearing made movement almost impossible. Realizing her predicament the elegantly dressed apparition trimly inched around the neighboring sofa, encouraging one of the sleepy inhabitants to slide to the left and gracefully handed her the glass while letting himself drop into the cushions with a sigh.
"Ahhhh, that's better, would you like some acid with the wine?"
Shaking her head she sipped.
His necktie was a curly strand of hair adorned with tiny jewels, illuminating the laced white shirt underneath.
His hands, slender as a girl's, lay lightly on heavy, purple brocade knickers.
"Would you like to do a fashion show to my paintings?"
She glanced at him questioningly.
A heavily powdered woman, balancing a white Louis XIV wig on her head, clumsily bent over to kiss the tiny man on the sofa.
"Darling, how are you doing, would you like some more wine?"
"No, my glass is still full."
The white powder with smeared red lips and a dark beauty spot, turned, greeting another guest with sharp tweaks of joy: "Darling! What a pleasure!"
"What do you paint?"
A tiny, polite finger pointed to the small collection of drawings she had examined when entering the space, the reason of her visit, an exhibition that had attracted her attention while reading the local paper.
"Those are yours? They're really good, all the details and strange little symbols, they are like a surrealist version of Bosch. I couldn't stop looking at them."
"I know, I was watching you, you were the only guest that took the time."
"How do you know I do costumes?"

"I've seen your shows and liked them very much, especially the elaborate ones with the flowered gowns and detailed hats."

"Thanks, that's an honor. I would enjoy doing something together with you."

Smiling he took another jab of acid.

"Would you like some?"

Politely she drank some more wine.

The couple lying on the sofa next to her slowly unlaced each other's bodices and meticulously powdered each other's breasts, delicately painting the nipples red.

A short egg-shaped woman well past the age of fifty recited a poem she was well known for, then rebelliously rejecting any aid bent down to kiss a blonde on her mouth and sinking back into her overflowing chaise lounge tossed her long white hair over her shoulder and murmured:

"Ah, I still have plenty of juice inside of me."

Male models dressed in transparent negligees reappeared, giggling airily behind dusty wigs, and sang to the piercing tape recorder.

"So should we meet tomorrow to prepare everything?"

"That fast?"

Staring at her impassively, he raised an eyebrow.

"Why not?"

BERLIN NIGHTLIFE

Berlin nightlife has always had the reputation of being excessive, the twenties already creating legends spinning with outcry as Anita Berber fainted during her languid cocaine performances or surrealist artists screamed scandals during wild drinking sprees. I felt comfortable in the extreme labyrinth of emotions, enjoying its antics, and taking pleasure in the fearless dance. Besides working at the Café Moskau, I waitressed at the Café Caiman known for live alligators, the Madonna, a rock haven, the Fischlabor, Dimitri Hegeman's first underground music café, forerunner of the Tresor and the Kloster, a beautifully designed bar inspired by ancient monasteries. I didn't mind getting up at 7 o'clock in the morning to serve coffee to people I had seen a couple of hours earlier at a gig or party and relished walking down "Maybachufer" at sunrise, kicking leaves and listening to the ducks quacking on the canal, opening the restaurant, setting the tables, receiving fresh "Brötchen" from the baker's man and preparing different breakfast possibilities with various selections of sausages or cheese, to then watch friends slowly drop in, pale-faced, red-eyed, sheepishly ordering a double espresso or another whiskey for breakfast, contemplating finally going to bed, meeting a business associate, or going to their studios. I usually got off work around 5 p.m. and strolled home, passing the colorful Turkish market stalls of Kreuzberg, buying ample purple eggplants, bright red tomatoes, and fresh fish for dinner, chatting with new acquaintances here and there about interesting parties or exhibitions that would open that evening, promising to call or come by, arriving at home, carefully fitting all of my purchases into our household refrigerator and preparing dinner with my roommates.

A couple of weeks after I had moved to Berlin, Claudia, my neighbor, invited me to the Ex'n'Pop. I had heard the name being mentioned a couple of times before, being the successor of the Risiko, a legendary dive in which the "Geniale Dilletanten" had hung out during the eighties, alternatively working behind the bar or celebrating wild speed parties in its small rooms. On the way to the venue I started feeling sick. I had eaten something bad and by the time we arrived I could hardly speak. Claudia told me to wait in front of the packed site so I sat down on the doorstep trying to focus on the people. I could see the bartender, a tall, handsome guy with spiky hair and a defiant expression, from where I was drooping. He seemed to know everybody, making comments on the side while serving beer and wine or doling out cocktails. It was a wild crowd, rough, boisterous men with slicked back hair, pointed cowboy boots and hats, wearing three-piece suits or leather pants, drinking straight tequila while talking and flirting with black-haired, heavily made-up women with snow white, powdered faces, dark cat eyes and brilliant lips. I sat slumped on the steps watching people popping pills and falling from stools, obviously on heroin or speed, until Claudia came back with a drink. She told me it would help my stomach. Thinking that it was a non-alcoholic beverage I drank ten of the small shots she'd handed me only to find out that it was not a soft drink. The world started spinning vehemently as the loud music and shouts from the bar receded and I was violently sick. The party continued as if nothing had happened, a couple of well-meant winks were sent my way by people carefully stepping over the puddle until the barkeeper appeared. He threw a pail of water over the mess, introduced himself as Johannes and offered me a glass of water. I had become an accepted member.

Johannes became a good friend. After marrying the singer Anita Lane and having a son with her, he stopped working in bars, founding his graphic agency "Minus Verlag" and designed album covers for Nick Cave, Einstürzende Neubauten, and Gudrun Gut. His enterprise later became so successful that he decided to move out of his home office, renting a large loft with many rooms together with Neubauten, inviting me to participate. Thus we shared lodgings for over eleven years, many a night spent working on deadlines and drinking coffee in the small kitchen, chain smoking cigarettes and nodding tiredly.

Back in 1986 the Ex'n'Pop was painted dark red and covered with pink plastic roses to hide peeling plaster. With swinging lanterns and very dirty toilets it was reminiscent of a rundown Mexican brothel. This club was, subsequent to the Risiko, the godfather of all Berlin bars, the personification of what made Berlin celebrated in the eighties. It was the favorite hangout of the Bad Seeds, Depeche Mode, Einstürzende Neubauten, Crime and the City Solution, even Iggy Pop dropped by occasionally. Club hours went from 11 p.m. to three days later, most customers arriving after a performance or tour, ready to relax or meet fans, ordering whiskey and vodka in large quantities, all set to make the evening a memorable one.

Here I met Nick Cave, drinking whiskey together with Johnny Klimek, speaking about their concert and planned tours, Mick Harvey and Anita clinking glasses with Alexander Hacke and N.U. Unruh, Gudrun laughing with Martin Gore, who tried sticking his tongue into my mouth, and Hugo Race ordering vodka for a fan.

Originally it belonged to Harry Hass, a lanky writer with light brown hair and a soft handshake. Jointly with Evelyn, a humorous, motherly woman, he gave shelter to a tight-knit group of rebellious entertainers, as excessive as his guests, compassionately defending their lifestyle, initiating wild parties and drastic dramas, the couple falling out of windows, fainting behind bars, and sobbing in the kitchen. Harry deeply appreciated ingenuity and would let his protégés get away with anything, breaking lamps or chairs, being sick in the rear rooms, fighting in the hallway, taking drugs in the bathroom, drinking for free, only asking for regular performances on the tiny stage as often as possible, letting them work behind the bar to pay off their debts. Thus the Ex'n'Pop financed a large number of musicians that would pour drinks for the stray, courageous tourist, daring him with scowls to participate in the madly moving, raucous rhythm of the evening. The fascinated sightseer would covertly watch the turmoil, leave town next morning with a bad hangover, and enthusiastically spread the bar's reputation worldwide, tempting other stray cats to come and participate.

Evelyn and Harry reigned untouchable for years, residing as underground royals, giving the music community a home and a means to survive, until they decided to sell the bar.

Jochen Arbeit, a member of the band Die Haut and guitar player in Einstürzende Neubauten years later, decided to take over the ownership in order to save his favorite hangout, and was joined by his girlfriend Tamara, a tough, buxom German girl. They took over organizing concerts and ordering liquor. I enjoyed popping by after waitressing at the Fischlabor, packing the last determined barflies into my small VW bug and wafting into the Ex'n'Pop together, knowing that they would be able to stay there for at least a couple of days until returning to my jurisdiction. Going to a bar where at least ten good friends are guaranteed to be found hanging out was always a stimulus and after ordering a drink and looking into the dark nooks and corners I would usually discover a group of them speaking, singing, dancing, playing table football, or just hanging out, and they would greet me with shouts and shots. Uli Schüppel was one of the regulars, a good friend and filmmaker, introverted, concentrated, soft spoken, always desperate because of an unexpected mishap; Petra Wende, Blixa Bargeld's girlfriend, known for her temperamental outbursts, causing brawls or heated discussions, covered by the dust of her marble sculptures or telling stories of the Jungle, where she was a popular bartender; Christoph Dreher, another Haut band member and filmmaker, tall and handsome, hanging out with his girl friend Ellen El Malki; Ed Czupkay, my favorite mandolin player and Hells Angels friend, forever ready to break somebody's jaw or crack a joke. It was difficult to decide when to leave: no matter how late or early in the morning, another great idea, story, or happening would inevitably occur just after one had left, the club spawning creativity with every breath.

After Jochen had managed the Ex'n'Pop for a few years, he decided to sell the bar to a group of employees, preferring to be a guest rather than the owner, tired of the constant responsibility and time investment. A collective ownership divided the costs and chores, helping each other financially and emotionally, organizing concerts, movies, video clips, and theater pieces, a stance that the Ex'n'Pop was especially proud of. Many of the musicians and artists inhabiting the smoke-filled rooms were from New Zealand, Australia, England, and the USA, attracted by

Berlin's reputation. Living costs were just manageable but any extra issue, such as needing a new guitar or drum skins, oil paint, canvas, or a trip home usually broke their monetary back. In this case a wild telephone interaction would commence, the lineup of a group show decided upon, newspapers informed, cheap leaflets made and distributed, with the result that, almost a week later, the destitute artist would have plenty of money to pay for his bills.

One of these memorable charity events was held to enable a musician to go back to Colorado. A guitar competition had been decided upon, all were invited to participate. Moritz Wolpert, a talented drummer, decorated the stage with 3D 1970s wallpaper, red velvet curtains and a jury's booth to give the place a glitzy atmosphere, everybody else distributed leaflets and called up friends. On the evening itself the club was quickly packed with onlookers, more lining the street, trying to fight their way into the small venue which vibrated with guitar cases, the smell of aftershave, hair wax or cigars, and the sounds of rustling silky blue and red embroidered suits, not to mention the huge lapels, colossal cowboy hats, silver rings, and neck chains. On stage, sweating performers crooned, plucked, strummed, and hit the strings, anything to convince the jury not to wave them offstage. The main judge was Rosa, an eccentric bearlike writer, known for his ruthless criticism and jeering remarks, coldly enjoying his power and randomly halting an act abruptly in the middle, bringing the perspiring musicians to a sudden stop with an especially pointed remark. After hours of listening to "Hendrixesque" screams and Bo Didley mélanges, Kristof Hahn, singer of Les Hommes Sauvages and guitar player of the legendary Swans, was proclaimed winner. Receiving a handmade trophy the champion was allowed to place the total collected entrance fee of the evening into the palm of the needy musician and the objective had been fulfilled.

The Ex'n'Pop lasted throughout the 1980s, 1990s, and even the aughts, frequently moving from one street to the next because of rental or noise issues, proudly upholding its style and reputation. This endurance of both owners and clientele was an unusual feat, with competition closing most nightclubs after three years. The fact that it never became commercial, instead remaining a haven for the ill-suited, poorly adjusted, and uncompromising made its existence possible, earning the club respect throughout generations for its undying loyalty to the underground.

TURBINE ROSENHEIM

Another influential club that initiated similar events with completely different music was the Turbine Rosenheim.

I was introduced to this significant institution on a sunny winter afternoon which I was spending with Gaby, my blond flatmate, gossiping about interesting hairstyles and extensions, taking an afternoon stroll in Schöneberg, a then-trendy area in Berlin with black-and-white checkered cafés, known for their fashionable clientele. Suddenly, my chattering friend stopped in front of the open door of a low building and enthusiastically whispered, "This club has the best dance music in town, it's the 'it' place to be." Pulling me into a dark room smelling of last night's cigarette fumes and today's detergents we were confronted by a tall, brown-haired man with twinkling eyes, who stood behind the counter polishing glasses with a soft red towel. After Gaby introduced me as her flatmate, he shook my hand politely and with a flowing gesture pulled out a front tooth from his mouth exclaiming, "Look what I can do!" I stared at the tooth not knowing what to say. Grinning, he stuck it back in, and that's how I met Motte. He was a carefree, reckless kind of rogue, good-natured and always ready for a joke or prank, with an attitude of unlimited curiosity, always on the look out for contradictions or odd occurrences. He was infatuated with discovering the extraordinary and the combination of this inquisitiveness paired with his deep integrity was an explosive, fascinating combination. We were attracted to one another immediately and after a couple weeks I was offered a job in his club serving drinks. The space was small, with chrome bars decorating stone walls, stairs to sit on, and a tiny space for dancing. Its main attraction was avant-garde dance music and lovingly prepared parties, organized by Falco and Daniel, a gay couple elaborately dressed in fin de siècle costumes, long extensions, and punk jewelry. They adored preparing special events and spent long nights cooking intricate buffets, weaving paper lanterns, folding hand-drawn invitations, sewing costumes, and helping us renew our own extensions for the different events. Here it was not so much about organizing concerts but rather about putting together inventive parties in which the guests themselves would partake in dressing up or being part of the show. Besides asking performance artists to mingle with the crowd and perform spontaneously, provoking shocked reactions or amusing interaction, we organized early Karaoke shows, basically unknown at that point, or theme parties with prizes for the most innovative costumes, visuals being as important as good dance music.

Initiating my first live installation I decorated one of the deep windows of the entrance, filling it with Japanese candles, porcelain dolls, and other Asian souvenirs my father had sent from his stay in Korea, dressing up as a geisha, wearing a kimono and mask, and stood in the window all night, moving only slightly every so often. Besides feeling faint because of the lack of air it was an intense experience of concentration and interaction, not moving for hours with people standing in front of the glass staring at me, wondering if I was a statue or real, knocking at the window, making grimaces, reminding me of children standing in front of gorillas in the zoo. The idea of humans turning into an immobile display case or robots had become popular in the international New Wave music scene and the Neue Deutsche Welle in Germany, Michael Jackson's "moonwalk" enthralling hundreds of clubgoers to copy the flowing movements, clubs in New York designing endless hallways filled with models reenacting still lifes behind glass, the Area in particular known for its choreography of outrageous scenes of sex and debauchery which would substantially influence the fashion and film world internationally, and the "Living Dolls" clients of my advertising agency in Cologne starting a fashion trend in training models to move like robots for fashion shows, fair exhibits or other advertising campaigns. The mesmerizing idea of where technology would lead our society was still very naïve. Mobile phones, high speed internet, ipods, DVDs, CDs or cable TV were as yet unknown and a pet theme of the underground was imagining a future society, envisioning people wearing plastic space suits, having metal limbs, or beaming each other from one city to the next, not realizing how fast technological development would escalate in the coming years.

The discipline in which electronic know-how became most apparent was music, and with it came the birth of a new style that influenced Berlin's next generation significantly.

Dr. Motte

Matthias Roeingh was born in Berlin, Spandau, an outlying area that had originally been a town of its own and, due to the Cold War, was part of the British sector until 1990. Its inhabitants consisted mainly of working-class families with a strong stubborn streak and modest means of survival. Matthias, nicknamed Motte, grew up with his single mother, an active, inquisitive woman, who was always interested in exposing him to an array of culture to broaden his mind, as far as was possible within her financial means.

Motte was lively from the start, loving music, bright clothes, and clubs. Initiating parties or experimental movements was his main goal and he set about organizing events and founding bands at a young age. After going through training in cement construction to earn a living and support his mother, he decided that a musician's life would be more appropriate for him and moved to Berlin Kreuzberg. There he worked in bars for a couple of years financing his career, inaugurated by performing in two bands: the Toten Piloten (1981–1984) and DPA (Deutsch-Polnische Aggression). Together with DPA he was one of the founding members of the Geniale Dilletanten movement. Tired of constant money problems he decided to open a club and the Turbine Rosenheim was quickly inaugurated after finding three like-minded friends.

Never one to be satisfied with day-to-day repetition, Motte became a versatile DJ, playing various styles of music in clubs all over the city. In those days DJs did not have the artistic recognition they do today, in fact a DJ was considered more of a craftsman or mechanic and was paid accordingly, seven Deutschmarks an hour, the equivalent of about three or four dollars.

Motte usually earned 110 Deutschmarks per performance; depending on how many hours he could hold up—Berlin nights lasting as long as five days. The work was grueling, some of the DJ booths so small he couldn't stand upright, frequently hidden behind the bar with no contact to the crowd and hardly a breath of air. To keep his enthusiasm he decided to initiate parties and DJ battles, curious to hear what his colleagues were playing, organizing parties in which DJs were announced as the main act, with no live bands performing. This was the beginning of a new culture in Berlin and with the emergence of techno his profession became a pathway to internationally acclaimed stardom.

We became a couple soon after our initial meeting, and moved into a cheap two-bedroom apartment on Lindenstrasse, overlooking the Berlin Wall, calling the area "world's end." With a watchtower staring into the kitchen and bathroom windows, East German border patrolmen controlling our movements with binoculars at all hours of the day, the atmosphere was apocalyptic. While designing my costumes and cutting patterns I could observe them speaking, eating and drinking, making phone calls, and leaving on regular rounds of the minefields with their watchdogs, a surreal setting silhouetted behind my sewing machine, influencing my color and design decisions.

In the distance an East German kindergarten could be seen, and the sound of children's laughter floated across the short distance in a ghostly manner, sending shivers up my spine regularly, making me feel as though I were a medium able to see two opposing worlds at the same time.

Our apartment was filled with books, costumes, old record players, a collection of rotting cheese and sausages in test tubes (Motte was examining the concept of decay), some of my father's paintings, Motte's three thousand records, and boxes of his self-recorded tapes. We had two spotted cats, Mickey and Minnie, a black leather sofa and a blue Turkish rug, in other words, we inhabited a typical Kreuzberg apartment of the 1980s. Besides working at home, composing music and designing costumes, we spent our time working in clubs, organizing fashion shows, early hip-hop events, 1970s disco dances, masquerades, some of first club events in town to play acid jazz, then acid house and techno music. This development within our projects was mainly due to Motte's unquenchable thirst for new sounds.

In 1988 he repeatedly complained of being bored by the music scene in Berlin, a mix of rock, early hip-hop, punk, New Wave, and leftover 1970s soul. He listened to hundreds of records sent to him by record companies until finally he felt a faint reverberation echoing over England's horizon. Newspaper stories about wild "raves," the "Summer of Love," police raids, forbidden events, kids taking ecstasy and above all a music form that was portrayed as the new avant-garde caught his curiosity and we decided to fly to London to visit an acid house club, an outing that was to change our lives and Berlin's music scene.

It was Motte's first airplane flight and we embarked excitedly, not knowing he would travel the world extensively in the future, presenting exactly what he was to discover on this first trip. After having arrived we made our way to a cheap Catholic nunnery on the outskirts of London recommended by my mother. The old building was surrounded by a lofty, impenetrable stone wall covered with ivy and bird nests. Its entrance, an intricately welded gate, held a loud bell, announcing visitors to the gatekeeper.

Not wanting to miss out on the food we dined with the nuns, politely bowing our heads to their prayer, eating their homemade bread hungrily, but when evening arrived we dressed up. My hair was carrot red at the time with ringlet extensions, and I was attired in my favorite look: bunched-up checkered skirts with suspenders and heavy boots. Motte preferred 1970s retro shirts and odd-looking ties. In this fashion we snuck over the thick stone wall, past the bell, into the abyss of the city's sinful center, anxious to finally meet the sound of the future. As both of us hadn't been to London before, it took us some time to find the club, catching double-decker buses and overpriced illegal cabs, peeping out at Westminster Abbey, the Tower of London, and Big Ben, all the while noticing brightly dressed clubgoers with flowery hairstyles, expertly hopping back and forth between streams of vehicles, listening to pumping rhythms on their walkman and wildly chewing gum while recounting undecipherable anecdotes. A friendly chap with green hair finally helped us find the club we were looking for. After getting through the body check, shaking our heads, not being used to any sort of detainment in Berlin clubs, we found ourselves in a huge factory space packed with hundreds of people dancing. The air was filled with pink smoke, eerily waving arms, and a dense atmosphere of excitement and adrenalin. A mad arrangement of electronic sounds and rhythms hit our ears in a new and violent manner, slightly comparable to early electronic bands in their tonal simplicity but completely different in the way they were put together. Just as punk and the Geniale Dilletanten had deconstructed music to create a new sound in the 1970s and 1980s, this was obviously the subsequent musical upheaval. I was lucky to experience it from its very beginning. I have always cherished moments of change and clashes, enjoying the emergence of new elements, innocent and dynamic, burning meteorites flung into further spheres, blazing their course vehemently until the span of time extinguishes them into cold stone. This was the feel of that memorable night in London. We stood, dumbfounded, listening and experiencing the dawn of a new era.

Not only the sound had developed, but the fashion, the colors—everything was brighter, more flamboyant, and obviously synthetic. Punk had revolutionized hair colors and styles, here they were suddenly being used in a freshly humorous, cheeky, more playful mode. In comparison to the explicit political background of music styles before, this seemed to have a different attitude of pure, hedonistic pleasure. The bright creatures were kissing and fondling each other in corners of the hall, even on the dance floor. Drinking didn't seem to be the cause of this intimacy and in spite of the signs prohibiting drug use posted on almost all the walls, people were taking whiffs out of small plastic bottles, snorting powder in the bathrooms, and obviously taking pills on the dance floor. Everybody was very friendly, smiling, answering questions in a helpful manner, not pushing or shoving and obviously having fun. The musical energy and cockiness was similar to early punk music, the harmony and friendliness closer to the hippie movement, the drugs to rock 'n' roll.

As soon as we got back to Berlin, Motte told his club co-owners that he was now going to organize weekly acid parties and needed a fog machine. His associates refused, not understanding the music and not liking it. They decided that Motte could rent time in his own club on Fridays and organize parties at his own risk. Motte agreed and we set about printing invitations, handing out about three hundred yellow leaflets with smiley faces throughout Berlin and calling all of our friends, telling them about the new music we had heard and inviting them to come and listen to the latest records Motte had purchased in England.

Curiosity never killed the cat—hundreds came and the parties were a huge success.

We used so much smoke the neighbors frequently called the fire brigade, worried that the building was burning down. The brave men would slowly file into the smoke-filled room with huge hats and rubber clothing protecting their bodies, pulling their lengthy fire hose, only to realize that again there was no fire but merely dancing people, enthusiastically screaming "more smoke" and "Aceeeed." Shaking their heads they would set about leaving again. We would watch the slow motion apparition time after time from the bar, waving goodbye before going back to work. The dancing lasted for days, a thrashing frenzy growing with every passing hour, the music wild but monotonous, flinging the guests into a rhythmical loop, losing their sense of time and reason. This music attracted everyone interested in musical revolution. One of the first guests was WestBam, a local DJ and experienced raver, immediately understanding the groundbreaking momentum. WestBam and his company Low Spirit would become the most profitable German "techno factory" in the nineties, releasing one hit after another and organizing Mayday, a mammoth rave in enormous sites all over the country with thousands of participants.

Motte organized acid house parties in his club for about a year. He had finally found music capable of expressing his innermost feelings, with an accompanying lifestyle.

For him life was a celebration and music its communication, this new "techno music" was what he had been waiting for all of his life and he wanted to share the experience with everybody. "We are so much happier than the sad, gray people scuttling down the grimy Berlin alleyways with typical German scowls on their faces, let's have some fun and a revolution, out in the open, in the middle of the street, I'm tired of hiding in broken down, mud-riddled basements." Of course, being a Berliner, he also enjoyed the idea of shocking people, confronting *Hausfrauen* out on their regular Saturday afternoon shopping sprees, and decided to organize a demonstration, a parade-demonstration advocating music, freedom of thought, and joyous festivity and decided to do it in the most obvious and anti-underground place in the city, the Kurfürstendamm, the main shopping street of West Berlin.

He called it the "Love Parade."

It was born one Sunday morning in our small kitchen in the Lindenstrasse. Motte had been DJ-ing at the Krik until 8 a.m. and while taking a short cigarette break outside with WestBam, came up with the idea of how easy it would be to organize a music parade. Back home Motte woke me up immediately, ready to start realizing the scheme and asking me to help him convince people to participate. Appreciating any clash of ideas or cultures, always interested in integrating visual aspects to music projects, and having a knack for organizing, I was easily convinced. Obviously we didn't have any money except for the small fees we were earning in clubs, so it meant asking for financial support, contacting companies and sponsors. After getting out of bed and having a coffee I started calling friends, telling them about our project, trying to convince them to play a part. It wasn't easy—the idea of walking down the Ku'damm on a Saturday afternoon, dressed up in colorful costumes and playing music that was just getting popular, in front of the black-suited existentialist crowd of the 1980s took guts, but a new epoch had arrived. Everybody could feel the restlessness in the air, old rules weren't enough anymore, years of introverted abstract thoughts and shapes had made brilliant colors and fake flowers interesting again. We started working on renting a truck for the sound system, contacting friends to help with the organization, legally announcing the parade to the police, printing posters and leaflets, and planning an after-hour bash. Nobody except for a couple of small local stores and friends really wanted to invest in the idea so we ended up financing it mainly by ourselves.

The first Love Parade was true anarchy: with a small truck, a record player and crowds of policemen protecting us from who knows what, we managed to traumatize the whole city. I was doing a lot of flowery fashion for performers during that period, my latest collection being vibrantly colored rococo costumes mixed with street-wear accessories, so for the parade I decorated friends in dazzling costumes covered with roses and appliqués, distributing platform shoes from a local shoe store. I also asked Fiona Bennett, a young hat designer, to bring some of her pieces and Christa Raspe, another designer friend, to wear her engraved metal shields and tank suits. Although most of the first participants were too embarrassed to wear colorful costumes on top of dancing down the street, the vivid apparitions of the different designers stuck in their mind.

For the next three years I continued styling different parts of the parade, designing T-shirts for techno clubs, sewing tight leather corsages, stretchy leggings with black shoelaces going up to the belts, fur bags with white leather appliqués, all combined with strangely formed sunglasses, hot-glued with jewels.

Throughout the afternoon of that first parade it rained and stormed, drenching the partakers continuously, but nobody really noticed. After the initial bashfulness of being stared at had been overcome, we were too busy moving and dancing down the street.

Today, now that similar dance parades and street spectacles have become common, it may be difficult to imagine what a scandal the Love Parade was back then.

Berliners, housewives, and underground avantgardists alike stood on the sidewalk with dropping jaws, shopping bags and appointments forgotten, leaning against light posts, between cars, not believing their eyes. It had been customary to be seriously meaningful, intellectually avant-garde, politically and culturally highly informed, or dramatically drug addicted in Berlin. And now, suddenly, brightly colored people of all sexes were screaming, "Let's have fun!" and the city stood speechless. With the force of a hurricane the parade publicized itself, becoming a phenomenon and before long one-and-a-half million people danced to the music. Newspapers, television companies, and politicians went wild, publishing critical essays on "Why do teenagers dye their hair green and go to the Love Parade—is this our next generation...?", " Is there a coherency to fascist demonstrations in the 1930s and a million teenagers dancing around the Siegessäule in the nineties...?", "Does techno music make brains shrink?" or "Peace loving generation comparable to Woodstock."

Berlin earned millions thanks to the Love Parade, finally having something to attract thousands of fun-loving young tourists, spending much more money in clubs, bars, hotels, and stores than those who went to see the somber historic landmarks. In the first year club owners did not immediately understand what was going on but after witnessing the crowds on the street and in the overflowing UFO club, which presented the "after-parade party," they quickly recognized the potential of our enterprise and registered their own trucks to participate the following year. Organizing parties to cash in on the fun, realizing that they could earn enough during the Love Parade weekend to finance their clubs throughout most of the year, a dream had come true. Soon after, the city began using the parade for their purposes and the event became a commercialized product, turning the underground scene against the procession and proclaiming it a sellout. Alternative parades popped up everywhere: the Fuck Parade, the Shit Parade, the Hanf Parade, the Sex Parade, the Schlager Parade, and the 1990s epidemic of parading spread throughout not only Germany but also all of Europe.

Throughout years of controversy, self-made millionaires and a constant tug of war between politics, finances, and ideals, the Love Parade became a blatant tourist attraction, losing its impact and initial innocence, but Motte never stopped believing in the combination of dancing and promoting peace. Even long after I had stopped participating and was singing in a hip-hop band, we would originate projects within the event, promoting the idea that art and music can have a social influence.

In 1997 I asked him if he would be interested in resurrecting his original stance by organizing a charity art event for an institution called Nordoff-Robbins, an conglomerate that uses music therapy to help mentally disabled children and stroke victims, via the Love Parade's notoriety and financial possibilities. Dr. Motte, as

Matthias called himself in the meantime, was all for it. We made a list of propositions and held a speech in front of the parade's committee, successfully receiving a yes and the backing needed. I set about asking twenty well-known Berlin artists, musicians, actors, and performers to paint pictures on public billboards three by four meters long on a busy street in the middle of Berlin, envisioning a street filled with art instead of advertisements, promoting something more than just products.

Not wanting to be engulfed by the parade's masses we decided to stage the event one day before, ensuring early tourists and Berliners the possibility of seeing the performance in peace.

On the morning of our "Brave New World" project the sun shone brilliantly, a surprise after weeks of depressing, never-ending rain, and by noon the billboards were being colorfully adorned with visual interpretations of what Aldous Huxley's story could mean for Berlin and how a commercial lobotomy of the city would look.

Strolling down the sidewalk, Inga Humpe of the hugely successful pop band 2raumwohnung, Jim Avignon, the initiator of U-Kunst, and Thierry Noir, the famous French wall painter, could be seen diligently working next to Lindy Annis, an American performance artist drawing black-and-white comic squares, carefully swinging her newborn child in a scarf around her neck, while Ben Becker, a Berlin actor, used his hands to spread the paint, politely doing interviews with Motte, whom he had just met. The twenty artists worked, laughed, and spoke to approaching friends, taking a break to look at each other's paintings respectfully introducing themselves without any sense of competition or distrust. Peacefully interacting in spite of very different tastes, lifestyles, and beliefs, they represented our original Love Parade aphorism of spreading peace through music and art perfectly. By observing Dead Chickens' artist, Breeda C.C., who came from a background of controversial Dada philosophy, always out to provoke, gluing monster collages onto the white-washed advertising board, or Wee Flowers, an artist known for her happy 1970s pop technique, pasting glitter briskly onto the wood next to the Tulip Enterprise, or a gay Dutch couple, printing pissing mannequins amid techno symbolism, the curious onlookers could witness Berlin's cultural magnitude, experiencing the coexistence and appreciation of many different elements within one community, evidence that diverging tastes produce versatile, inspiring horizons in contrast to Huxley's "new world," which promoted mass similarity, very similar to what our fashion and lifestyle industries try to achieve today.

Individuality is vitally important. Human beings need to be able to express themselves to be happy. It has been proven in psychoanalysis that distinct uniqueness in a person or relationship provides security and durability because it allows one to tailor one's life to one's own needs. Blindly following a mass-produced dictum, trying to squeeze millions of different shapes and colors into one form, can only result in unhappiness and neuroses for most. The question and challenge for all of us is how to achieve this peacefully and without anarchic chaos.

By initiating this event we had explored the possibilities of how to do this in the realm of art, one known for a high level of disorder in general. The experiment of having one theme in which very different visions of reality could be expressed within set boundaries, in an atmosphere of mutual respect and appreciation, proved successful from the very start.

After everybody had worked for hours and the billboards were covered with the first layers of drying paint, colleagues began serving homemade sandwich rolls to the performers and growing audience. Cake and cookies popped up, water was distributed and Radio Berlin, one of the first Cheap Art galleries in the city, sold "Hemingways," sweet, orangey cocktails in small tumblers, to celebrate the day.

DJs took turns on the small turntable placed on a cardboard fruit box, presenting various records, and children danced to dub or easy listening, twirling lazily in the afternoon sun. Curious pedestrians, friends, tourists, Love Parade followers and other artists had gathered with people hanging out on the street, which had been cleared of cars, watching the artists at work, commenting on their themes, making jokes, speaking to journalists and getting to know DJs.

By evening we had finished the compositions and put together a small "Art Parade," carrying the billboards in a long row to the nearby academy with storage space.

The silhouette of the huge canvases quietly moving along the darkening sky turned into a silhouette, a collective recollection of an unforgettable day. While helping to gather paintbrushes I accidentally ran into a stop sign, cutting open my eyebrow and giving my brain a good dose of concussion. After making sure that the art was safely stored in a locked room I was put to bed in the Hotel Adlon next to Brandenburg Gate, and continued watching the Love Parade on television with an ice pack on my forehead.

Motte and I had been booked rooms in the deluxe institution for the event by the parade's committee, giving him the possibility of moving around quickly in the overflowing city, rushing from interview to interview on a motorcycle, DJ-ing in different venues and hurrying back to the Siegessäule to make the closing Love Parade speech.

It was odd lying in the clean, starched sheets, holding the cold package to my face and watching the parade on TV, its noise concurrently throbbing through my window. Experiencing the event as a mirrored virtuality was the interesting completion of this event in my life. Watching the many similarly dressed thousands of participants, dancing to the same repetitive beats, seemed eerie after having launched our small alternative version. What had started as a parade of individuality had become a mass march of replicas. Aldous Huxley seemed to smile knowingly at me from above.

I never went to the Love Parade again.

A week later I was back on my feet, working in my small studio space, making phone calls and sending out information.

A large museum in the south of Germany, the Staatsgalerie Stuttgart had agreed to host the Love Parade charity event in their main hall, helping us organize the project by sending out official invitations and press releases. We rented a small truck in Berlin, covered the billboard canvases with bubble wrap and one of the artists, Kai Teichert, who was scared of flying, drove the seven hundred kilometers down to Stuttgart.

Insuring the art during the exhibition would have been too expensive, so the museum invited the artists to protect the art themselves, covering their travel and hotel costs.

When Kai arrived in Stuttgart, pulling up in front of the museum's back entrance, the other artists had already arrived. Word of the appearance spread quickly through the museum and different curators gathered in front of the door, having heard of our unconventional method of transportation, and watched incredulously as we pulled out one billboard after another, merely covered with a thin sheet of bubble plastic, and carried them inside.

We tiptoed through their storage rooms, balancing our vast packages past work by Picasso, Anselm Kiefer, and Gerhard Richter, hardly daring to breathe, an unforgettable moment.

In order to be able to present our work in depth we had agreed with the museum to show an additional small collection of art next to the billboards and spent the day unpacking boxes, carefully hanging objects on movable walls. In the evening when everything had been arranged and the room was starting to relax happily, a curator from the Modern Art department suddenly entered, loudly calling out to a group of admirers behind her, "Well, let's take a look at the Berlin Underground crap and then go home." The heels of her designer shoes clicked loudly as she arrogantly walked towards our assemblage. Being used to this kind of feedback and devaluation from academic institutions, none of the underground artists reacted, instead they merely watched her move through the room quietly.

After inspecting the first pieces, frowning as she bent towards the art, her expression changed, obviously charmed by DAG's jaunty, unconventional rhythm paintings, Jim Avignon's cardboard drawings, and Kai Teichert's impressive clay busts, and she loudly asked, "And how much would it cost if I bought two of these?"

After buying a couple of pieces for the museum and even more for herself, everybody was deliriously happy, our enterprise had already born rich fruit and we went to our hotel rooms to change. By the time the museum doors opened, an eclectic mix of artists, collectors, Dr. Motte fans, and rich socialites had gathered in front of the entrance, curious to witness the event within. Elegantly dressed women in evening gowns, men in tuxedos, and artists in fur costumes could be seen mingling among the rows of chairs when Ben Becker began conducting the sale, in synchrony with a professional auctioneer. Ignoring the initial wariness of the prudent Swabians, the two dissimilar merchants managed to seduce the audience into buying all of the billboards, cracking jokes, spilling inside information on the artists, their biographies, and facts about the therapeutic institution, resulting in a donation of 40,000 DM to Nordoff-Robbins.

Encouraged by the success of using the Love Parade's promotional power for a good cause and helping to support a positive foundation, Motte and I initiated one more charity event the year after, in 1998. This time we invited international artists to participate, specifically from other countries that had a Love Parade of their own: England, Austria, Japan and Israel. Due to not having the financial means of covering travel costs, we could not invite the artists themselves to participate, simply asking them to donate pieces of art. The response was overwhelming. Within weeks our office was crowded with elaborately packaged canvases, boxes, and bulky parcels from all over the world, accompanied by letters expressing support. The auction took place in a reputable gallery, the Haus am Lützowplatz, and was held simultaneously on the Love Parade website. Realizing that the internet was becoming a huge means of communication, we were curious to see if a supportive community could be created on this virtual pedestal, interested as we were in discovering new realms of exchange. Three internet designers sat for days figuring out the logistics, trying to make the site look and operate as efficiently as possible. Although the parade's committee had agreed to finance the project, their interest was marginal and as with a neglected child it became rebellious. While working out virtual complications, the hype of our project had attracted destructive characters as well as supportive ones, and the expensive, rented computers were stolen from under our noses, throwing everything into a chaos of burglary, confused emails, and police. Shocked by the unwelcome intrusion, our small group of optimistic workers dealt with the insurance companies, computer programmers, and distraught curators but the atmosphere of positivity had been permanently undermined. After a packed opening and many fascinated internet viewers, every piece of donated art had been sold, giving us the possibility of financially assisting Nordoff-Robbins with another large sum of money.

But the financial result had only been a small part of what we were trying to achieve. The response of the artists, the input of the gallery, and working together with Motte had been another inspiring and moving experience, but the fact that none of the Love Parade associates had come to see the show clearly portrayed a lack of interest. Having learned that out-of-the-ordinary results can only be achieved by an honest, in-depth commitment on the part of all participants, I decided to find institutions whose aspirations were clearly within social and cultural realms instead of consisting of mere commercial interests and said a final goodbye to the parade, giving up on turning it into a broader platform.

Motte continued performing as a DJ, traveling the world, became internationally known and participated in many charity projects. The parade's new profit-making sponsors mocked our original ideals, and cooperation became difficult, leading to uncomfortable clashes, and finally resulting in his resignation. It was a difficult step to take, since the Love Parade had been our child, but it had turned into a ghost, empty of meaning and seduced by uninspired commercialism.

Watching Motte come to terms with this and starting new collaborations with unknown artists instead of becoming bitter was touching, demonstrating an acceptance of change and evolution, staying true to his Berliner heritage of not bowing to conventional standards, even after having tasted the addictive sweetness of international fame, financial gain, and the power of success.

1989

They slid to a stop in front of the first border control station. Not a soul could be seen in the thick, billowing snow, the wind whistling ominously amid low metal buildings.

"You think we can just drive through?"

"I don't know ... let's wait for a couple of minutes."

The checkpoint remained silent. Pictures seen the day before reemerged in front of her eyes, transforming the quiet pathway into a labyrinth of screaming masses, waving flags, crying children, and crowded streets filled with pastel colored Trabis. The Trabant is an automobile that was produced by former East German auto maker VEB Sachsenring Automobilwerke Zwickau in Saxony. It was the most common vehicle in East Germany, and was also exported to countries both inside and outside the communist bloc.

"The Berlin Wall has fallen." Headline news covering all channels with excited reporters standing among cheering housewives and drunken bus drivers, her boyfriend calling, sobbing "it's over," friends laughing wildly over the phone then suddenly hanging up, the models and designers huddled in front of the television, listening speechlessly, Austria's mountain landscape in the background.

"I think we can go on, nobody's here."

The frosty landscape reappeared as they apprehensively crawled through the first border crossing, accustomed to unfriendly patrol guards running out and screaming commands.

"How can they have just disappeared in such a short time?"

"Dunno, it's great not having to wait for hours though."

"Yeah."

Berlin's lights slowly came into view, fog disintegrating their steady shine into soft, glittering tear drops.

"Where is everybody?"

The throbbing city had disappeared, frozen shadows revealing dim lanterns, illuminated, mud-covered sidewalks, trash containers filled with overflowing garbage and cars wildly parked on curbs and in alleys.

"I guess everybody's sleeping off their hangover."

"Well, it is pretty early, they probably celebrated for hours, I'm pretty knocked out myself."

"Yeah, it was a long drive, I'm glad to be home."

"Hmmm, home? I wonder, will it ever again be the same as the place we left just last week?"

The Fall of the Berlin Wall

During my first years in Berlin I spent countless hours in front of my kitchen window, gazing onto the barren landscape surrounding my apartment building, contemplating the cement snake cutting through the city's districts, self-righteously splitting buildings, families, and lifestyles that had previously been one. It consisted of two parallel constructions, one that passed in front of my door, leaving only a small space through which to enter the hallway, the other about one hundred meters behind it, coiled in the same constructed rhythm, both topped with barbed wire, isolating a strip of muddy land in their midst, home of countless watchtowers. The fact of being in the midst of an enclosed country never lost its bizarre impact, forever confronting onlookers with the harsh reality of political terror and confinement. Newspaper articles ceaselessly described frantic East Germans trying to escape by arranging unimaginable getaway routes, visiting forgotten relatives in the West or paying for a marriage. It was an inexhaustible confrontation comparable to the perpetual fear on New York's streets in 1980, where the dread of holdups, rape, or murder was a disquiet I had grown up with and was used to, almost appreciating its perpetual alarm, preferring to be faced with ruthless realities instead of rocking myself to lullabies and denying anguish in a safe middleclass haven, a common experience for middleclass teens in the Western world.

In Berlin the poignancy of sadness and despair constantly touched all of us on either side of the Wall, casting a shadow over our existence. This melancholy was an ingredient of everyday life, Germany still rent by a common sense of guilt. Berlin had stayed a postwar division, a city speckled with cavities, a desolate wasteland, full of architectural ruins and industrial debris, a monument of the past, apprehended in the petrifying position of being split into four districts of different nationalities to ensure neutrality, sternly reminded of its past crimes and terrible sins.

As an American it was possible to meet other artists while visiting the East, smuggling art supplies, magazines, and other desired objects through Checkpoint Charlie. Collective projects were more difficult to realize because of the quarantine, regardless of friendships formed and interaction initiated. In East Berlin people were mainly committed to surviving under the circumstances, trying to deal with disinformation, malnutrition, and the Stasi. In West Berlin, a city filled with defiant housewives, poor artists and men fleeing the army, most people were concerned with either just getting by or deconstructing the past to be able to find a future. In comparison to comfortable German villages or wealthy cities like Hamburg or Munich, Berlin was a vessel overflowing with dirt, drugs, suicides, fires, and controversy, a haven for politically minded youth or questioning individuals. I thought it was the most beautiful city in the world, but my father was shocked when he came to visit, gazing at the crumbling postwar architecture and sparse department-store window decorations, exclaiming how ugly everything was. I tried explaining the beauty I saw within the destruction, a space for new possibilities. He said I was crazy and should come back to New York. I refused, having met far too many people I felt close to, in fact wishing that I had made my move even earlier to have experienced the very beginnings of my favorite phenomenon, the Geniale Dilletanten.

This group of musicians and artists had celebrated being amateurs since the early 1980s, boycotting any form of academic education. Not interested in learning how to function for a preconceived world, they insisted on inventing original forms of art by deconstructing and recreating instruments, sounds, forms, and language. Einstürzende Neubauten, Sprung aus den Wolken, Mark Reeder, Frieder Butzman, Gudrun Gut, Leben und Arbeiten, Beate Bartel, and Die Tödliche Doris belonged to the initial group. Most of the participants prided themselves on being avid readers, writers, painters, or designers besides composing music, deciding on what they considered trustworthy and believable, creating a universe they felt comfortable in, using the leftover debris lying around in their city to give birth to a stubborn, innovative consciousness and way of life.

This was the atmosphere that prevailed throughout the eighties, a mirror of my own estrangement to common attributes, welcoming me to display talents otherwise scorned or misunderstood. When the political situation started crumbling in 1989 everybody held their breath, not daring to believe that this long occupation could be over, not yet realizing that this incomparable anarchic and cut-off semblance of a city would disappear, as quickly and as completely as the Wall. When the Iron Curtain fell it was the end of an era, the end of the petrified, incomparable timelessness that had reigned since the war, the end of depressing black-and-white GDR television shows, the end of checkpoints and scary body searches at the border, the end of the Cold War.

It was also the end of "sitting in the same boat." Capitalism with its insatiable entrepreneurs crossed the city's threshold within weeks after the political upheaval. Self-assured grins introduced a new mandatory law of survival: "each to his own," and welcomed us into the new Cold War of commerce, erecting a wall as relentless as the one before, but this time invisible.

Surprisingly I was not in Berlin on the celebrated weekend of the Wall's collapse. Sometime before the historical occurrence I had moved my sewing machine into a large studio belonging to the hat maker Fiona Bennet. The dark basement space located on Kreuzbergstrasse, around the corner of one of Berlin's few hills, the "Kreuzberg," was situated underneath an alternative theater, large enough for both of us to move around in, exhibit our designs, and store patterns or new fabrics.

I had met Fiona during a fashion show in the parking lot of the KADEWE, a luxurious department store overflowing with exotic foods, expensive make-up, jewelry, one-of-a-kind designer handbags from Paris, and detailed window decorations. Its multistory garage had been closed for the day, filled with installations of bizarre objects, phosphorus lamps, intricate metal drawings and sculpture, furniture forged from industrial residue and jagged jewelry, highlighting the dark shadows produced.

I had been invited to participate with a procession of silk brocade gowns and layered hats, taking Motte along as my main model, heavily powdered, wearing a wig and stoically pounding a drum. With ashen faces and Oliver Twist-like movements my small group marched up and down the winding runways of the parking lots, passing interested onlookers, hidden exhibitions, and flickering lights, the steady beat echoing eerily against cement walls and metal signs. After my défilé had strutted for hours I released them from their responsibilities and wandered through the booths, watching presentations, and ended up in front of a high pedestal showcasing Fiona's designs. She was obviously a perfectionist, elegance not only visible in her intricate headwear but also in the way she presented herself. Reminiscent of Coco Chanel, flitting back and forth, adjusting hats, her flirtatious, erotic manner was enhanced by dark, straight hair, a curvaceous figure, and exquisitely penciled eyebrows. Appreciative admirers could be seen helping her carry the smallest hatbox backstage and her gorgeous models obviously imitated her slow, laidback femininity onstage, followed her every movement with envious delight and fluttering lashes. To witness Fiona was like catching a whiff of expensive, seductive perfume floating by on a summer's night, an elegance not found often in Berlin.

We met behind the scenes after the show, drinking champagne, gossiping about common preferences, curiously acknowledging a mutual attraction.

In comparison to her carefully designed, precise collections I was an anarchic whirlwind, churning out pattern after pattern, disregarding practical issues of wearability or economic values, solely interested in expressing emotions. This amused Fiona, who commented on the speed with which I could cut a pattern in comparison to her slowly stitched craftsmanship. But in spite of her regal elegance and perfect style, Fiona was nonetheless a real Berliner and appreciated individuality, contradiction, scandal, and surrealism as deeply as myself, so after doing a couple of photo shoots and realizing how well we got on we decided to combine our talents and create a different sort of atelier. Moving into the cellar she was occupying with her then-boyfriend Ralph Meiling, I set up my sewing machine in a corner, draping my latest designs onto two figurines next to a bizarre hat stand one of our friends had made for Fiona, a box filled with cement heads that could be turned on to bob up and down. We settled down to work, chatting lightly while preparing one show after another. Our enterprise attracted the attention of many and we participated in countless fashion shows, installations, and fashion shoots, considered to be one of the most promising fashion collaborations in Berlin. A trip to Austria was the result of this partnership.

Lisa D., a knitwear designer, originally from Graz, keen on becoming part of our team, had told us stories of soirées in her apartment, presenting innovative dresses to the readings or recitations of her husband. She proposed doing something together with us in her hometown, inviting us to Graz. As Fiona and I had been chosen to participate in the Vienna fashion fair we decided to combine all elements and began asking models to come along, inviting Judith Förster, another Berlin knitwear designer, to participate, finalizing our new female musketeers collaboration.

To test the compatibility of our different design styles, we initiated an exhibition of our newest collections in a small fashion gallery in Berlin. Lisa sent us her gowns from Austria, not being able to come herself. Envisioning an installation rather than a show, Fiona, Judith, and I spent days on the lighting and draping of fabric, perfuming the floors by covering them with lavender, rearranging the display dummies for days. Finally it was time for the opening and exhausted we watched the crowds move in, wandering from one spotlit garment to the next, discussing the ideas, sniffing the perfume. After the delighted crowd had praised the results in highest terms, we were convinced we should restage the endeavor in Graz. I was happy to be collaborating with such a promising group and prepared my designs at breakneck speed, working double shifts at night to earn enough money for the upcoming trip.

Vienna is a beautifully morbid place. I remember a hot, sweaty bar with squeaky spiral stairs leading downwards into a subterranean floor, with walls covered by long forgotten photos, worn-out sketches, faded pastel paintings, and torn notepads left by distressed writers and despondent philosophers as payment for a late beer or salty sausage.

Fine dust, the smell of leather, tobacco, and sweat held every object in the room firmly embraced. The bartender/owner, a spectacled, obese man, sang operas when asked for a drink. Verdi, Wagner, Puccini, his repertoire was limitless. As the night progressed his concertos became thunderous, a nervous vibrato added for effect, making conversation difficult, everybody shouting at the top of their voice and laughing at the madness.

The fashion fair in comparison was the usual ruthless mass market of booths and salespeople competing for potential customers. I hate trade events with their countless onlookers ambling past, consuming mustard-drenched hot dogs, cold beer and bitter coffee, commenting on displays with outbursts of laughter, spluttering, burping, and yelling:

"Hey, Liz look at this! Don't I look cute?" And dirty fingers ruining painstaking work within seconds.

I would usually disappear from my booth and spend time examining other designer clothes to distract myself, leaving more destitute than before, with a stale taste lingering in my heart, wondering if I would ever fit in.

After arriving in Graz, the opulent atmosphere experienced in Vienna disintegrated into provincialism as an unexpected nightmare slowly became apparent. Lisa had organized a waitressing job for me at the annual fair, the Steirischer Herbst, so I would be able to survive, as the tour had swallowed my meager financial means more quickly than I had expected, and although again it meant working double shifts I looked forward to this possibility of meeting interesting authors and earning extra cash. Disappointingly the enterprise turned out to be exhausting, running from one neon lit hallway to the next, collecting empty glasses, comforting depressed authors, mopping up vomit from the night before, and endless further unromantic tasks, resulting in my being late for show rehearsals and not sleeping. After a couple of days I fell ill with a peculiar rash covering my body, pinpricked with nervous pain and ended up lying miserably in bed listening to the designers and models preparing the fashion show. Envious of my friendship with Fiona from the start, the group quickly began mobbing me, their nasty comments audibly wafting into my sick room, complaining that I was not making enough effort and abusing the group's endeavors. I had never been undermined this way before and lay there sadly, helpless prey to the group's whispers and acid comments, disenchanted, hungry, and inert. Ironically it was the first time in years that I had the time to think about my life in general and while watching the bonfire of vanities passing in front of my bedroom door, I gradually came to the conclusion that fashion, with its stylized cattiness and artificial flowers, was not what I had been looking for, as unconventional as it was in Berlin, realizing that my main obsessions had always been music, literature, and art, and that I considered the superficial fashion aspect an accepted but annoying part of the deal. Now I suddenly realized that if the fashion facet were turned into the "accessory," or even dropped altogether I could concentrate on the other areas more freely.

A moment of clarity initiated by pure misery.

After transporting the clothes back to Berlin, being the only girl with a driver's license who couldn't afford a train ticket, I set about packing my belongings into boxes and emptying the studio as quickly as possible, barely noticing the upheaval on the streets. The Wall had fallen two days after our fashion show and the city was full of ecstatic East Berliners roaming the streets, lining up for their first Western money, drinking beer in overflowing bars, speaking to strangers, and buying exotic fruit. Oblivious to the historic events unfolding around me, I pensively transported the fabric, sewing machines, and patterns back to my apartment and sat back to contemplate what to do next. The experience of betrayal had given me the necessary strength to alter the direction of my life and I wondered how the journey would continue.

A Roman artist had organized the party on "die Insel," a small island surrounded by the river Spree. With an arched bridge leading to the venue, the "castle" had been a popular place for unusual concerts or parties during the East Berlin communist regime.

The surrealist, known for his tarot photo sessions, acid experimentation, and black magic inspired installations, had asked her to participate as the main fairy tale figure, performing the transcendence of enlightment in different stages, the first of which was to stand on the castle's balcony overlooking the lake and greeting the arriving guests with a ballad and white feathers.

Having agreed to participate she now stood on the narrow rim, wearing a raven black wig curling down to the ground far below, encased in an antique white ball gown, singing shaky arias in spite of the army of mosquitoes hovering around her, ready to enter her mouth with every tone.

The peculiar, transfixed figure on the castle's balcony, spotlit with bugs and flying insects, wearing a strange black wig and throwing feathers that didn't float down but instead seemed to hover slightly above her head, told the crowd that this event was not going to be an everyday occurrence.

She stood on the balcony for three hours, throwing feathers, waiting for the arrival of a donkey that was to be the next part of the performance and the end of her predicament.

Finally she saw it arriving on the other side of the bridge, a tiny creature obviously unwilling to cross the water. She anxiously watched the owner trying to lure him with carrots, petting his ears, alternatively pushing or pulling, even trying to carry him but nothing worked. The animal repeatedly managed to escape and resettle in the same spot.

Finally the donkey was taken back to his farm.

Not wanting the performance to fail, the director grabbed the donkey cart, ordered her down from the tower and asked two blondes to pull the vehicle.

Precariously positioned in the wooden object, she was led along the island's earthy pathways, waving to an imaginary crowd, the real one having moved to another part of the island where drinks were being sold and music could be heard.

The moon rose and in silence the procession moved on, each participant secretly yearning for its termination, not daring to mention it to the enthusiast Italian walking alongside the cart chanting mystic choruses.

Finally a small forest appeared in which part three of the performance was to be inaugurated, and she was draped onto a cool "tombstone," a stone bench with a guard wearing armor there to protect her. The blondes disappeared quickly, the organizer wandered off into the bushes, leaving her alone with the guard in complete obscurity. The sound of laughter and techno could be heard faintly, magnifying the silence they were in and after a short moment the guard mumbled something about coming right back and disappeared, not to be seen again, leaving her with the occasional bat flying by. While contemplating desertion she heard unexpected footsteps. "Ah," she thought, "somebody has remembered me." The steps stopped and a sudden splash of liquid splattered next to her head.

Snow White jumped up screaming, scaring the pissing innocent out of his mind and ran to the party hall dragging her dress behind her, feathers flying wildly, cursing performance art, and swearing to get at least one bottle of free champagne from her tripping host.

1990–1995

No Man's Land

The fall of the Wall was an event of unimaginable historic import. After the relatively peaceful upheaval, Germany was reunited, families and friends brought together, with twenty thousand East Berliners crossing the opened borders on the 9th of November, 1989, after twenty-eight years of suppression. The strongest symbol of the East/West conflict had collapsed, opening doors for countless future developments within Europe.

The fact that all of this happened without a war, without weapons or bloodshed, is amazing. That the complete structure of a country, the GDR, disappeared without a single house being bombed or tank rolling in, is a fact that should be mentioned more often. Instead of governments considering war and bloodshed as the only solutions, the possibility of change without bloodshed was proved possible. Experiencing the sudden disappearance of a political system and the positive change of not only a city but a country was comparable to being thrown into an anarchic whirlpool, overriding laws and regulations, with cheerful chaos reigning, inhabitants dreamily roaming unknown streets and studying the foreign planet that had been their home.

The Wall had always been a tourist attraction. Millions of people took pictures of the world's largest graffiti canvas and its wooden overviews, offering a bird's eye perspective of the fenced-in country on the other side. Now a new swarm of souvenir hunters arrived, armed with drills and hammers, quickly named "Mauerspechte" (Wall peckers), hammering away at the Wall day and night, collecting small pieces of colorful cement to take home and place on their wardrobes. Living next to the edifice, the constant sound became symbolic of the new times. Strangers demanding electricity for their roto hammers rang my house bell on a regular basis.

Some of the legendary drawings that had been rendered on the rough cement surface would later be auctioned off in Berlin and Monte Carlo, bought by the CIA, the Vatican, the Peace Museum in Caen, France, and the Imperial War Museum of London, saving some of the more beautiful pieces from the just-commencing renovation of the city, which had decided to rid itself of as many mementos as possible, keeping only six small stretches of the Wall as a memorial. The idealistic initiative, "The Eastside Gallery," was one, maintaining a section about one-and-a-third kilometers long of 106 paintings by international artists, making it the largest open-air gallery in the world. Its impressive exhibition of bold art attracts visitors even today. I have ambled past the tourist buses often, happy to see the pictures being admired, remembering the time when they were first created.

During the aftermath Berliners often got lost in the former white spaces of their maps. Landmarks were torn down and entire street blocks vanished. I recall trying to find my regular gym, walking in circles for hours because of three streets having been redirected, their drab apartment buildings gone and a colossal building site shooting out of the ground where an old fountain once stood. Real-estate ownership was a mystery—until, that is, it became apparent that studios, clubs, shops, and apartments could easily be acquired simply by breaking into the empty spaces and putting locks on their doors. Deserted buildings were everywhere: huge factories, forlorn office structures, apartment buildings, crumbling and decrepit churches, spacious lofts with creaking hallways, subway tunnels, bus depots, and entire train stations. Underground clubs and bars were set up at breakneck speed. Vacant hair salons, flower shops, drugstores, and restaurants, left to rot by their former owners, were discovered by enthusiastic party organizers and filled with crates of cheap drinks and installed with video screens, intermingling GDR relics with commercial and technical BRD accomplishments. The opening of these temples was announced by word of mouth, resulting in an atmosphere of secret societies and hushed entrances, code words, and dusty basement dance orgies. It became fashionable to discover especially bizarre spaces to stage happenings, a competition in which dozens of trailblazers outdid each other, effectively turning a city known for its melancholic, heroin-riddled, post-war atmosphere into a throbbing party.

I met the expat Carl Alexander, a black gay man who was born in England, but grew up in the United States, during one of my night shifts. We immediately bonded, enthusiastically discussing rituals, hair extensions, voodoo happenings and art, becoming good friends and collaborators. He modeled for my fashion shows, I served him drinks for free in the clubs I was working at, as is the usual custom for artists, who are always in solidarity with one another.

Although I worked every night of the week, I also made a point of getting up as early as possible in the afternoons to spend the day working on art and taking long walks together with Carl to discover new shops, galleries, or interesting event locations. He had organized theme parties in the USA and his chief goal was to combine out-of-the-ordinary locations with particular costume themes to create surreal atmospheres.

We were mainly attracted by large, abandoned industrial sites, climbing in through the already-broken windows and gazing at deserted, sunlit rooms filled with leftover office books or furniture in awe, wondering why some of them had been abandoned so hurriedly, with the pen still lying next to the log book, the sentence unfinished. Trying to imagine the individual story layered beneath the dust was one of our favorite pastimes. We spent hours sitting in the immense, silent ruins, comfortably smoking cigarettes and drinking water.

The first locality we decided on for a party was the basement of an industrial site so huge we never did discover its borders. The maze of grimy tunnels, tiled shower rooms, rotting stairways leading to deserted cubbyholes filled with mysterious, indecipherable manuscripts, contained multiple trap doors and double windows, some of them sending shivers up our spine. It seemed soundproof and therefore perfectly suited for an underground event. After decorating the space with white tulips and a wooden bar, Carl decided that the theme would be "dress in black and white." Beer was bought, along with some cheap champagne, a small record player was finagled and leaflets were photocopied. We advertised by word of mouth and distributed the cheap invitations everywhere, handing them out in cafés, subway trains, galleries, department stores, bars, and private homes, warning each recipient that they would regret not coming. I spread the news at the clubs I was working at and the amount of people arriving punctually the night of the event was more than we had imagined in our wildest estimations.

Mainly being interested in the artistic aspect of the evening, Carl and I were especially pleased by the effort everybody had put into their appearance, the hours spent combining black and white in an unusual way, which metamorphosed the party into more than just a rave. A fantasy world emerged, blooming within the building's rotting carcass, merging joyous creativity with melancholy ghosts. Our goal was achieved.

We were so delighted we decided to organize another similar event on the roof of the same building, covering its floor with roses, asking the guests to "bring a rose and wear a hat," curious to see what the crowd would come up with. About five hundred people arrived wearing colorful bonnets, boaters, fedoras, and caps, handing us perfumed flowers at the entrance and dancing all night or standing on the roof drinking cheap white wine in the early morning hours, quietly speaking while looking over the sleeping city and watching the sun rise. Word spread and we were told that a well-known party organizer from NY had flown in just to participate, telling everybody back home that it was one of the most amazing evenings she had ever experienced. The parties quickly became too large for us to organize alone, and friends were asked to participate, with people lining up in front of our doors, eager to partake in the adventurous secrecy of underground festivity. Thus with the combined efforts of countless other organizers, Berlin's reputation as a party metropolis grew, attracting thousands of young tourists, boosting the city's meager economy and bringing in money for all. Obviously the business world quickly realized the financial possibilities of our entertainment and sent out trend scouts to figure out the best possible takeover. To prevent this exploitation, many party organizers became professional club owners, officially renting spaces to maintain control, so they could promote non-commercial music and artists they valued instead of bowing to greedy enterprisers and chart music.

Idealistic club managers are not common. As a performer I have experienced the opposite in many towns, most proprietors arguing that due to high rents and many employees they cannot afford to be naïve. The fact that the innovative Berlin clubs would continue to be exceptionally successful, in spite of paying decent fees to unknown performing artists and hardworking bar staff, managing to cover higher rents and costs in spite of the increase of these expenses over the years, proves that it is possible to be idealistic and commercially successful simultaneously and that cutthroat calculation is only due to excessive financial greed.

A good example of this stance was the WMF, known for its innovative music and dependable avant-garde design taste. Its first legendary location was at Potsdamer Platz. This plaza had been the busiest traffic intersection in Europe until it was totally destroyed in World War II, leaving a barren wasteland throughout the Cold War era. The club's entrance was a hole in a large, metal, empty garbage dumpster standing solitarily on this deserted terrain. To reach their destination, the guests had to crawl through the hole and down a precariously steep ladder leading to the narrow, tiled labyrinth of the former public toilet, now throbbing with loud music and pink smoke. The claustrophobic sensation of having to exit the same way one had entered added to the general atmosphere of thrill and adventure, resulted in the guests drinking and dancing for hours to postpone their departure. After finally daring to exit into the early morning sunshine, they would emerge crawling out of the container onto the silent and vacant piece of land, not a sound to be heard from the overflowing underground club below.

I enjoyed the exploratory aspect of these times, it was the eve before reality hit the city and the short span of chaos among the bureaucrats had an astonishing result. Not being confined by the usual regulations the residents took over the responsibility of deciding how to go about doing things and although property was taken over, it was property that had no official owners. It was never damaged, quite the opposite in fact; instead it was carefully renovated and put to use, improving its worth for future landlords, in contrast to moldy ruins left to decay.

Another impressive aspect of the underground was how former East and West Berliners interacted, curiously meeting each other in clubs, forming collaborations in which no hierarchies existed, organizing venues and cultural centers collectively with everybody earning an equal amount of money for the same amount of work. It was only later, when bureaucracy had a better overview of the situation and the usual biased commercial restrictions were put into effect that vandalizing parties got started and right-wing propaganda became popular among clearly neglected East Germans. The epoch of bedlam after the fall of the Wall was one of the last times in which I experienced true comradeship among a large mass of people, with nobody pushing or enviously watching others, curiosity and tolerance reigning strong, with a communal sense of having achieved the impossible and helping each other to acclimatize.

They had discovered the forsaken gas station by chance. Overgrown by wild shrubbery and weeds it stood alone in a deserted part of West Berlin, forgotten by all.

"This is perfect for our next party," they whispered, carefully squeezing through the half-open wooden door into the dark and cool space within. The dirt floor was covered with broken glass and garbage, remains of various bums and overnight visitors, who had obviously slept on the old newspapers carelessly left behind. Discovering a staircase in back they carefully climbed the rotting steps to discover yet another room as large as the former.

"This is perfect, look at the window front, we can actually look out on to the street and watch everybody arrive!"

"Yeah, let's do this one to the max. The theme will be 'everybody wears white' and this time we are going to hang video monitors in every corner of the room, turn it into a real art event. I want this party to go down in history..."

The next couple of days were spent cleaning up the location, sweeping the floors, washing the windows, transporting TV monitors and buying beer. Invitations were by word of mouth only, whispering complicated instructions to friends about meeting at a subway station, to then be picked up by a sentinel who led three or four guests at a time to a distant landmark, to another guide on a bicycle, who stood waiting to bring them to the final, secret destination.

Standing at the window on the first floor, dressed in a white ball gown with pale beige lilacs in her hair, she watched the groups in white costumes arriving furtively, eagerly searching the area with their eyes to discover the hidden vicinity, lighting up with pleasure after having discerned the deserted station.

"People are arriving early," she called to a friend arranging the last glasses on the bar.

"I can't believe how many they are, I think we're going to have to let them come up soon or they'll cause a riot!"

Suddenly the night was lit by sirens and blinking headlights as a line of police trucks came around the corner, ordering everybody to "Stay where you are!" over loudspeakers, screeching to a stop in front of the building. The peaceful white figures that had been waiting in the driveway immediately scattered in small groups, running off in all directions, followed by policemen waving heavy torches and handcuffs. As she stood watching, the area in front of the party zone turned into a military base with people dressed in evening gowns, feather boas, sailors costumes, lacquered shoes, and Marlene Dietrich *polyester pant suits being thrown on the ground, carried into the trucks and interrogated rudely.*

"The police were told by some old lady that we are a religious cult about to make an offering and they will throw mace into the building if we don't all come out immediately."

F. had come running up the stairs, panting and sweating.

"I can't believe this is all happening before the party even started, all the effort gone to waste."

Sadly she climbed down the repaired stairs to find all of the organizers and helpers standing in the dark back part of the lobby whispering and laughing.

"What's going on?"

"Well, we just decided that if they think we are a cult we'd better act like one to get just a little fun out of this disaster," someone whispered back. "We're all going to hold hands and stand in a circle when they come in and shout boo very loudly."

Hearing the muffled voices of policemen coming closer, the twenty friends silently took each other's hands and stood in a circle, listening to the careful tread of heavy boots.

"I can't see anybody."

"Maybe we've got them all."

The front door was thrown open and the figures of three policemen could faintly be seen beyond the strong beam of their flashlights.

"Can you see anything? Oh my God there's more in here, hundreds and they're standing in a circle! This must be the core group."

Immediately the room was filled with uniformed figures carefully marching ahead in lines of seven, slowly inching towards the silent circle.

Bursting out with laughter she yelled, "Boo!" and ran towards the door among the other participants now rushing around wildly, evading cops like in a game of catch.

After having searched all the rooms in vain for dead animals and registering names and addresses, the police disappeared hours later leaving a small group of costumed partygoers despondent on the sidewalk.

"Well, I guess that was the last party we've organized, it's too much effort to get busted that quickly. Let's go to the 90° and celebrate the decline of anarchy."

Nodding thoughtfully they headed off in a new direction.

THE 90°

From the outside, the 90° was nothing spectacular: a square, white one-story building hidden in the curve of a rural neighborhood street, surrounded by shrubs and garbage containers. It consisted of two medium-size rooms and a small back area for storing beer kegs and wine bottles.

Bob Young, an American ex-pat who organized various parties, had rented the space to stop moving around, not realizing the popularity he would achieve in the ensuing years. His main interest was good house music combined with intriguing environments, and he invited artists to create decorations at regular intervals.

Thanks to Berlin being a club-oriented city, this kind of backing and presentation was equivalent to being supported by a curator, helping to develop new ideas and working on promotion until a real gallery or label discovered the artist and took over. Nightlife not only represented entertainment but an invaluable and important hub for many different art forms over the years.

By hiring particularly imaginative artists and musicians to not only work behind his bar but also decorate his club, Bob offered a tempting environment for designers, curators, and collectors from the Charlottenburger high society, a crowd with money. By adding a dash of gay savoir vivre he attracted countless attention-grabbing, extroverted individuals to twirl on the dance floor and become his regulars, initiating outrageous appearances comparable to New York's Studio 54, but on a smaller scale.

Similar to Turbine's homosexual couple Falco and Daniel, Bob enjoyed treating employees as family, organizing cozy dinners in his apartment with elaborate dishes and candlelit music, encouraging everybody to brainstorm, creating a tight-knit loyal community.

His hiring as manager Hille Saul, a beautiful blonde with pale gray eyes, was a stroke of pure genius. Experienced in working for bars and cafés, she took over the mothering. Hille was the one everybody confided in if unhappy or broke, she was also the one that could out-drink or out-party any of the guests, daring them to try and stay up longer than her. Talented in attracting DJs to come and perform for little money, she also convinced introverted, intellectual writers to work the door, thus having an intelligent bouncer choose a high-level crowd. During the early days of post-wall Berlin a waiter could almost have the same status as a pop star. Serving drinks or mixing cocktails in a popular club was considered an honor which only few could achieve, being an artist or musician on the side was almost part of the job requirement, giving the club an "insider" reputation that lasted for years. Multitudes of DJs, artists, designers, and filmmakers started their careers behind the 90° bar, serving drinks, spinning records, or working the cash register.

After Motte left the Turbine, tired of being a club owner, I started working at 90°, enjoying the inventiveness and warmth of the employees. If we weren't planning a new mode of decoration or themed celebration we would hang out together at home, go boating along the Spree or discover new clubs and music together. Johannes Boehnke, an introverted jewelry designer, became my closest friend. Together we gossiped about fashion, design, and necklaces into the early morning hours after working a shift. He helped me finish costumes with meticulous perfection and helpful feedback. The bond has never broken and he has has designed all my jewelry over the years—including my wedding ring.

Besides paying good salaries, 90° was always entertaining. The rooms would fill quickly after the doors opened and while pouring cocktails or beer we heard countless stories of interesting art openings or intriguing premieres. The eclectically dressed crowd came to hear new dance songs, moving passionately to funky beats and cheering to Madonna's "Vogue," which had just been released. Kaspar Kamäleon, a renowned entertainer, commenced "After Hour" raves on Saturday mornings, parties that started at 7 a.m. after the actual club evening was over, and were made up of a group of daintily dressed, music-loving queens jiving and finger snapping well into the afternoon, resplendent in white feather boas, perfect makeup, large clouds of expensive perfume, pink tutus, sparkling glitter, or rhinestone jewelry. Their humorous, outrageous love of beauty shone in every detail.

When techno music took over in the 1990s, pushing aside the lighter house music, the gay look turned more macho, and short crew cut hairstyles and military clothes became popular. But in the late 1980s their look was much more playful and sparkling. Together with Motte, who loved dressing up and dancing to motown or house music, we would often hang out at the homosexual strongholds of SchwuZ or Kumpelnest 2000, twirling on the dance floor with Bev Stroganov, Ades Zabel, Bob Schneider, Petra Krause, Ichgola Androgyn, Püppi Foster-Jenkins, Melitta Sundström, Gérôme Castell, Kaspar Kamäleon, Tima, Lotti Huber, and Poppe, cheering at "Ladies Neid" performances and clapping endlessly during the premiere of the Teufelsberg film production *Drei Drachen vom Grill*, a satire of a popular German TV series about three elderly, proletarian women working in a chip shop.

There was a strong identification among this crowd with the Berlin "Trümmerfrauen" (the rubble women who reconstructed Berlin brick by brick after the war) or the "Hausfrauen" the down-to-earth Berlin housewives—Prussian dominas who did their chores in curlers while smoking cigarettes and admiring their greasy husbands drinking beer and watching soccer games. Instead of trying to impersonate elegant Hollywood divas they preferred speaking in the old-fashioned Berlin dialect, wearing ratty, oddly shaped wigs, gaudy jewelry, and lumpy dresses with torn silk scarves or asymmetrical evening gowns. The queens also enjoyed playing the "Mutti," or the unemployed working girl with broken fingernails. Berliners' rebellious identification with the maladjusted yet again became strikingly apparent.

I became good friends with the beautiful Gérôme Castell. We worked together at various bars, spent long afternoons speaking about gay politics, discrimination, broken hearts, the horrors of HIV, and finding good bargains. Warm-hearted and motherly, with perfectly plucked eyebrows and fake eyelashes, Gérôme gave advice on how to fasten wigs professionally and make your breasts look larger, screaming with joy at every dirty joke thrown his way by incoming guests.

The lesbian scene was as individualistic. Lena Braun, a local kitsch'n'trash sovereign with a long history of gallery curating and event management founded an open space "art installation" known as the Boudoir, after successfully launching the gallery Loulou Lasard in the 1980s. Both environments were known for surreal, glamourous experimentation with plenty of red velvet, feathers, and scandal. On these evenings one could strip, dance, sing, or get a new hairstyle besides flirting with the bar girl or looking at the objects on display. The Boudoir was situated beneath one of my later studios and was one of the first places in which Gudrun and I organized all-girls performances in the 1990s. The lesbian scene was playfully colorful and imaginative, keeping alive the free reign of the dance and performance culture of the Anita Berber tradition, celebrating the female body, accentuating the nonconformism of being a trespasser and proud of it.

The gay crowd of the original 90°, in comparison, was influenced by the many African-American expats who were still enamored with Hollywood, more inclined towards glamorous accessories than trash culture, performing choreographed dance routines perfectly, dancing to the Pet Shop Boys, wearing feather tiaras and expensive designer wear, thus attracting a more distinguished, less politically inclined crowd than other gay clubs.

Things started changing for the 90° after DJ Jay Ray (a bashful, soft-spoken man, with whom I later recorded a couple of songs) discovered hip-hop. He began featuring Rakim, Dr Dre, and other popular rap stars during his set. Hip-hop was just becoming popular in Berlin, and there was no specific place where one could go to hear it. Although quite a few DJs had become interested in the new rhythms, the fact that it was a gangster-oriented, American genre mainly attracted crowds of Turkish gangs, happy to have somebody speaking about issues of prejudice and anger. Word quickly spread that the 90° was playing this music and within weeks the club's crowd completely changed. Instead of feathers and make-up, baggy jeans, greasy hair, and heavy silver chains became de rigueur. Mobs of Turks stood in front of the small entrance, lounging in the street and showing off their muscles, threatening each other with stares, insults, and weapons. There were about fifty different gangs at the time in Berlin, made up of Turks, Croatians,

Russians, or Arabs. Most of them dealt with drugs and crime, usually as an outlet for their discomfort and unease with having to live in a foreign country. A lack of decent job opportunities and unfamiliar cultural norms produced seemingly unbridgeable barriers, forcing the immigrants to develop their own communities and job prospects. But going out and having fun remained a problem. Turkish clubs were nonexistent, since the use of alcohol or mixing among different genders was frowned upon. Most other clubs refused entry to these guests, fearing fights and sexual harassment.

After discovering hip-hop, the American voice of the suppressed and ignored, the Turkish youth in Berlin had a type of music they could identify with. Bands that mixed German lyrics with oriental sounds spoke out against racism and intolerance. Any club that dared to play these songs would immediately have hundreds of young Turks standing in front of their door, causing a ruckus inside and out.

After a couple of weeks it was obvious that not all of the people in line would be able to enter the 90°, and a war resulted to decide which gang would become the "protector" of our club, a situation comparable to West Side Story or Romeo and Juliet—except without the lovers.

I was working as the cashier for Bob, and after about two weeks I had seven bodyguards standing next to me instead of one. The bouncers consisted of an ex-cop taking anabolica, two gang leaders of opposing groups that could give us insight into their mentality, a kick boxer, our club manager, the brother of one of the gang leaders (who was killed during the ensuring riots), and our original bouncer, a Swiss philosopher and intellectual. My task was to collect the entrance fee and all weapons. Soon I had a mountain of knives, guns, and knuckle rings piling up next to forgotten umbrellas and boas from former times, and had become an expert on different brands of mace. The situation was a nightmare. We had hooligans lined up in front of the club every weekend. Dogs barked and men fought, threatening to shoot, club, or knife each other to death. Women and drag queens completely disappeared from our vicinity; any attempt to invite them was met by horrified grimaces. Raids were constant. I grew accustomed to policemen rushing in and Turkish gangs rushing out right in front of my desk.

Then I was attacked in the bathroom. Six Turks kicked down the door and tried to grab my breasts and the cash box. Johannes exploded a bottle of champagne into the crowd, grabbed the register from my frozen hands, and screamed, "Follow me to the back!" After that the club closed.

We decided to restructure the program and play different music. It took almost six months to get the original crowd back, but the initial innocence of the club had been permanently destroyed. Bob took the opportunity of renovating the place while it was locked up, adding a modern sound system and professional equipment. He was now interested in earning more money, hiring trendy DJs to attract a commercial crowd in contrast to the previous artistic one. It became a rich kids' playground, with millionaire sons driving up in expensive cars, and celebrities knocking on the door instead of artists and drag queens. The crew had also taken a nasty hit during the Turkish riots and even Hille, complacent and laidback as usual, felt less comfortable. Although a couple of interesting characters would pop up every so often, in general the commercial feeling became dominant. One of the last remarkable encounters was with Marusha, a soon-to-be important part of the multifaceted Low Spirit family. DJ Dick, WestBam's brother, brought her to the 90° early one morning around 6 a.m., proudly introducing her as his new girlfriend. She had just moved to Berlin and I remember being impressed by her fresh skin and sparkling eyes, which seemed to change their luminance with every flick of her very long, shining, and brown hair. With her natural friendliness and enthusiasm she quickly became a well-known DJ star in Berlin.

After her first smash hit, she catapulted into the role of Techno Queen of Germany.

But in general, beside a few interesting events, the guests had become boring and pompous. They asked for cigars or expensive wine, ignored the decoration, and had little to no interest in inventive music. The general dissatisfaction among the crew grew.

Hille and her boyfriend Andreas Rossmann had been thinking of opening a club of their own for a long time and after finding a suitable space they decided that it was time to open up their own venue and resigned, leaving Bob to run the club on his own for a couple years. After realizing that money alone is not enough, he decided to go back to his roots and manage a gay institution, the GMF. This place was more politically oriented; it was a meeting point for all the different homosexual groups in Berlin, actively participating in gay conferences and demonstrations to minimize prejudice, combining entertainment with serious goals, a combination more suited to Bob's intelligence and wit.

The 90° was sold to new owners who lived off of the club's history for years and continued attracting rich kids. It became a VIP club with international pop and TV celebrities visiting frequently, dancing to commercial music in designer clothing, far from the original crowd who had initiated the scene.

1991

He was sitting next to a stunning redhead, beautifully arranged in a pale silken dress, proudly showing off her impressive bosom.

Playfully trying to flirt he winked but received no response.

The creature daintily arranged her pearls and pointedly turned her head away.

Annoyed, he looked around to see if there were other possible attractions, when she ordered a drink.

Her voice was deep, better suited for a drunken sailor than Coco Chanel. Curious, he appraised her more openly, noting her large hands, broad shoulders, narrow hips, beautiful thick, wavy hair and very long legs.

The lady ignored him.

After taking ecstasy together with the barkeeper, K. was silent for a couple of minutes, sipping his wine pensively. Then, after the drug had set in, he determinedly gazed at the silent damsel once more.

"Hi, K.'s the name and you are absolutely gorgeous. May I enquire how you developed your beautiful breasts?"

Receiving no indication of having been heard he tapped her shoulder and repeated his introduction. The slim figure turned and fixed a furious stare slightly above his eyes.

"I beg your pardon?"

Happy to have received a response K. smiled shyly and repeated: "Hi, glad to meet you. I'm K. How did you make your tits grow?"

Hissing "Fuck off," the beauty pointedly ordered another glass of champagne.

Surprised, he politely nudged her elbow, and spoke candidly to her back.

"I'm sorry, I didn't mean to be rude, I just feel very honest right now and would like to find out about growing breasts. How did you do it?"

Turning smoothly she elegantly poured the fresh drink into his lap.

For a couple of minutes he sat, looking bewildered. Then, unperturbedly catching another glimpse of her magnificent décolleté, he repeated his question once more, politely leaning forward to catch the answer.

She smacked him over the head with her golden purse while simultaneously ordering another drink for herself in his name.

K. pulled the barkeeper aside, loudly informing her, "I am only asking a polite question, why is she reacting so violently?"

"Maybe you should leave her alone if she doesn't want to answer."

"I'm feeling a little wobbly, is my face really blown up? It looks strange in your back mirror."

"You look fine, maybe you should try dancing, it really does the job if you're high."

"I'm not really much of a dancer... but if you say so maybe I'll try today."

K. left his seat, politely smiling to the immobile damsel and jauntily walked to an area filled with sweating dancers, waving their arms in exhilaration, cheering to sudden breaks and moving their hips to the beat.

Tentatively he started moving, waving his arms in a similar fashion to his neighbor and watching her professional moves furtively.

"Hey, you want to go skiing?" Turning he saw A. standing next to him swaying to the music and smiling with a glint in his eye.

"Sure, why not, it's my night out, I've been in the studio for days."

Following the jean-clad figure he delicately went down a deserted hallway to a muddy corner from which A. removed a brick and pulled out a large plastic bag filled to the brim with white powder.

"Wow, that's a lot of cocaine."

"Shush, it's my secret stash, here, we'll take enough to last us a for a while."

Pouring a portion into his silver cigarette case, A. put the bag back into the secret hiding place and pulled K. along the corridor to a back room.

Entering the large space in which dozens of polyester-clad ravers lounged, A. slid down on one of the pink cushions lying around and started laying out long lines of cocaine.

"I can't take all that."

"Hey, what's the fun of drugs if you don't share!" A. laughed. "Look at all the friends we have!" and pointed at the pale figure coming closer.

"It's the foxy woman from the bar, hey, good to see you, do you want some coke?"

K. stood up, chivalrously making room for her on his cushion.

Smiling, the figure sat down, arranging her Chanel jacket carefully over her long legs.

"Sorry about the drink I spilled on your lap before, I wasn't sure if you were an asshole or not but if you know A. it's fine."

"That's ok, I just really wanted to know, how did you make them grow?"

"Well let's have some of this delicious candy and then I'll tell you everything. Oh, and wait, do you have any more of that ecstasy?"

The Planet

Although I worked and hung out in clubs and bars during most of the 1980s and early 1990s, meeting interesting new contacts or friends, I never mistook this part of my life as my main focus. It was only a means of achieving my most important aim, to express myself creatively. Having a knack for connecting and inspiring people I was often offered commercial, managerial jobs, which I reluctantly declined, knowing that they would change my financial situation radically but leave no time for development of my art. Because of this I turned down the chance to be an official Love Parade "board member" or co-partner with Hille on her successful clubs. I preferred to work at the cash register a couple of nights a month and help decorate, not delving too deeply into the financial and economic realms or having to stay up until midafternoon on Sunday, taking care of guests who were high on ecstasy and out of their minds. This way I had time, freedom, and enough cash to spend on exactly what I felt like, which was designing costumes, drawing, or composing music.

Because of this conscious decision I never earned the large amount of money that some of the entrepreneurs did during the time when techno music was at its most popular, but I never regretted having taken the difficult path of committing to my artistic endeavors. It has been a long and winding road with many ups and downs and numerous difficult obstacles, but in hindsight the nightmares make more sense then they did at the time. I consider myself lucky to have experienced many unusual events and states of mind which I may not have experienced had I chosen another path.

After Motte and I drifted apart, essentially because of different timetables, but remaining good friends, I continued living in the Lindenstrasse with our two cats, the green leather sofa my father had sent me from NY after visiting me and being horrified at my empty apartment, and two thousand books my former roommate Roland Wolf had deposited in the hallway after losing his apartment while being on tour with Nick Cave.

My timetable was always full; since I was not able to depend on jobs coming in, I made sure to be out there generating them, speaking to potential customers, working night shifts, doing interviews, meeting new acquaintances, hanging out with girlfriends, planning collaborations and events to hype my work and that of friends.

After leaving the 90° Hille and Andreas opened a new club, Planet. But I had started singing in a band, taking voice lessons from Jayney Klimek, and was writing lyrics as often as I could, so not much time was left for partying after late-night Planet shifts.

Due to this tight schedule I saw the close-knit family of the Planet crew less and less during the day. Happily this didn't diminish our friendship and I continued being part of the creative crowd, working at least once a week at the entrance of the club.

The first Planet opened its doors in a charming, deserted factory on the edge of the Spree river. The combination of wooden floors and crooked brick walls with a small tower made it look like Sleeping Beauty's fortress, hidden by ivy and old weeping willows. Domenico Zindato, who was known for his surreal art installations, immediately set about decorating the interior with trees and branches, hanging heavy golden frames between the twinkling leaves, through which he would take portraits of the dressed up audience. Within days people lined up for hours to have their picture taken, medieval knights, fairytale princesses, or black s/m dominas pierced up to the eyeballs and dragging their slaves behind them.

Thanks to the large, overgrown courtyard in front of the club I could sit outside in the summer, next to the three bouncers protecting me, under a pretty straw roof, sipping cocktails with Hille, chatting with friends, and collecting the entrance fee.

In the winter we had huge barrels filled with wood burning brightly to keep us warm. I enjoyed the camaraderie of the bouncers, most of them rough guys, who joked with each other and drank grog while listening to hip-hop music on a small portable radio. Many were from Bosnia or Serbia, trying to earn money for their families back home, and buying expensive watches and cars from their leftover earnings.

They had experienced almost every illegal profession imaginable: weapon and cigarette smuggling, drug trafficking, extorting debts, guarding gang leaders, Mafia blackmailing, underground box fights, or gambling. They trained their bodies to enormous muscle-bulging lengths and carried at least five to six weapons at all times. I prefer honest, direct characters to pretentious ones, and I enjoyed listening to their remarkable stories of families living in small wooden huts the East European countryside, brothers fighting in the war, adventurous escapes to Germany, hiding in trains, walking for days, or stealing bicycles to arrive at the yearned-for destination, being hired as private bailiffs or debtors, and learning how to adapt to being an illegal immigrant far from home.

Working in underground clubs was never boring; the place was regularly raided by police or gangs and drug squads or simply robbed by jealous competition.

Everybody working there had to be on their toes at all times, ready to stop a fight, resuscitate a guest from a drug overdose, or mop blood and vomit off the floor. On top of taking care of the money, I had to deal with a constant stream of visitors expecting free drinks and special treatment. I also had to ensure that the crew wasn't stealing, report to the manager after my shift with the night's total, keep smiling, and look pretty in spite of staying up all night. But all of these duties are commonplace for anybody that has worked in a club.

The reason why I continued doing this for years was to witness the roots of our society. This often-neglected area was the site of most occurrences and developments. Not only artistically speaking, but even more so in human and social terms. Nightlife is the gray region in which everybody lets loose, showing their true face and yearnings. I have drunk and chatted with politicians, diplomats, scientists, journalists, and biologists for countless hours and have been able to get to know them in an undocumented, unlit environment. It was much easier to understand how their worlds functioned there than had I met them in a regulated and controlled work atmosphere. This was where one could hear about hidden motivations, secret dreams, well-concealed prejudices, ambition, fear, greed, and shortcomings. The lies and corruption that smooth out the cracks in our society were revealed, boasted about, or justified, the mask lowered and a glimpse into the true mechanics could be perceived. Besides being continually fascinated by the psychology of motivation, this insight was vitally important for my art. To create a vision with depth I always felt I had to surround myself with the lines and wrinkles of my fellow man; Botoxed faces reveal nothing of the soul.

A party was not only an event that caused bodies to move, nor simply a meeting point for friends; the underlying deeper interaction influenced everything. The lower the standard of entertainment, the more primitive the society becomes, its basic needs reduced to sex and money, and it is dissatisfied if it cannot have them. If creativity and ingenuity are included, proving that there is more to life than just profit, society's perspective becomes broader and the inhabitants more content. It is like an invisible scale.

That is why the creative clubs of Berlin were so important. Nightlife influenced our city just as much, or maybe even more, than the events mentioned by history books. Human nature can best be perceived without light.

After the Planet had existed for some time the owners were told the space was going to be renovated and that they would have to find a new venue. Andreas loved discovering new sites and spent most of his time driving around Berlin unearthing interesting landmarks anyway, so this was no big problem. He quickly spotted an interesting piece of real estate on a peninsula in former East Berlin. It was a deserted, rectangular ground floor building with walls made from plywood, and was covered with large, green ivy leaves. Although it had an adjoining courtyard, the atmosphere was not nearly as magical as the original space on Köpernicker Strasse, but it would do for a short-term transition. Situated in Alt-Strahlau, on the outskirts of the city, it also took quite some traveling to get there, so I reduced my working shifts even more, trying to get by on a small amount of money to concentrate on my art.

When Hille called me a couple of months later, I had almost completely given up on working at night, but after she told me that they had found an even better space and were moving to an amazing site, I was intrigued. The new venue turned out to be the building in which Carl and I had done our first underground theme party and was in fact five minutes from my apartment so I cheerfully accepted a job as a cashier in what was to become one of the largest and most successful techno clubs in Berlin during the 1990s—the E-Werk.

1992

He disappeared for three months, not calling anybody, neither his mother nor manager. The meaning in life had disappeared and he decided to stay in bed until it came back. After buying enough groceries to last for a long time he set about waiting.

He didn't read, didn't watch TV, and tried not to think.

In the outside world his gigs had to be cancelled, tours delayed, with worried friends calling each other, asking for news.

Then, after three months, he woke up one afternoon and knew: "The only meaning my life will ever have is the one I create," suddenly understanding all the implications of not relying on anything or expecting happiness from anybody. Looking around his room he heard books shouting out that he had never read them; they seemed to wave at him, promising support.

He read like a man starved, devouring words and sentences, filling himself with thoughts and ideas: he was surprised at how easy it had been to find the unexpected.

Then, finally, he felt the urge to leave his cave, curious to see how he would merge the inside and the out. So after shaving off his impressive stubble, he showered and left the small apartment.

It was December and the city lay in a bed of snow and ice, the temperature having sunk to 5 degrees Fahrenheit.

He didn't notice.

The old mushrooms found in the corner of a cupboard enveloped him in a light, buzzing world of his own.

Walking from Kreuzberg to Mitte, he enjoyed the crisp, quiet atmosphere of a sleeping winter city, admiring snowflakes, the silhouettes of buildings and cars until he ended up in front of the huge and famous club.

Entering quickly, past friends and acquaintances he only said "Hi" to the bouncers and went straight to the dance floor, packed with about a thousand raving techno fans moving to P.'s music. Heading directly to the DJ he told him that he had something to say to the audience. Before P. could react he turned down the volume, tore off his clothes and swung himself all the way to the top of the monitor mountain. There he stood up straight, fully naked in front of the astonished crowd and said: "There is no meaning to life. You have to create it yourself!"

In the silence he then sat down, put his head in his hands and said: "Let's meditate together, do something different than following a purely hedonistic pastime."

P. grabbed the chance to put on another record and restarted the music. After about five minutes the meditating man jumped down from his airy peak, tore the needle off the record again and yelled:" Try to find the light with me!" running into the courtyard of the club, into the snowflakes. At this point friends became a little worried, trying to convince him to go home. Instead he found his clothes and walked for three hours to tell his surprised and sleepy mother he loved her. Then he walked for another three hours back to his apartment in Kreuzberg and fell asleep.

The next morning, fresh and clear-headed, he jumped out of bed, ready to go about creating his future and doing everything he had neglected before, not worried about failure anymore, his fears having disappeared.

THE E-WERK

Architecturally the E-Werk was difficult to supervise. Hundreds of rooms, tunnels, and stairways led to unknown labyrinths, winding down through Berlin's basements, climbing up hidden staircases and towers and ending in trap doors too heavy to lift. We soon got lost during every try. Going from one floor to the next revealed unexpected settings, illuminating but a small slice of what the building had been occupied as generations ago. On the first day of throwing out old junk we discovered a round room reminiscent of a *Star Trek* stage set, with bizarre rows of old computer contraptions decked out with large buttons. Fascinated we sat on the decrepit wooden chairs behind the rusty tables, carefully looking through drawers, but not finding any puzzle pieces to reveal the secret of the dusty, faintly lit room. The future dance hall was covered with cracked white tiles which could have turned into a sound problem but when the first "Evidence" party took place in February 1993, with DJ WestBam spinning records, the sound was surprisingly dry and the crowd roared its approval, kicking off the birth of a mega club into techno orbit. In time the many hallways were investigated room by room by the crew, who came back with reports of odd coincidences, finding charcoal drawings smeared on the walls, black magic symbols, seeing an apparition behind a dead window, hearing curious sounds in vacant hallways. In the end, a white witch was asked to carry out a ritual to get rid of the ghosts. Countless birthdays were celebrated in the small side rooms. We watched the sunset from the rooftop and initiated exhibitions, fairs, and after-show parties of a hitherto unknown magnitude.

The impressive building was a universe of its own.

After the balcony of the main hall had been renovated I often stood looking down on the masses of dancing and sweating bodies, again and again amazed at the amount of people dancing to the DJ's music for days on end. DJ Clé, West-Bam, Woody, Jonzon, Disko; Derrick May, Juan Atkins, Kevin Sounderson, Dr. Motte, Carl Cox, Laurent Garnier, Sven Väth, DJ Hell, the young Paul van Dyk, anybody considering themselves a serious Disc Jockey wanted to perform in this remarkable space.

The asset of its overwhelming size, numinous atmosphere, and great management were not the key reasons for its success. The creative and affectionate input invested by almost every staff member was its most important quality, and having fun and breaching restrictions were the common denominator. Elaborately costumed drag queens doing playback performances, gorgeous go-go dancers sweating on large blocks of cement between hundreds of visitors, presenting elaborate dance movements, body contortionists bending backwards covered with emeralds, avant-garde cave women dressed in furs with fake animal teeth glowing through their lips swinging from the balcony on wire chairs through the masses, avant-garde piercing and branding events glowing menacingly through purple smoke, second-hand fashion shows choreographed to pounding live concerts of local emerging electronic bands, art events covering huge portions of the ceiling with early video installations and computer set ups, light installations illuminating the dark corners of back stairs and basement nooks, briefly exposing naked bodies having sex or being sick from too many cocktails, the bathrooms overflowing with cosmetics and put to use by screeching transsexuals or platform-heeled women, the doors covered with black-and-white photocopy art, late afternoon, laid back, after-work get-togethers with everybody telling each other the most outrageous or hilarious stories of the night before—this was what the E-Werk magic consisted of.

Protecting the castle from unwelcome aggressors were reliable friends, all in the charge of a muscled security gang; Angela Mettbach, the mother of Alexander Hacke's first child, Ali Kepenik, Mac, and Alexandra Dröner, all of them admired throughout town for their cool, laidback attitude, decided on who would be given permission to pass through the gates of our paradise. Having passed this test, the guests would arrive in my domain, the cash register, where they would undergo a thorough inspection of bags and style while being regaled by jokes. Only then, after having been approved by all, could they finally enter the courtyard, filled with small booths selling homemade food or light long drinks and immerse themselves into the throbbing, perspiring miasma.

The E-Werk was situated on Wilhelmstrasse, at the center of Berlin, a cross-road of the former East and West. It was close to the "Bannmeile," a security area surrounding government buildings in which another set of laws ruled.

It was around the corner from the "Topography of Terror," a museum documenting repression under the Nazi regime, on the site of the former headquarters of the Gestapo and the SS. During World War II the E-Werk building had remained upright in the midst of the last battles, when the SS and Wehrmacht retreated from the Red Army, leaving bullet holes in the thick walls that could still be seen next to the "Stolpersteine," stones which were later positioned in the courtyard in commemoration of deported Jews. The building had been constructed in 1928 as the largest electrical powerhouse in Germany and continued functioning until 1946. Then, due to heavy damage, the E-Werk was forgotten during the Iron Curtain regime and was deserted until the Wall fell.

Only after the adventurous Andreas had rediscovered the momentous architecture did it return to life, metamorphosing into an underground icon.

In general, history could be felt everywhere in this neighborhood. "Unter den Linden," the main boulevard around the corner from the E-Werk, was originally conceived in 1648 after the Thirty Years' War by the Elector Friedrich Wilhelm, who wanted to beautify the destroyed countryside with a thousand linden trees.

After the trees had started growing, painters, attracted by their splendor, painted landscapes of the area, and as the future monarchs built operas, theaters, and academies around it, the avenue became legendary. Known for its grandeur, it was nonetheless almost completely destroyed during World War II, which left a desolate city on its knees in 1945. By the end of the 1950s many of the buildings, with the exception of the palace, had been rebuilt. The architecture often had a distinctly Russian flavor, thanks to the occupying nation, and the Soviet embassy was added to demonstrate the connection to Russia. After 1961 the GDR regime continued the renovation by adding the asbestos-riddled Palast der Republic in the center of the boulevard as a monument of their success, a construction that was declared a health hazard in 1989 and finally torn down in 2008. After the Wall had come down and the renovation begun, an unparalleled, dense historic merging of sites occured in the center of Berlin, amalgamating very different pasts with the present, with endless layers of stories lying next to each other, impossible to ignore. On the way to work, my footsteps would follow what had been the former "Todestreifen," or Death Strip, the territory which had existed between the two parallel cement constructions of the Wall. Before being able to use the central real estate and allow roads or buildings to be built there, authorities had to have the area searched for bombs and mines, cleverly hidden in the dry earth to ensure security for the communist regime. As I lived directly next to the Wall, I witnessed the deserted area, which I had watched from my kitchen window for years, turn into a thriving neighborhood with international architects constructing prestigious temples of modern commerce and design that had formerly housed Nazi headquarters, replacing the watchtowers and gunned guards as quickly as possible with parks and galleries. It took some getting used to, walking among these speedily changing landmarks; Checkpoint Charlie, my halfway point to the E-Werk, and even now sends shivers up my spine, has resurrected its toll booths and barbed wire fence as an exhibit for tourists.

The fact that I had instinctively chosen a place to live from which the progress of events could be watched so closely amazed me, and on the early mornings, after my night shift was over, while slowly walking down the long, dusty pathway leading away from the club, passing hundreds of tired ravers lying in the grass, sitting on the cobblestones or in their parked cars, red-eyed, flabby-faced, and smelly, I would ponder the drastic changes this city had gone through, feeling as if I was walking over thin layers of bone and stories, lightly dusted now by this short phase of fun and excess, young people celebrating life, and marveled at how fast things can change. I deeply appreciated the fact that this neighborhood, which I had chosen as my home, demonstrated the rise and decline of events so clearly, sweeping aside any false pretensions of security taught elsewhere, with the waywardness of life keeping all of us on our toes continuously.

The E-Werk's popularity was similar to the Love Parade's success. Its events became huge, with big companies moving in to cash in on the hype. International advertising agencies called to book Massive Attack, Versace, and the MTV Awards, attracting celebrities like Björk, Tom Jones, Naomi Campbell, or Bono, who hung out on E-Werk's balconies, dancing in our carefully decorated hallways and leaving the vicinity in huge limousines, impressed by German creativity and Berlin's unlimited excess that we had brought to life. Along with the Tresor, another techno insignia down the street, the area had added yet another layer to the city's history, this time with a more positive result than that which preceded it, receiving international admiration instead of disdain.

"Here's the key, you'll be alone most of the time, except for the cleaning staff. They'll be upstairs in the main hall and toilets."
The key chain was heavy with old-fashioned metal objects, bent and blemished by time.
"If you need branches or shrubbery to decorate the cellar, take it from the garden. That's the back door over there."
His finger pointed to a small entrance in the shadowy part of the long hallway.
"Is there a phone in case I need to reach somebody?"
"Not down here, upstairs, all the way in the back, there's one in the small office but it doesn't always work, phone lines in this part of town are taking their time."
"Oh ok, I have friends that told me it took years for them to get a connection in the former East but I thought it had been taken care of in the meantime."
"If you go out on the street there's a phone booth there. I have to go now. Let's meet for dinner tomorrow evening and you can tell me how things are going."
Attaching the keys to her belt she waved goodbye, carefully placing the plastic bags filled with scissors, paintbrushes, a glue gun, boxes of nails, nylon thread, heavy hammers, feathers, and light bulbs on a small stack of faded newspapers next to her feet. The room was dimly lit by naked light bulbs, elongating bizarre shadows of iron bars and metal drawers on the dirt floor.
The walls she had been asked to decorate seemed moldy and crumbling. "Nails are going to have a hard time here." Touching the moist plaster wasn't comforting, indicating the need for a lot of work.
Silence had spread. The room was blanketed by dust and a strange smell of rot, which seeped into her pores with impressive speed.
Shivering, the realization of being alone in the basement of a deserted building crept up her spine, projections of horror movies flickering in the background of her mind, jumping at the slightest noise. Turning, there was nothing.
"Stop it, don't start imagining things, the week will be a nightmare otherwise."
Her voice seemed small in the dark tomb of eavesdropping silence.
"Let's go look at the garden and let in some air and sunlight. That'll chase away the ghosts."
Straightening her shoulders she decisively walked to the small metal door and started shoving different keys into the rusty lock. It felt uncomfortable standing with her back to the room, the obscurity behind her body increasing in volume, invisible hands lightly touching her hair, making it rise on her arms.

Finally the lock turned and the door creaked open, gradually revealing a narrow set of stone stairs leading up into green and thin rays of sun.

Jumping several of steps at a time she was brought to a stop once more by a stained gate protecting the building from outside intrusion. Fumbling, none of the keys seemed to fit, the lock stubbornly remaining shut. Hearing another slight sound she jumped, gasping with fright; the empty staircase grinned into her face.

"This is ridiculous, there's nobody down here so stop making a fuss, find the key and get on with it."

Speaking loudly seemed to help and she finally discovered the right fit, pushing open the stubborn metal and stumbling out into a softly lit Friday afternoon. After her eyes had become accustomed to the brightness she discovered a small dirt path, which she followed, relieved to be rid of the clammy silence and heavy air below. Breathing out the dust she had swallowed, she sucked in the fresh smell of earth, flowers, and sunlight, cleansing her soul and body. Small bushes entwined fragile ferns, ancient oaks resided next to twinkling silver birches, ivy competed greedily with weeds for space to grow. Reminiscing about the children's book The Secret Garden, *one of her favorites, she slowly walked along the path enjoying nature's unruffled composure, feeling the warmth on her face until she found a small sunny space among an old bed of flowers. The dried leaves and earth whispered as she sat down, enfolding her into a world of silent worms, beetles, and scurrying ants. Sighing she closed her eyes, relaxing her back into the nest of flora.*

"I love nature, there's nothing as reassuring as its neutral, pragmatic growth, all that city noise and hub is just exhausting. Thank god Berlin still has plenty of weeds crawling through the cracks of civilization."

Moments later, realizing she had almost fallen asleep, she sat up quickly readjusting her hair and removing twigs from her T-shirt. Glancing at the tree opposite from where she was sitting a feeling of peculiarity struck her. The tree was bent, obviously having started out growing straight up into the sky but had then changed its direction, now growing almost vertically towards the right. "That's strange, I wonder why it has changed its direction like that, I can't see an apparent reason."

Glancing at the other trees and bushes she suddenly realized that all of them were growing in a similar fashion, bent over and pointing in the same direction.

"I wonder if it's due to the sun coming from a certain angle."

Turning, a sudden shiver ran down her spine, elusive and swift as a lightning bolt.

All of the trees were pointing towards the decrepit building, in fact, directly toward the door she had just come out of.

The Tresor

One of the first large techno clubs to open and survive for years was the Tresor club, settling in the vast ruins of the Wertheim department store. Originally the space consisted of many small rooms intertwined in a maze of hallways ending in an immense subterranean vault, filled with heavy metal doors, large strong boxes and heavily rusted bars. It was exhilarating to discover the different rooms, wandering from one dark space to the next, unearthing stories covered with dust. In general the 1990s seemed to be filled with long excursions through spider-web covered subterranean tunnels. Dimitri Hegeman, the innovator and owner of the Fischbüro, a futuristic bar of the 1980s, had discovered the space in 1991, rented it immediately and transformed it into a laboratory of music, the club becoming legendary not necessarily because of its raves but for the quality of the electronic music. I spent years working for this venue, enjoying the collaboration with a management that was always interested in supporting a high standard of music or art, attracting a serious-minded creative crowd to plow the way into the electronic universe, analyzing, experimenting, and researching in many areas. Tresor aways seemed more of a laboratory than a club, scientifically working on projects with the goal of reaching a higher level of expertise under the supervision of Dimitri Hegeman, one of my strongest supporters and patrons in the years to come.

DIMITRI HEGEMANN

I was introduced to Dimitri Hegemann by Motte on a sunny afternoon in spring, after a coffee at Café M., where I pondered what to do for the rest of the afternoon. After contemplating the different possibilities Motte suddenly decided: "It's time for you to meet Dimitri." As we sauntered down the street I imagined him as a tall Greek with a huge black mustache.

I had heard about his first bar, the Fischbüro, a popular meeting place for intellectual anarchists hammering away on typewriters or planning Dadaist manifestations, arguing about Timothy Leary recordings and drinking huge amounts of beer. Dimitri had been the initiator of the first Atonal festival at the SO 36 in 1982 presenting bands such as Die Tödliche Doris, Liaisons Dangereuses, Einstürzende Neubauten, Laibach, and Psychic TV. I expected him to be an aggressive, ambitious character.

When we entered the Fischlabor, Dimitri's new and second bar, a venue with two rooms, the front one long and narrow, the back one small and cozy, I was surprised to be introduced to a blond, pale, and soft-spoken man, seemingly shy and very polite, asking us how we were, listening carefully to our stories and nodding quietly.

As we spent the afternoon sitting in the sun and drinking champagne, I was reminded of Andy Warhol, whom I had met once at a party in NYC. He had radiated a similar feeling of vulnerability combined with crystal clear alertness, immediately registering anything of interest in his meticulous internal bookkeeping, portraying an uncanny instinct for detecting relevant, groundbreaking talent, news, or ideas.

I was to find out that Dimitri had a similar intuitive Midas touch for the truly avant-garde, living the contradiction of being an excellent businessman and a persistent dreamer.

Steadily pursuing his goals he opened commercial restaurants, carefully finetuning the food, design, and music until they became successful and generated money for his more idealistic endeavors, supporting artists, founding experimental clubs and originating avant-garde festivals. The list of musicians and artists featured and discovered by Dimitri Hegeman is endless: Jeff Mills, Blake Baxter, Juan Atkins, and Paul van Dyk are but a few of the better known. He was always interested in new developments, his legendary club Tresor in the Leipziger Strasse, a techno icon, reigning from 1991 to 2005, and his record company Tresor Records becoming one of the largest independent labels in Germany that promoted techno music.

After being introduced we became close friends, tossing ideas and madcap concepts back and forth, enjoying outrageous results, planning ludicrous co-operations. From the very start he was extremely supportive of my artistic work, offering me a job at the Fischlabor to survive on with a position of absolute freedom in how to serve the drinks. Being a first-rate business man he obviously knew that my knack for combining interesting characters and thirst for contradictions would guarantee an out-of-the-ordinary crowd, so the deal was a fair exchange of assets. I did my best to turn the bar into a hot spot, showing black-and-white Super 8 movies, making popcorn, buffets of salmon bagels, or homemade quiche, inventing colorful drinks, printing hand-drawn flyers, distributing them throughout Berlin, inviting my friends to special pre-evening cocktail hours with free drinks and pretzels, initiating drag-queen photo shoots, elaborate fashion soirées, organizing press conferences, label meetings, and after-show parties.

My Monday shifts attracted a variety of innovative artists drinking, performing, and mingling: WestBam arriving with his then-girlfriend Rose Zone, a contortionist, clinking glasses with Inga Humpe; Johnny dropping by with Gudrun; listening to Hartwig Masuch, BMG's future boss, lamenting a complicated love affair; Die Fanastischen Vier celebrating an international hit, and Alexander Hacke and Roland Wolf presenting their most recent music demos.

These evenings were not necessarily a financial success for the bar. I would serve far too many free drinks, but Dimitri repeatedly whispered that everything should be considered an investment for the future. He had acquired an enormous amount of debts because of his various enterprises but instead of becoming worried or depressed he was convinced that this was the only possible way of pursuing his ambitions without having inherited a large sum of money or having other financial means. His faith in his future success was impressive.

Not everybody liked him. Like Warhol, he was blamed for using people's creativity to further his own success. He had strange quirks of whispering crucial sums during business meetings, and would become introverted, moody, or haphazard when an enterprise was not developing as he had anticipated.

If crossed or not taken seriously he could become cynical, in a very covert manner, ridiculing other people's weaknesses or insecurities, using his power to infuriate the subject of his irritation.

As is true of any artist, it was easiest to deal with him by not being dependent on his whims. He was too capricious and hated being nailed down, and liked being surrounded by open-minded, independent individuals, and joint ventures.

Due to our friendship I merely had to hint at an idea for him to envision its realization, thinking up ways of making the endeavor possible. After watching me labor in various bars for years, he surprised me with a grant of ten thousand Deutschmarks, a silent donation initiated and bequeathed once a year to artists he considered dedicated, talented, and professional. The grant made it possible to survive for months without having to take on handy jobs.

After Dimitri discovered the underground vaults of the former Wertheim department store in Mitte and decided to turn it into a club, he asked me to help embellish some of the decrepit rooms and create an out-of-the-ordinary atmosphere. I spent weeks painting floors, plastering black-and-white drawings on the bathroom walls, and decorating the bars, hot-gluing plastic roses and leaves onto the banisters.

Besides working behind the bar, accompanied by my Space Cowboy band members, playing tapes from a tiny ghetto blaster, attracting a jumbled mix of rock 'n' rollers, electronic music fans and fashion designers, I spent hours walking through the halls listening to Dimitri's ideas and dreams.

After he had finally decided that the musical direction of the club would be techno, the Tresor was yet again completely renovated by a professional handyman, giving it more of a neutral, minimal touch, in line with the electronic concept that was emerging. The smaller rooms were torn down to create a large dancehall, and a sliding door was added so the room could change in size. Nevertheless he continued to enjoy and rely on my company as he built his universe, due to our combined appreciation for pursuing new creations.

In 1993 Dimitri mentioned that there was a large room on one side of the Tresor that could not be used for anything other than a side bar due to noise limitations. I proposed organizing photography exhibitions in the space. I had collaborated with diverse photographers throughout my years working with fashion and art performances, and had admired their skill and wondered why their work was never shown in galleries. His reaction was enthusiastic. He asked me to set a date soon and promised to pay a small monthly commission for invitations and costs.

The exhibitions opened the first Saturday of every month. I would arrive at 12 a.m., bringing the framed pictures, kicking out drunk barflies, switching off the fog machine, cleaning left over glasses, distributing flowers to cover up the smell of old cigarette smoke and spilled wine, sweeping the floor, rearranging bar stools and generally making the space presentable and suitable for an art crowd. As the walls were extensive, the chosen photographer could present a large amount of work, so there was always a rush to get everything on the walls within six hours. The artists would arrive around 2 p.m., after I had beautified the room, sometimes bringing assistants to help hang their work, so that we could all set in hammering nails, arranging and rearranging frames, dusting the chairs, and fixing the lights until the show was perfect.

The photographers would then go home to change into their evening wear while I put together the buffet I had prepared the night before in my kitchen. Since my cooking skills were limited, it would usually be the broccoli-and-cheese quiches my father had taught me how to make, sweet cakes, or lox sandwiches. I put the food on red tablecloths, next to silver paper plates, and plastic forks and knives. Around 6 p.m. the musicians or DJs responsible for the music would arrive and start the soundcheck while the bar filled with people. A little later the bouncers ambled to their posts and while the last ashtrays were distributed, the first knocks on the door could be heard. The first few minutes when guests arrived provided me an opportunity to change into glamorous design outfits, which I had made especially for the opening and usually consisted of red or white shiny plastic two-piece suits, stiletto heels, and a beehive with false ringlets curling down my back. Dimitri habitually arrived just before the live music started, quietly entering the room via the back door, giving himself the opportunity to get an overview before anybody saw him. Then he would politely greet friends and associates.

The exhibition series was a success. Large crowds came to look at photography by Domenico Zindato, Martin Schacht, Ilse Ruppert, Kerstin Ehmer and Stephan Maria Rother among others, and sometimes someone would even buy a piece to the delight of all. Dimitri loved having art in his club and defended any decision I made, even when his barkeepers threatened to boycott Miron Zownir's exhibition of dying Russian Mafia bosses and drug addicts, saying that the ravers would be distracted from the music. Dimitri told everybody that art cannot be censored and that the show would go on.

After I had organized the Aurora Lounge, as it was called, for nine months, Dimitri decided I was a born curator and that I needed a gallery of my own. I wasn't convinced, since I considered myself an artist who liked supporting her friends, but he continued insisting for years.

Dimitri Hegeman has influenced and inspired Berlin and its music culture in countless ways. He is one of the few businessmen I have met who kept the dream alive of investing in idyllic and non-commercial projects even after having become successful financially. His practice is an example of how business can be an inspired art form that enriches and fertilizes culture as well as making money. He supports both older artists and younger, making their dreams and goals a reality by giving them the chance to develop their ideas and execute them professionally. In this way he rejuvenated his community continually with audacious, madcap projects and ideas. Dimitri's financial ventures survived much longer than his competition thanks to this stance, proving that a society is stronger not only socially but also economically if it invests in the arts.

After having decided to shift my focus from fashion to art, music, and literature nothing much happened for quite some time. I continued working on my commissioned ballgowns to earn money, organizing events, and working in clubs, meeting friends and hanging out at night, sure that something would pop up and I would feel prepared to take on a new calling.

The day I was asked if I felt like singing in the band Space Cowboys was therefore a memorable one.

I learned how to play piano at the age of four and violin at the age of ten, sang in a children's choir for years, usually taking over the soprano solos because I was able to span three octaves. I went through a phase of singing sad Edith Piaf songs at the top of my voice for hours at the age of twelve, which annoyed our neighbors. But I never seriously considered performing music because of a nightmarish piano concert I experienced when I was seven. During this first performance I entirely forgot the prelude I had laboriously learned by heart weeks before, and left the stage in anguish, walking back to my seat through a silent, embarrassed audience, initiating an onset of terrible stage fright. The thought of singing, which meant not being able to hide behind an instrument, seemed radically impossible and more horrifying than anything else imaginable. So after Boris stated his question I immediately said yes, especially because I felt I could never do it.

Boris worked at the Turbine, where he was the bouncer, taking money from newcomers or throwing out drunken troublemakers. With his long brown hair and beaked nose he looked like Geronimo, and being soft-spoken and friendly, he was usually surrounded by pretty girls. Boris was also a drummer and had played in a band for five years, known for their charismatic singer Alfred A. Jones. The Space Cowboys had won a couple of prizes and landed a record deal, making them local heroes of the then rock-oriented crowd of Schöneberg and Kreuzberg.

Five years later Alfred decided that literature was more to his taste, quit the band and opened a salon in his apartment, which was soon known for its odd assemblage of readings, performances, and scandals. Although I liked Alfred and appreciated his taste, I seldom went to the small apartment, always feeling smothered and ill-at-ease from the bad air and extroverted performance artists. Once a poet almost hit me with an ax that he was using to split open a wine bottle.

After Alfred left the Space Cowboys, Ottmar, the former guitar player, decided to become the lead singer, influencing the band to combine rock with hip-hop beats to support his rap lyrics. Mike Vamp, an outgoing Italian and known solo artist in the 1980s took over the guitar, bringing a lighter touch to the otherwise heavy rock riffs they preferred. Chip, the keyboardist, came up with the main backup sounds and sequences. At the point when Boris called me they had decided that they needed a female element in their music and after having hearing Motte's record *Buddy Electric*, called me, not knowing that it was a woman named Daniela Sonntag who had sung on my former boyfriend's record. I was surprised to receive the offer and accepted, hoping the experience would cure me of my stage fright.

The first performance was to be one week later and I spent the entire stretch of time thinking up different excuses to cancel my agreement. After finally mustering the courage to call Boris so I could back out, he said it was too late and I would have to perform no matter what. We rehearsed once in their tiny studio room next to the local airport, Tempelhof, from which airplanes would leave at regular intervals, turning our music and performance into silent mimicries, which otherwise were eardrum-popping loud. I had to scream: "There's life on Mars!" as piercingly as possible into the microphone. This was easier than I had expected and the boys seemed pleased with the effect.

On the evening of the show I wore a very short and very flared skirt I'd designed, and a tight top with knitted sleeves and a black wig, which I layered into a beehive.

The concert took place in a club called Villa Kreuzberg, known as an alternative cultural institution housing a stage, a farm with animal shelters, children's playgrounds, and rooms for workshops in the middle of Berlin's Victoriapark. I screeched throughout the show, losing most of my angst as I looked at the astonished faces in the crowd, who weren't used to the new rhythms the boys were playing, the lyrics Ottmar was singing, or the sounds I was emitting. I enjoyed performing with Mike who spontaneously arranged choreography for both of us and by the end of the show the crowd was cheering and clapping, the Space Cowboys had been reborn and I was part of it.

Things moved very quickly after that. We recorded a new album, took press pictures, shot a playback video, did interviews—and I went on my first tour of Europe. I loved the traveling, sitting in the small kebab bus, which still smelled of old grease and peppers, cramped among the musicians, the tour manager and the driver Andy Jung, a former cab driver who was also our engineer, tearing through the Alps at breakneck speed and telling each other stories of embarrassing performances we'd experienced. Over the years I remained frightened of going on stage but mainly due to Mike's friendly coaching we worked out an entertaining stage show that took away the awkwardness of what to do with my arms. I became a tambourine maniac, hitting my legs and knees so hard that they would turn blue and then red after the show, developing welts, until our tour manager bought skater's apparel to cover my legs with and fingerless leather gloves to cover the bloody blisters. The band became larger and more professional, with Mike Parker playing the bass, and even a trumpet player participating at a couple of shows.

My lifestyle transformed, now everything evolved around music. Besides listening to records for hours and going to see other bands play, I learned how to discern individual instruments, got to know historic bass lines, different percussion possibilities, and what a Fender guitar is. I enjoyed writing lyrics, rapping with Ottmar and singing with Mike. The interactive nature of music, the way it combined sound and language was enthralling, exactly what I had been hoping for. It expressed my thoughts and feelings more precisely than the design of a perfect shirt pocket. Over time I became more self-assured and was an increasingly prominent part of the show, developing from background singer and tambourine player to the front woman, rapping or singing next to Ottmar. The combination of our crossover music style, Mike's Italian charisma, Boris's stoic good looks at the drums, and my eccentric stage wear was magical, and our fan base grew ecstatically.

Noticing the hype, large record companies became interested in signing us, offering colossal sums of money and luxurious tour offers, asking us to join their labels and leave the one we already had: Rough Trade. Sadly, due to our everlasting financial crisis, we couldn't resist when MCA England offered us a generous contract. Behind Rough Trade's back, an act I am still embarrassed of today, we were flown to England, invited to a thousand-pound sushi dinner by a smiling A&R man, and we signed a record contract that let their lawyer deal with the label that had been loyal to us through all the ups and downs, convinced of our value. When we signed the new contract we were penniless, staying at the house of our friend David Harrow, the producer of the Dub Syndicate. He was a good friend of Mike's, and invited us to breakfast knowing we were too poor to afford even that and wished us luck when we left, hoping that good fortune would finally come our way. Back in Berlin, we were contacted by the infuriated Rough Trade team, informing us that we were idiots and wishing us all the worst, which quickly became a reality when we were told out that our new A&R man had been fired, leaving us with a contract but no representative, the death of many a band.

In despair we decided to ask around for advice, not making any progress until Johnny Klimek proposed a meeting with K.P. Schleinitz, the former manager of Terence Trent D'Arby and current agent of Alphaville, Bobo In White Wooden Houses, Nikko & The Passion Fruit, Rausch. The meeting took place in Charlottenburg not far from the man's office and went badly. After having shown him our records, photos, videos, and describing our plight he bluntly asked us why he should want to manage us? Knowing that live performance was our strongest asset we invited him to experience one of our concerts before making up his mind.

KP was hesitant but finally assented, giving us enough hope and energy to organize a gig in the U Club, a known hip-hop venue at the time, branded by its many Turkish gang wars.

I built stage sets with huge banners and golden Space Cowboy logos, designed an entire hip-hop collection for men, and sent out elaborate invites to make sure the club would be full on the important evening.

We had done so much publicity that when the night came hundreds of people stood in front of the club waiting to be let in. Jubilantly I collected the entrance fee, happy that for once we would earn some money, and went backstage to put on my make-up and costume, a short silver skirt with a silver leather corsage I had finished making the day before.

The concert started as soon as KP entered, with the fashion show initiating clapping and stomping, so when we finally got on stage to play an uproarious first song, dancing, jumping, and rapping, the crowd cheered madly, jumped up and down, almost hitting the low ceiling with their heads in their enthusiastic frenzy.

The second song had a prelude for which I had to rap alone, standing in front of the band with a megaphone. Usually the band would set in after, but that night they didn't.

Turning I saw my fellow musicians frantically crawling around on the stage looking for something. I ran to Ottmar, worriedly whispering, "What's wrong, what are you doing?"

He had stepped on a cable, pulling it out of its socket and erasing all of Chip's stored loops that had taken hours to load. At the moment they were looking for the cable but the terrible fact was that the loops had to be loaded again which would take at least one-and-a-half hours.

Chip had forgotten to make backup copies.

We looked at each other, horrorstricken, imagining all of the money we might have to give back and KP leaving forever.

After a panicky moment, I went to the microphone and said, "We are sorry to say that every electronic musician's nightmare has just happened to us, our samples have been erased and we need to reload them which will take about two hours. If you are willing to wait and save our evening the drinks are on us, otherwise we will give you your money back." Half of the audience there that night were musicians just discovering sampling themselves and their compassion resulted in everybody staying and dancing to the music that a DJ provided, happily becoming drunk and virtually causing a riot when we finally restarted two hours later as they screamed their welcome, some of them getting sick in front of our feet. KP had stayed and drunk with our fans, watching us deal with the chaos and congratulating us at the end of the show, showing more interest than before.

During the next couple of weeks we met him a couple of times to speak about our dreams, his possibilities, and finances in general. Our company, BMG, was willing to finance a record, the boss being a fan of Space Cowboys, and although we couldn't pay KP, the band had become so popular that none of us doubted we would be able to sell a large amount of records and find a new record company in short time. Little did we know that this was but the last step to our final downfall.

After agreeing to represent us, KP started flying in photographers from London and producers from Los Angeles, dropping names like a dog does fleas: Madonna, Queen Latifah, Compton's Most Wanted. We were flying among the star-studded heavens, feeling the whiff of potential fame and money.

Then he called Jamie.

When Jamie R. arrived in Berlin none of the bands he was going to work for realized that their careers were to be warped forever by this short, heavily built man from California.

The first time we met, he was exquisitely dressed in a furry white cap, an elegant purple pinstriped suit, shiny black patent leather boots, a heavy wool coat, momentous silver rings, and a beautiful handbag filled with fashion magazines and Mary J. Blige's newest CDs. Jamie had been hired to be our official stylist. Within a very short period of time he had stripped Boris of his beloved jeans and sweatshirts, replacing them with a pink-striped suit topped with light beige safari hats and heavy gold chains; Chip, the shy guy in the band, bashfully appeared in a heavy patchwork fur coat, his hair braided into tiny Jamaican extensions, sporting a sleazy green three-piece suit underneath. Ottmar was transformed into a white-clad jockey and I was forced into tight, sexy skirts, in which I could hardly move. Most importantly, we were not allowed to wear shoelaces or socks.

In comparison to Rausch, who were forced to cut off their long hair and ultimately lost their record deal, ending up with a debt of a hundred thousand Deutschmarks, or Alphaville, who were thrown into a Mexican jail during a video shoot organized by Jamie and his assistant, we were lucky. Instead Jamie only succeeded in undermining of our self-confidence to the extent that it completely disappeared.

Jamie was convinced that not only we were inept fashionwise, but that our music lacked the essential ingredients needed to become successful in the international music world. Being black and coming from LA was, as he told us in great detail, the only way to create truly good music and he would gladly help us with the encouraging hand of his idol, Mary J. Blige. Jamie adored Mary J. Blige and carried her CDs around with him constantly. We had become so insecure and depressed thanks to all the advice being forced upon us that our instincts withered and died. We ended up in the absurd situation of being locked out of our own recording studio, while Jamie, who was inside, arranged our music with as many Mary J. Blige samples as possible. "Terrorist," our "should-be" hit single cost over a hundred thousand Deutschmarks to produce. There were six different versions by various producers, all directed by Jamie, but none were ever released.

My first freakout occurred after being asked to look at our new posters in KP's office, printed for the South by Southwest festival in Austin, Texas, and discovering that Jamie's bald head formed the center of our promotion, blown up enormously on the poster with an "A" for Anarchy painted in white on his forehead. I had worked in a club the night before, serving drinks and cocktails to a crowd of rich cocaine addicts and was already in a bad mood. After being told that Jamie had been chosen to represent us on our poster because he was the most beautiful, I loudly asked if everybody had gone insane. After being told that he was thinking of coming on stage with us to rap a little I completely flipped, tearing off my wig and screaming: "Over my dead body." The band shuffled their feet and looked embarrassed, but were also happy that somebody had finally taken on the role of revolutionary. That I was the girl and could easily be written off as hysterical made things easier. But we were beyond redemption; a couple of weeks later Jamie and KP once more suggested that Jamie become part of the show, if only to keep us from being a purely white band, since there was now a black man on the poster. My choleric tantrum was worse this time, causing a serious rift between the band and the management. The performance in Austin, Texas was to be our last. We had managed to keep Jamie off the stage but after trying to perform the songs he had so badly mutilated, in front of a few confused onlookers, the project fell apart. Noticing the decline, KP tried convincing Ottmar and myself to go solo, with the result that Boris, the good natured backbone of the band, gave up and turned in his resignation. Mike Parker was the second to go, Mike Vamp and myself next.

It was a difficult decision; in spite of all the difficulties and obstacles we had all secretly hoped for a positive outcome, since we had invested all of our time, energy, and money. But it wasn't meant to be.

In hindsight I think it was the fact that we had become so insecure throughout years of poverty and bad luck that we believed Jamie's bullshit and let him go through with it, forgetting that the band's strength lay in the individual members, their characteristics, and taste. Our bridges had been lowered too far, the enemy had been allowed in to slaughter all inhabitants and leave an empty shell with no content.

It was a hard but important lesson; be very careful whom you give the power to make decisions for you, in every aspect of your life.

1994

It had been their last performance, the hall filled with dancing fans screaming to the music and swaying to the heavy hip-hop beats. Watching the animated faces from the stage while singing and following the choreography, she felt sad that everything had gone so badly, wondering if the bad luck could have been thwarted in any way.

After packing the instruments and saying goodbye she took a cab home to the empty apartment.

She had kicked out her last lover the day before, packing his belongings into boxes and carrying them out into the street, calling his best friend to help him transfer them.

Enough was enough, the dream had died a long time ago and the constant violence had caused a nerve in her face to go numb, resulting in an expression of bewilderment, which was appropriate to the state she found herself in.

Dropping the instruments and bags, she sat down on the green leather sofa in her living room and started counting the money she had earned, folding the bent bills carefully. While mulling over the new situation, she realized with a jolt something was wrong.

The hair on her arms was standing upright.

With increasing unease she glanced around the room, trying to find the cause of her reaction when she saw the brown body hanging from a curtain rod.

When their eyes met it started flapping large wings and flew straight towards her, sharp as an arrow and as fast.

Yelping, she jumped and turned in midair, running out of the room as fast as possible, slamming the door shut.

"How on earth did that get in? All of my windows are closed, what is a mammoth bat doing in my living room?"

After a couple of minutes and silence she furtively opened the door a crack, trying to see where it had landed, and hearing the flapping again, crashed the door shut once more.

"I can't believe this is happening. I don't even have a bed, the apartment is empty, my band has split apart, it's 3:30 in the morning and I'm huddled outside of my living room with the sofa I was hoping to fall asleep on now unreachable because an enormous bat is terrorizing me. I thought they don't attack people?"

Not wanting to sleep on the floor she tried opening the door repeatedly, always hoping the animal had left, but the bat was ready, obviously waiting for her, lifting his heavy wings and swooping towards the door as soon as it opened an inch.

Finally giving up she constructed a small mound of kitchen towels in the empty bedroom and fell asleep shivering with repulsion.

The next afternoon the doorbell ringing woke her up.

It was B. coming by to pick up drumsticks he had forgotten in her tambourine bag.

Asking for help she slowly opened the door of the living room. No movement was apparent.

After scouring the room, B., who was armed with a broom, discovered the mammal hanging onto the back of the television set and with a careful maneuver managed to throw it out the window. Outside the animal seemed to want to re-enter the apartment, circling in front of the windows' three times and knocking on the panes in front of her horrified eyes.

Finally it turned and flew off into the horizon, a black shadow in the clear blue sky.

B. looked at her thoughtfully.

"I hope you aren't superstitious..."

Ta-Coma

After our band's separation I felt lost. For the first time in my life I was unprepared, not having found the urge to change my direction. I had come to love performing, enjoying the companionship of musicians and their down-to-earth way of life. My interest in fashion had completely disappeared; it turned out to be nothing more than a short love affair. Not wanting to give up on music I decided to create a band of my own and look for musicians interested in the music I felt like writing. As Berlin's creative population consisted of a huge crowd of possible applicants I decided to try out different constellations that resulted in mainly working on songs for compilations.

Die Haut, a Berlin band known for their instrumental music, invited different singers to write and perform their lyrics, and was one of the first to ask me to sing on one of their records.

I felt honored to be to joining an illustrious list of participants such as Alan Vega, Arto Lindsay, Kim Gordon, Debbie Harry, Jeffrey Lee Pierce (The Gun Club), Blixa Bargeld, Anita Lane, Kid Congo Powers, Lydia Lunch, and Nick Cave, and hoped it was a sign of my future success.

Jay Ray, the 90° resident DJ, invited me to participate on *Divamania* a compilation of music by women, a couple of weeks later, teaching me how to compose music on a computer instead of with a band, and after I had received Gudrun's old Atari and "Cubase" to work on I started writing scores and recording odd sounds with my Sony walkman. I had been writing lyrics and poetry ever since learning the alphabet in school, secretly planning to become an author, and now trained myself to put pen to paper a little every day, using an intriguing technique I had read about in Anne Sexton's biography. She recommended opening a dictionary with closed eyes and pointing at words randomly, using them as the first and last points of a sentence. Surprising results would occur, which incorporated my original choice of topics but constructing them differently than I would have originally done, resulting in a fresher, unexpected manner.

After experimenting with different musicians and working possibilities I decided my preferred style would be mixing live and digital recordings inspired mainly by the British bands Portishead and Massive Attack, which I had discovered while working in a record store. Their use of different media and slow rhythms felt perfectly in tune with what I wanted to express. Having its roots in hip-hop and dub, trip-hop was not dominant in Berlin in the early 1990s. Fetish, my favorite Berlin DJ, who was always years ahead of his time, was one of the first to play the music in clubs, leaving me breathlessly excited, listening to the melancholic, voodoo-esque sounds, standing speechless during one of his WMF performances that introduced me to this form of expression.

Finding musicians was not easy, in general putting together members of a band is difficult if it doesn't happen naturally. It's hard to find others with the same taste, aspirations, and musical goals.

Deciding to randomly experiment with friends and let things happen intuitively I spent time working with Jayney, both of us singing, writing music, and designing elaborate costumes, but her taste veered towards pop and dance music. With Motte I tried writing a techno hit which quickly made it obvious that this was not what either of us wanted, and with Paul Browse, a former Clock DVA member, I composed an electronic, experimental track, which was inspiring but lacked the live instrumental element.

Finally deciding to go back to my roots I collected all the unused lyrics, rhythms, and melody ideas I had written for Space Cowboys and invited two longtime friends, Jacki Engelken and Ulrik Spies, to play guitar and drums for my new project, which was to be called Ta-Coma.

Bent on fulfilling my dream I courageously rented a studio to rehearse in and asked BMG for a small loan. Hartwig Masuch, the manager and a loyal fan of the Space Cowboys, surprised me by consenting, happy that one of us was continuing in spite of the band's downfall.

Thus I was able to hire a technician.

The sound engineer was very interested in participating and offered to organize a recording studio on the cheap, as long as I would pay for the catering and drinks. He also mentioned that he could play guitar and had wanted to do his own solo record for years. His eager anticipation should have awakened my suspicions, but again, it all happened too fast. The first days were spent recording my lyrics, Jacki playing slide guitar and Ulrik playing drums. I was exuberant to be working with friendly, supportive musicians and friends, composing music and singing my lyrics, a dream come true.

On the fourth day after discussing a certain chorus line which I wanted done very simply, in contrast to the engineer who wanted a multi-voiced choir, he ended up declaring that he was my producer, and, very similar to Jamie, after I reminded him that this was my project, on which I was spending my money, he threw me out of the recording room to arrange the music as he had wanted to, locking the door behind me. The disempowerment was so complete that I had no idea what to do. If I had been a man I would have punched him out of the studio but my musicians didn't want to confront him, worried that we would lose the studio and any other possibility of mixing the music, after already having spent all my money on the rent, the technician's fee, and catering. They decided it would be better to finish the recording badly and at least have a demo to distribute, rather than nothing at all, and took turns trying to influence him positively, but as he had the keys of the studio, the recording of our music, and a ruthless attitude he ignored any plea to stop kidnapping somebody else's dream and continued his rape without hesitation.

Deeply shocked I couldn't believe that the exact situation I had been in before was repeating itself. As a result I had a nervous breakdown. Stuck in bed, riddled with misery, unable to go the studio, I tried to direct the musicians by phone, telling them I did not want choirs or endless guitar solos ruining my songs. After shakily getting back on my feet on the last of the seven rented studio days I was confronted by the musicians handing over the twenty-four tracks with my poorly mixed music.

I was devastated.

1995

The break of day twinkled onto the golden stockade, reflecting glass in crystal clear sparkles, dazzling her eyes with their brilliance. The home of one of the largest media conglomerates in Germany meant her weary legs had almost reached their goal and promised the much-anticipated act of going to bed. Munching on a fresh croissant bought at Café Adler, the halfway point between work and home, she felt the warmth of the morning sun touching her tired face, its soft fingers gently mourning her skin's exhaustion.

Deafening rhythms, squeals of laughter, and slurred voices lingered in her ears as she progressively turned toward the Lindenstrasse, reflecting on the small talk she had made while collecting cash at the door, the furious face of the journalist to whom entry had been refused, and the many drinks downed.

A numbing wave of exhaustion clutched at her throat, how she longed to stop doing night shifts and concentrate solely on her art. Fumbling for keys in the small red bag bought the day before in Schöneberg, the wave of panic, a standard response to the mechanical repetition of her life, was unexpectedly interrupted by a slight movement in the corner of her eye.

As she looked up, the hair on the back of her neck stood upright in shock. She saw a large white form standing on the set of steps leading to her door. Gasping and staring speechlessly at the silent apparition, her numbed senses and instincts came alive with a jolt.

A pair of black, shiny eyes stared back unblinkingly.

In her favorite Ennio Morricone-scored movies, with Clint Eastwood in the leading role, this would have been the memorable scene of the final countdown with Eli Wallach crouching in the forlorn desert cemetery, both men about to pull their revolvers, an unmistakable Morricone music-box melody pointedly crying out into the echoing canyons and a sequence of memories depicting lost loves, crying children, and dead friends floating past the heroes' stonefaces. Comparable to this Hollywood version of a near-death experience, a wild array of faces, music, and memories swept through her mind, with an earsplitting mass of voices threatening, pleading, crying, and fading into a chess game of questions, morphing finally into the most urgent: which way to turn. The utter absurdity of not being able to go on walking nor turn back because of the figure blocking the entrance broke when a whirl of dizziness, resulting from the long hours of work, flung her into a spin of nausea, and afraid of fainting she moved to find a place to sit down. Finding a stone post close to the sidewalk she collapsed, burying a sweat covered brow in the soft cotton sleeves of a jacket thrown over the lacquered combat suit hours before *and breathing slowly the lump in her throat grew smaller, the roaring in her head fainter.*

"Maybe I should go back and get one of the bouncers to help me," she thought, slowly straightening up and peeking towards the house's entrance carefully. The huge swan had disappeared.

Confused she stood up and warily inched towards the door.

Nothing. The metal fixture stood as always, encased in the grey cement walls of the apartment house she had been living in for almost ten years. Staring at the cold front door, the image of the magnificent creature which had stood on the top step, its snow-white feathers softly moving in the morning air, the red feet firmly placed on the doormat, the long, elegant neck questioningly turned in her direction, in a posture of curiosity and proud defiance, ready to attack or relax, a warrior angel shining brightly, she suddenly felt she had missed a vital puzzle piece, the one she had been searching for.

"Come back! I need you to give me the answer!"

Running behind the building she expectantly turned right and left, hoping to catch a glance of the messenger.

But the extraordinary sentinel had disappeared quietly, leaving nothing but a feather on the doormat.

The Transition

The slaughter of my solo record not only left me distraught but also penniless, and to earn some money on the side I continued working in the record store, spending my time listening to new productions, remixes, and DJ recommendations. Walking home after work in the late afternoons the city seemed strangely desolate, the sky white and remote, stretching endlessly, as if something was shifting or lost. After the Space Cowboys' separation I had managed to disentangle myself from a violent and dishonest boyfriend, whom I had naively let into my life, not having had bad experiences with men up to then, and the distress of these combined betrayals and fear had shaken the definition of support I had always taken for granted. Not only was the group of friends, my family of almost five years, now divided, I had loved the wrong man and lost my main means of income. Jacki and Ulrik decided to join Ben Becker's Zero Tolerance Band after the producer chaos within my project and I was left on my own again, without a band or certain future.

Licking my wounds and trying to think up schemes of how to redirect my life toward a more positive direction, I turned to appraise and reevaluate my surroundings and was confronted with an estranged community, an ever-growing wave of commercialism and a new generation of DJs, artists, and entrepreneurs from outside the city that I had never heard of. Feeling slightly alarmed and overrun I decided to get back into touch with reality and spent weekends scrutinizing new clubs, listening to unknown DJs, visiting club owners, catching up on the latest gossip, visiting museums, galleries, curators, and, most of all, getting back in touch with old friends.

Roland Wolf

Born in Bonn and raised in Greece, Roland moved to Berlin in the early eighties, lured by the music scene of the Geniale Dilletanten. Within a short time the talented musician was asked to play keyboards for Nick Cave, catapulting him into that musician's heaven and hell. Being able to play almost any instrument or tune, composing classical music or symphonies on the side, brooding over George Crumb's intermezzos, Hank Williams's slide guitar, or Arvo Pärt's compositions were his favorite pastimes but his introverted, highly complex personality did not mesh well with the ruthless world of entertainment.

After I initially moved to Berlin, I didn't meet Roland for quite some time. The friendly community of fun-loving characters I lived with provided constant entertainment and I had become accustomed to the comfortable evenings with Gaby and Claudia cooking dinner, telling each other stories about parties and jobs, inviting friends over to watch a movie. Marcus would appear randomly, bringing a bottle of wine and additional fellow students, the large group of people laughing and arguing loudly, drinking, chain smoking, cooking pasta at four in the morning and slurping Gaby's delicious chai until sunrise.

It was on one of the mornings after such a party as we were washing dishes and cleaning our large wooden table companionably, that the apartment door unexpectedly opened and a man carrying a couple of guitar cases and a huge suitcase strode over the threshold. I was surprised, having forgotten that there was one more person paying the rent and looked at Gaby and Claudia questioningly. They in turn had become unusually silent, watching Roland drop his luggage and throw his coat on a small chair next to the door. After mumbling a gruff hello and throwing a sharp glance at me with piercing blue eyes, he walked off to his room, dragging the suitcase behind. The mood changed in our abode.

Roland did not emerge from his room for days and Gaby reacted by canceling appointments and standing in front of his door silently, her ear stuck to the wooden frame, trying to catch any signs of life. Claudia reprimanded her in regular intervals to leave him alone and let him sleep, taking a neutral stance, and Markus disappeared completely, staying over at his girlfriends.

One morning after about a week, coming home from my café shift, I found him walking about in the telephone room, unpacking guitars and placing them next to the other fifteen instruments displayed there. Ignoring my shy hello he continued tuning his twelve-stringed telecaster without acknowledging my presence until, annoyed, I turned around to go to my room. It was then that he hoarsely asked: "Who are you?" Whirling around to explain that I had just moved in, I caught a full glimpse of his face, which was usually hidden by long, light brown hair. The mixture of shyness and defiance in his expression took my breath away and for a long moment we stood contemplating each other, then simultaneously turned, one of those moments you never forget.

During the following days and weeks I slowly became used to Roland's lifestyle, an unorthodox schedule of playing loud guitar solos at three in the morning, disappearing for days and then suddenly joining us at our chai-drinking sessions in the evening. He would sit at the table, head in hands, hair covering his face and every so often suddenly contradict somebody's blithe comment in a precise and cutting manner. Nobody dared answer except Gaby. Laughingly making a joke to lighten the atmosphere and shaking her head at him she would get the conversation going again, but his presence remained intimidating.

I was intrigued by the things he said, not daring to answer, but thinking about them for days, looking up authors he mentioned or listening to the records left lying around.

Sometimes as I sat watching TV in our large, empty entertainment lounge he would walk in silently, sit down on the red sofa, and look at the program with me, leaving a couple of minutes before it was over, not saying a word.

On a rainy Sunday afternoon, months after Roland had come back from tour, I sat sifting through his extensive record collection in the living room, poring over names I had never heard, inspecting the dark, raw covers depicting eerie scenes of underground clubs or strange instruments, when his rough voice suddenly asked from behind me if I knew who Diamanda Galas was.

I had been convinced that he wasn't at home and jumped with fright, worried he might be annoyed that I was looking at his belongings, but instead he sat down next to me, pulling out his favorite albums, playing certain songs, explaining their background and philosophies in a modest but passionate manner. I could have sat there forever, hoping he would never stop, his words a stream of stories I felt I had been waiting for all my life, philosophies I had tried discovering, finally introduced to the deeper meaning of the uncompromising mystic search for truth and provocation that this dark and ravished city of contradictions could both offer and attract.

After a couple of hours he left as abruptly as he had appeared, leaving me in a state of transfixion.

We tried and struggled to find a way to interact for months but the tension remained and the endeavor was doomed to fail. An unbreakable barrier kept us from being able to relax when we were together, a pressure we were not allowed to name. Once in a while he would abruptly appear in my hallway where I sat painting and softly say, "I can't take you where I'm going," leaving me to cry for hours. At one point we stopped speaking to each other, not being able to cope with the situation, everybody in the apartment tiptoeing around silently until he went back on tour. By the time he came back I was gone.

For years we would see each other sporadically. After he had stopped playing with Nick Cave and experienced a short and unsatisfactory tryout with P. J. Harvey, not getting along with her manager, his life became increasingly solitary.

The Ritterstrasse community broke up because of rising rents and he moved into a small one bedroom on the ground floor of an apartment building in Schöneberg, overlooking an immense graveyard. He would sit for days composing complicated modern symphonies. Known as a gruff and ruthlessly honest man, never willing to make a light excuse, uncompromising (often unbearably so), unerringly loyal and trustworthy, he was respected and admired from afar but most people were unsettled by his straightforwardness.

At times he would visit me at the bar I was working at, staying for a drink and telling me what he was up to, bringing an invitation or putting me on the guest list for a concert and we would make careful conversation, evading difficult personal themes, lingering on cultural or political topics, carefully clinging to the barriers we had built, waving goodbye sadly in the end and returning to our everyday life.

Seven years after meeting for the first time, we bumped into each other late one night at the Ex 'n' Pop. It was unusual for Roland to go out at all and I was astonished to see him sitting alone on a bar stool, apart from the crowd. He looked worn and depressed. I went over to say hello, asking how he was. Obviously in a bad state he avoided looking into my eyes, gruffly muttering that he was not very well and tried turning away from my gaze despite obviously being happy to see me.

Worried, knowing what an extreme character he was, prone to excessive drug abuse and guns, I scrutinized the sunken figure, noticing his slender, intelligent fingers shaking and his face covered in sweat. Picking up my courage I asked him to finally give me a true answer, tell me what was wrong and how tired I was of our cat-and-mouse game. As if pulled by a string his head slowly turned towards me and for the first time since our initial glance years ago, he looked into my eyes for more than a few seconds. The beautiful blue eyes with dark lashes had acquired dark shadows and once again I was rendered speechless, and with pain and defiance, this time he asked why he should trust me, challenging me to give the right answer, scornfully accepting disappointment.

Overcome by empathy for his unadjustable stance I began telling him why he was so important to me, causing surprise and then a growing light in his eyes. Concentrating on my words he hesitantly started speaking, obviously not accustomed to baring his soul, but the stumbling stream of expression grew stronger, turning into an avalanche and finally breaking the damn, flooding away inhibition, fear, or prejudice and accepting the dare of revelation.

We forgot the world and sat in the dark bar talking for hours. When the crowd grew too loud we stood outside, under a roof, protected from the wind until I started shivering, ending up in his tiny apartment around the corner and catching up on the rest of the last decade, now that we were finally able to speak to each other.

Being there in his room that first evening was odd. I knew almost every one of the hundreds of books surrounding us, including their metal shelves and smell, having had them stored in my apartment for years. I had often sat looking down at the handwritten, scribbled notes written in between the Beckett, Burroughs, Kierkegaard, or Cormac McCarthy texts, imagining Roland reading the book in a silent, dark room, smoking Gauloises cigarettes without filters, writing comments next to a sentence that had caught his attraction, while listening to music by Burt Bacharach, Morricone, or the Swans, in complete, fulfilled solitude.

Lying next to him in bed was even stranger; sharing intimacy with somebody I had thought about so intensely was confusing, making reality and dreams whirl into a waltz of unbalanced steps. Watching him smoke and listening to his thoughts about the consequence of influences, rummaging together through boxes of homemade tapes, playing our favorites, listening to his description of lyrics, structure, and morbid biographies, I felt as if I had arrived in a dark, quiet cave of my soul, my spirit flattened out on the thin pillows, exhausted but happy, another missing link finally apparent.

The first weeks of our liaison were spent in the dark room, lying on the narrow cot with rays of light falling through the curtain, speaking of childhood, parents, the many tours he had gone on, addictions, food, our taste in music and art, sharing dreams and aspirations, listening to music for hours, setting tarot cards, looking at antique books and trying to deal with our new familiarity. Roland agreed to give up his longstanding drug habit and mentioned wanting to compose music together with me, loving the same unfamiliar sounds, uncommon rhythms and forlorn atmospheres. He planned to concentrate on working together with the three most important people in his life: Blixa Bargeld, Alexander Hacke, and Ghazi Barakat (Boy from Brazil), jokingly calling them his "three magi," explaining that each one was responsible for a different part of his personality: the intellect, the soul, and the body.

Blixa and Alexander I had met, Ghazi Barakat was new and as Roland wanted me to like him as much as he did, the good-looking Palestinian singer of the Golden Showers became somebody we met with regularly, hanging out in his apartment looking at bizarre videos and unusual art pieces.

Ghazi loved anything that was deviant, his rebellion against placid, fake morals or corrupt bourgeoisie far more excessive than anything I had experienced in friends before. Bondage art, documented eye or heart operations, freak forms of sex, death cults, heroin philosophies and morphium relics, anything he discovered within these realms was eagerly examined, smiled, or laughed about and integrated into his lyrics, styling, or cover art. Some discoveries would make me feel sick, and I would leave the room and come back after the film was over to find Roland chuckling over the ludicrousness of what he had just seen, his black sense of humor appreciating the contradictions and Ghazi watching with a gleam in his eye, happy to have a friend who could match his excessiveness, both of them laughing at my queasiness, and then we would all go off together and eat something at the local Indian restaurant.

Blixa Bargeld, the charismatic vocalist of Einstürzende Neubauten, represented an utterly different realm for Roland. They would meet regularly in the morning after breakfast, to work on theater and music compositions, exchanging intellectual views on music, literature, and minimalism while composing, playing the piano or guitar, two unconventional loners sharing a deep pleasure of perfection and crystal-clear observation. Roland, quite a bit younger than Blixa, loved him as a friend and father figure, appreciating his opinion, sharp humor, and taste in clothes. Blixa on the other hand cherished Roland's candid honesty, impatient intelligence, and startling talent. This intensely personal and bonding relationship was a well of strength and support for Roland, who was much weaker and more vulnerable than I had expected him to be. Frequently he would mention the fact that similar to himself, Blixa woke up every morning thinking "Why go on?" and that the reason why both continued was reassuring. I was never told the reason.

Alexander Hacke, the bassist of Einstürzende Neubauten and the third musketeer in Roland's group of soul mates, was the heart of all matters. This bearlike figure, with his good-natured chuckle and expansive gestures, was the opposite of Roland's introverted character. Fearlessly taking dares, a hurricane bursting through concerts and relationships, constantly surrounded by clusters of fans, groupies, and envious entrepreneurs, a natural skipjack, bouncing up immediately after a blow, not bothering to contemplate the cause, instead, instantaneously heading off to the next adventure, popping pills, kissing girls, drinking bathtubs of whiskey and beer, throwing jokes out at breakneck speed, he challenged anybody to stop or deter him. He considered himself Roland's friend and protector, loving him deeply as a frail but cutting-edge genius, roaring with laughter at his dry jokes, cutting comments, and grumpy idiosyncrasies. After Roland had stopped playing with Nick Cave, Alexander decided to put together a country band "to entertain himself" between Neubauten sessions, called Jever Mountain Boys. He invited Ralf Strunz and Jochen Arbeit to play guitar, Moritz Wolpert drums, and Rumme Beck bass. Shortly after, Strunz fell in love with the Neubauten tour manager Jessamy Calkin and decided to move to London with her, so Hacke asked Roland to join the band with his slide guitar. Alexander himself is an incredibly talented multi-instrumentalist who plays guitar, bass, and drums, and had decided to sing only weeks before. Stumbling home he had encountered an ex-convict on the edge of the Spree river, contemplating what to do with his life. Upon seeing a guitar in Alexander's hand he asked him to sing a song, possibly a country or blues tune. To his great embarrassment Alex had to admit that he didn't know any by heart, as it had never occurred to him to memorize lyrics. In what was later called a "moment of clarity," he went home to teach himself Hank Williams and Johnny Cash evergreens, then and there deciding to create a cover band as homage to the music he had grown up with, when he listened to AFN, the American Forces Radio, as a small boy growing up in the Neukölln district of Berlin. The band formed in 1991 and after rehearsing for a couple of weeks the wild alliance performed at the Graf Joster on the 25th of December.

Although it was Christmas Day, a difficult date to catch a crowd, the band was an instant success.

Alexander Hacke turned out to be a natural born singer, his strong voice, charismatic appearance, and madcap stage persona had star quality, the kind of presence that brought a gleam to all eyes watching him. Combined with Roland's melancholic slide harmonies, the unconventional swing/rock beats that Moritz played on his drums, and Rummie's sexy bass playing it was a perfect combination. Enrico Croci, Neubauten's Italian booker, immediately organized a tour, getting a slot as supporting act for the Swans, introducing them to a larger, more international crowd. In 1994 they recorded their first record *Bury the Bottle with Me*, released by Mr. Dead & Mrs. Free, a local record store, and the eagerly anticipated product quickly became a cult object for their large fan base, singing, screaming, and dancing at the first glimpse of the band coming on stage. The shows were persistently packed and a "must-see" among the Berlin underground, catapulting the musicians into well-deserved success.

Even so, because of his former, longstanding drug abuse, resulting in deep depressions and panic attacks, Roland was consistently experiencing strange accidents, worrisome for all his friends. Either he slipped in the shower, disconnecting his shoulder, shot himself through the tip of his tongue during an illegal gun competition on a deserted farm, or drove into a stop sign on his bicycle, giving himself concussion, or almost crashed the Neubauten bus filled with instruments he was driving from Berlin to Conny Plank's studio in Bavaria.

Being a complicated personality it was difficult to fathom what was going on with him, or help him. The extreme recluse repeatedly muttered that nobody could help him, that he was an evil person who had committed unspeakable crimes, and that everything was hopeless. Just when I was about to despair he would suddenly fall into loving descriptions of music, speaking about rhythms, sounds, and melodies for hours, his eyes sparkling with enthusiasm.

Our relationship remained a surreal experience, recording music, watching bizarre movies, and reading nihilist philosophies, visiting abstract theater plays or just lying around our apartments. Roland was all I had imagined, but his extreme character accentuated the dark side of an addict trying to get the monkey off his back, combining sudden, furious outbreaks of desperation with paranoid telephone calls, sometimes thirty-five in three hours, asking me where I was, paired with violent crying. The situation was comparable to a state of madness far beyond anything I had anticipated. Our liaison was a constant mix of desperation and magical understanding, the typically romanticized rock 'n' roll relationship along the lines of Sid and Nancy, Curt Cobain and Courtney Love, Kate Moss and Pete Doherty, which in reality is almost impossible to maintain, being a heartbreaking mix of drugs, alcohol, and confused and disheartened personalities trying to find the solution of their misery in the other person, not realizing that no matter how strong the actual love is, the problems need to solved before being able to deal with any kind of rapport. Tragically many of these idolized figures end up dead, too exhausted to confront life in a promising way.

Roland was willing to try, eating healthily, hardly going out to clubs, proudly abstinent, indulging in long bike rides and inspiring projects. Trying to find a solution to our topsy-turvy relationship we decided to start seriously recording music together in a friend's studio. Concentrating on the same goal and uniting artistically seemed to be a positive and fulfilling endeavor. After my bad luck with working on music I had become very cautious but Roland was so enthusiastic, preparing and collecting strange, rusty sounds of carriage wheels and squeaking wood, that I decided to put aside my fear of being betrayed once more and trust his integrity.

We had arranged to start recording on the 26th of March, 1995, both looking forward to getting our project rolling, borrowing studio material, instruments and recording machines from friends to save costs. I deejayed the night before, earning a little money in one of Dimitri's clubs by playing a 1970s soul and hip-hop mix, happy finally to be entering the world of music again, this time with a true friend and anticipating the different songs we had discussed. When Roland came to see me, kissing me happily before leaving early, not wanting to be too tired the next day, I felt that we were on the right track, relieved to have found a solution at last.

The next morning I was woken at 7 a.m. by his sister crying on the phone, saying Roland had had a car accident and was unconscious in hospital. I listened in shock, my brain not functioning, not knowing how to react. After hanging up I sat, staring at my cats, remembering his departure the evening before: whispering "See you tomorrow," flashing his lopsided grin, twinkling his beautiful blue eyes, flipping a cigarette carelessly in the corner and turning to leave through the door, ignoring the sweaty dancers and drunken women, turning back once again to wave, his intense glance slipping over my face, to be gone the next minute.

Gone. The word seemed to ring hollowly, scaring me to tears; jumping out of bed I called Ghazi. Surprisingly he answered at the first ring. After hearing my tears and news he rushed over immediately and we went to the hospital together, holding hands in the subway, consoling each other and, promising that everything would be OK upon our arrival. Finally there I met Roland's parents for the first time and was confronted with the news that he had just died.

I left the hospital not knowing where to go or what to do. I spent hours silently sitting in the subway unable to leave the dark, comforting tunnels of Berlin, Ghazi at my side.

The rattling of wheels, screeching metal, monotone travel announcements, shuffling footsteps, and muffled speaking masked our tears. Wooden platform benches and plastic-covered subway seats became sanctuaries, catching our turmoil within a lurching world, twisted into a senselessly rushing transportation vehicle, hastening through a city, on the way to nowhere, faster and faster, unbearably loud, screaming, a soul lost in the midst of a black void, a film of déjà vu sequences flashing past, encased in the blurred windows: Roland walking into the Ritterstrasse, his memorable eyes, rough voice, carefully pitched, softly explaining intricate rhythms, dark three-piece suits carefully hung, the vast collection of tapes, hats, Australian cowboy boots, guitar strings, composition paper, our bodies lying next to each other on the narrow cot in the shadowy room, listening to the silence, dark blond hair curling behind his ears in soft ringlets contradicting his impatient macho stance and brusque brushing off of silly, superficial chit-chat, his favorite ring with the black stone, the soft sound of a piano playing Burt Bacharach at four in the morning, Arvo Pärt melodies in the Ritterstrasse on Sundays, his slide guitar and favorite drones accompanying Ghazi's singing, knees bent with concentration, the smell of aftershave, the old-fashioned desk covered with ink scrawlings, long phone calls while he was on tour, descriptions of cities and countries seen, hopes and dreams hesitantly mentioned.

With each passing moment, memory, subway station, and tear, another layer of flesh was ripped off, tearing my heart to shreds.

Roland's parents decided that he should be cremated and fixed the date to one month after his death. After calling Alexander, who was working with Neubauten in Munich I fell into a nightmare, unable to sleep or speak. My brother and sister took turns watching me, when they went home my friends came by constantly. I started hearing voices, experiencing strange daydreams of Roland wounded and bleeding, the sensation of the top part of my head slipping off, sidewalks and buildings seemingly rolling in the wind with sounds amplified to a roaring volume, forcing me to wear earplugs constantly. I was either avoided by people, not able to deal with my situation, or held tight by the courageous ones that could. Sometimes I would go out with a group of friends and try to drink away the shock but was incapable of becoming drunk. Soberly I would watch strong musicians drunkenly cry and reminisce, incapable of connecting with anybody. As the weeks went by and my state became worse I became the communal responsibility of Berlin's underground, Gudrun taking me to her home, turning her sofa into a comfortable bed, cooking meals and drying my tears, Motte, who had become a Buddhist, introducing me to prayers, Johnny trying to lift my spirits by cracking jokes and inventing funny little excursions, Ghazi calling at all hours of the day, Bob Rutman playing steel cello whenever I appeared, Dorothy Carter giving me healthy kefir mushrooms, Jochen hugging and crying with me, their worried faces watching me walk backwards down the street horrified of being attacked by a ghost or stabbed in the back by other imagined dangers and protecting me from eager psychologists recommending that I be locked up. The only friend who had completely disappeared was Hacke, who drank himself into oblivion, unable to cope with his friend's demise.

When the dreaded occasion finally took place a large group of helpless, shaken friends stood waiting in the cemetery.

After we had been sitting in a small chapel staring at the urn, the priest finally came, and a procession began winding down the pathway to the gravesite. The walk seemed endless, the wind blew softly in the graveyard, which ironically was stationed directly beneath Roland's former apartment. The crypts we were passing were the ones we had gazed upon often on late Sunday afternoons, happy to be alive, making jokes about which one we would choose later on. As I looked up toward the window an unbearable sense of solitude, a feeling of being cut off from all human connection, encased my heart. I walked alone behind the urn carrier and Roland's parents, each subsequent step seeming impossible, nobody daring to walk next to me and fill the empty space. With tears dropping from my eyes I suddenly felt a strong hand under my arm, catching my downward fall and looking up I recognized Blixa handing me a Kleenex, looking straight ahead but nodding his head reassuringly. He held my arm throughout the long march and together we walked to the grave, watching the urn sink into the earth, listening to the few words spoken, following the long line of pale and drawn mourners, stepping up to the burial place and silently bidding farewell to a friend and an era slowly being lowered into the dark, cool earth.

With Roland's death, the underground scene of the Geniale Diletantten I had hung out with, the celebrated and admired anarchic, existential, 1980s character of the Berlin I had loved so much received a heavy blow, throwing its members into the four winds, stumbling, trying to regain their balance, only to realize that the communal feeling was disappearing. Berlin had evolved, the new make-up hardening into permanent features and by 1995 we stood alone. The latest rules and regulations were opposite to the ones we had been used too, with prices rising, wealth becoming more and more important, VIP adulation, silly game masters and reality shows popping up, actors pretending to be rock stars, cheesy cabaret events, slick fashion shows sponsored by Veuve Cliquot or Mercedes Benz, luxurious Rolls Royce car rentals, *Playboy* spreads on local celebrities, and buffets with politicians making sleazy jokes or propositions. Berlin had entered the real world.

Pictures

1: This is a picture of my father's family in Egypt. My father is second from the right. I used to love listening to the stories he told us of his childhood—they were always filled with admiration and respect towards his parents. Sadly they died when I was four—his father of cancer and his mother two years later of a broken heart.
Photographer: unknown

2: The day of the "Schöne Neue Welt" charity art project was magical—here you can see me painting my picture for the project early in the morning. It was the first sunny day in weeks.
Photographer: Pico Risto

3: This is the window of my first room in Berlin.
Photographer: Danielle de Picciotto

4: This is Motte in our first appartment in Lindenstrasse. You can see some of his hundreds of record stacks behind him.
Photographer: Danielle de Picciotto

5: This photo of the Tiger Lillies, Hacke, and myself was taken in Hamburg in front of the "Schmidts Tivoli" theater in which we were performing *"The Mountains Of Madness"*.
Photographer: Fritz Brinkmann

6: I like this photo of Roland, he looks relaxed and happy. A rare state for him to be in.
Photographer: Danielle de Picciotto

7: This photo shoot with Space Cowboys was fun. We did our own styling—the bird kept on slipping but otherwise everybody felt comfortable.
Photographer: Uwe Arens

8: This is a picture of the third part of my "Dornröschen lacht" exhibition. It is a short film loop of my niece Kira waking up and laughing in a bed of roses.
Photographer: Danielle de Picciotto

9: The castle in Senzke illuminated by Skudi Optix looked amazing from a distance set in the sober landscape of Brandenburg at night.
Photographer: Anno Dittmer

10: I took this picture of Gudrun Gut and Anita Lane for their *Oceanclub* single.

11: I took this picture one day during the mid 90s—it portrays the magical, timeless feeling associate with the Berlin I fell in love with in 1987.

6

7

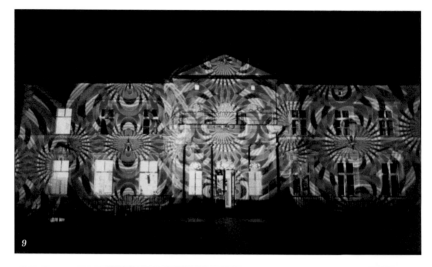

9

10

13

14

15

16

17

18

SERVUS, KAISER. EINE MODENSCHAU

LISA D. JUDITH FÖRSTER
FIONA BENNETT DANIELLE DE PICCIOTTO
SEPPO GRÜNDLER — MUSIK

LISA D. , GRAZ, BERLIN
FIONA BENNETT, BERLIN
JUDITH FÖRSTER, BERLIN
DANIELLE DE PICCIOTTO,
BERLIN, N. Y.

*SERVUS, KAISER
EINE MODENSCHAU*

*Musik: Seppo Gründler
Text: Anette Berr
Bühne, Licht: Hermann Schapek
Frisuren: Alcazar*

Sa., 11. Nov., + So., 12. Nov., 20 Uhr
Festsaal im Meerscheinschlößchen
Mozartgasse 3, Eintritt: S 120,—/100,—
Karten an der Abendkasse

19

20

21

22

unsere lieblings pLatten

RADIO
Knorr

Im Goldenen Hahn PÜCKLERSTR 20

22 UHR DO 8. SEPTEMBER

GENIESSEN SIE IHREN AUFENTHALT.

23

12: This is a picture I took of Motte and a model wearing my clubwear. I actually made the jacket for Motte. The back of the girl's top is an application of the queen of hearts I stitched by hand. It was a lot of work. The applications were always made of leather and very hard to pierce with a needle. But the material allowed for very precise images.

13: This is an installation I did at the Maria club. It was a mixture of filmloops and slide projections moving randomly.

Photographer: Danielle de Picciotto

14: This was my first installation of the Tresor club's bathroom which was always an exciting place during the early 1990s.

Photographer: Danielle de Picciotto

15: This is the installation I did in Hong Kong for the "Vision of Light" festival. I was impressed at how quickly they had built the pavilion specifically for the festival on a parking lot and how beautifully the floors and partitions were designed. I had gone through an extended phase of painting oriental portraits for years before I went to Hong Kong. The inspiration probably stemmed from my father working in a Korean orphanage when I was four and having sent me Korean dolls and kimonos which I wore throughout my childhood.

Photographer: Danielle de Picciotto

16: I took this picture from my kitchen window in Lindenstrasse.

17: I took this picture of Alexander Hacke on our first trip to Mexico.

18: This is Alexander in Fredrick Nilson's studio in L.A. I took the photograph during our road trip for *Sanctuary*. It gives a good impression of how mobile his studio was—small and handy but very professional.

Photographer: Danielle de Picciotto

19: This is the invitation to our fashion show in Graz which I was at whilst the Wall came down in Berlin.

20: The *Sanctuary* tour lineup. From the left: Sugar Pie Jones, Danielle, Alexander Hacke, Ash Wednesday, Gordon W.

Photographer: Thomas Ecke

21: This is the press photo for the album Alexander and I recorded together in 2010 in which I sang, played piano and autoharp, and did visuals. It was a dream come true to write music together with the man I loved.

Photographer: Tina Winkhaus

22: Alexander Hacke took this picture of Fiona Bennett and myself in Hamburg in the Elb Lounge where we were celebrating my new installation of pictures and statues.

23: This is one of the many invitations I designed over the years—I have always liked collages. On that evening Gudrun and I DJed our favorite songs—focusing specifically on female vocalists. It was set in the Goldener Hahn, a small Italian restaurant initiated by Dimitri Hegemann.

1995–2000

The Tempest

Shortly before Roland's death and the demise of the Jever Mountain Boys, the band had acquired a new fan.

Ben Becker, the adopted son of iconic German actor Otto Sander, had returned to Berlin after living and working in Stuttgart for a couple of years, learning theater techniques and acting in a couple of films. Immediately falling in love with the Jever Boys and their tough cowboy stance, which included wearing huge hats and pointed boots, dressing up in Mexican wrestling masks that Hacke had obtained during a Neubauten tour, drinking madly and partying wildly with hysterical fans gathering around them after each successful show, he followed them from performance to performance, trying to become a member of the crowd, method acting to recreate Alexander Hacke's every movement. The musicians, used to fans, accepted his admiration matter-of-factly, accepting their different artistic responsibilities with respect and distance.

After Roland's death and the ensuing confused, lost state of all of his friends, Ben was suddenly in the position of offering them the support they needed. Knowing Roland but not being a close friend, he was able to participate in the burial rituals without being as shaken as the rest. During the weeks before and after the burial, my friends sought each other out constantly, trying to find comfort by being together, not wanting to stay at home with dark thoughts, hanging out in bars or restaurants or sleeping over, happy for anybody to take over the lead, telling them when and where they should meet and what would happen. Alexander Hacke, the former head of the pack, was too distraught by the death to be able to deal with responsibility; in fact, his excessive drinking had become so bad that people were worried he would go next, as they observed with rolling eyes and shaking fingers. The youngest of the Neubauten crew had never had an easy life, death had often been a part of it, but this one he could not digest. His behavior was horrifyingly erratic, the man only cared about his next drink or distraction, anything to block out his pain.

Ben's assets in comparison were money that bought drinks, a family offering elaborate home-cooked dinners, and a project to distract us. Ben had decided to produce a play in which he could combine his world of theater with that of Alexander Hacke, an authentic, rebel outlaw. He convinced us by saying that all of the friends in mourning would play a part, asking me to design the costumes and stage settings. To make it as authentic as possible he decided to set it in the Ex 'n' Pop, home of all outlaws, promising that it would be a huge success and ensuring financial support for all. The play he had written was to be called *Sid und Nancy;* the story of the infamous heroin rock 'n' roll couple, with Alexander playing Sid, and Ben's sister Meret as Nancy.

This theater piece introduced a new setting to the Ex 'n' Pop scenario. During the first weeks of rehearsal I prepared the costumes and stage settings in a sticky cloud of misery, breaking down and crying constantly, only too happy to have something to do and people to meet, not noticing or caring about the details or strange temper tantrums being acted out on stage. The warm companionship of the crew helped in being able to cope with a world out of sync and I suspect the endeavor was the only thing keeping me alive during the first few months after Roland's death.

Soon we'd completed the construction of a small wooden stage covered with a red rug, a metal bed, lamp, and small bathroom. The stage was set so that the entrance of the club was blocked and had to be taken apart every evening after the show, which meant vacuuming the rug, taking down all the furniture, collecting the costumes, set items, make-up kits, and the beer boxes from under the stage floor that held the weight of the performance as quickly as possible and storing them in the back. Pepi Streich, an eccentric Berlin figure, known for bicycling through Berlin with a homemade wagon, turned out to be a reliable, matter-of-fact hand for these unusual proceedings, making the show possible from a practical point of view. The premiere was sold out, filled with celebrities and friends. We all stood on stage, bowing, holding hands, entwined in the combined effort, happy that the experiment had worked out, once more having found a den in which we could lick our wounds while supporting each other.

When on the second evening Ben decided to only allow the "V.I.P" actors to go on stage and take the applause I finally woke up and reacted immediately, fiercely defending the other participants and insisting that everyone should take bows every night for their work, otherwise I would have been robbed of the only thing that made sense for me in the dark, endless abyss of pain and loss, standing together with a group of friends, being in the same boat, existing in a community in which the sole thing that counted was friendship and shared enthusiasm.

Because of my "widow" status Ben tolerated my first and last tantrum and further appearances were concluded with everybody on stage at the end of the evening, but the comradeship had been split into "V.I.Ps" and "Non V.I.Ps," and the boat I had imagined saving me sank quietly. After-show dinners were spent in restaurants which only wealthy people could afford, leaving friends outside, sadly peering through the windowpanes. Press releases mentioned names already known, ignoring the combined effort that had made the show possible in the first place, and salaries paid were not related to the actual labor nor were they split equally among everybody, as we had usually done, but instead according to the "degree" of one's fame. Considering that this was a tiny performance, taking place in a bar that would not hold more than one hundred chairs, the strength of these rules seems amazing in retrospect.

Shortly after the last performance Dimitri asked me to meet him for dinner. We had developed a nice little ritual over the years, meeting in unusual cafés for Sunday lunch to brainstorm on music, art, and literature. The theme of the last meeting had been Neapolitan tango music, which Dimitri had discovered; this time he once more proposed renting a gallery for me, convinced that this could be a more professional way of my promoting other artists as I had already been doing on the side for years, and getting to know the art world from another perspective. I hesitated, worried it would take too much of my time, but Dimitri was so adamant about financing the whole venture, including paying the rent, a small salary, and funding a catalogue for each exhibition, that I seriously started contemplating the idea for the first time.

It would be a good way of not having to work at night any more, something I had decided on after Roland's death. Nightlife had become entirely dissatisfying, I found the constant repetition of drinking, dancing, and coupling depressing after experiencing how quickly life can be lost.

In general, the experience of my boyfriend dying so unexpectedly had changed my life entirely, to an extent I would only grasp years later. Looking back I see that my life has been split in half: before and after Roland's death.

During the aftermath, with the shock wearing off after many years, all I could do was survive. Depression, panic attacks, fear, self-accusations, a deteriorated self-esteem and distrust of life in general took over. All interest in designing colorful cloths, looking eccentric, making an effort with my hair or wearing jewelry had completely disappeared. In contrast to my extroverted former appearance, wearing a beehive of hair extensions, fake eyelashes, strong make-up with white powder and bright red lips, strings of necklaces, earrings, rings, and many bracelets, tartan skirts, striped stockings, silver bodices, appliquéd jackets, lace up, lacquered boots, I now for the first time in my life entirely wore black.

Because of the inconceivable change within the city and within my circle of friends, of my not working at night any more, hardly going out, and my music career having come to a complete halt, I became a recluse, preferring cats to small talk, finding social life difficult to deal with, not understanding the implicitness my surroundings had retained. I would go to the Ex 'n' Pop to participate at social gatherings once in a while, performing with friends, but in general I felt distant and misplaced. I don't know how people deal with losing families during a war; the amount of time it took for me to come to terms with the bereavement seemed endless.

Then I was flung into the next abyss. My father was diagnosed with leukemia. He had been a great support after Roland's burial, flying me to New York and his comforting arms, trying to offer distraction with trips to the Metropolitan or Modern Museum of Art, shyly introducing me to the only relief that had helped him survive concentration camps, war, death, exodus, persecution, racism, madness, divorce, prejudice, and loneliness: art and his love of it. Knowing how broke I was, he worried about my wellbeing, buying me trunks full of clothes, books, and oil paints to help me survive in Berlin, transferring a small amount of money each month to help me pay my rent. His Sunday afternoon phone calls and compassionate conversations on the newest exhibitions or cultural trends was a ritual of ours for years. In spite—or because of—his attacks of paranoia, during which he would rant about how his neighbor was trying to kill him, his hairdresser had almost cut off his ear, and the drug store around the corner was being run by a spy, this small, frightened man completely understood how life can tear you apart, offering compassion and help at any time of the day or night, a warmth I could feel no matter how far away he was. Not wanting to worry us he didn't mention his state of health to me or my siblings until it was too late. Then my brother, an architect in Hamburg, was called long distance by a doctor who informed him that our father would die within a couple of days. Charles flew to New York immediately, my sister Simone and I managed to get tickets for a flight two days later. I tried bracing myself for yet another death but when we arrived nothing could have prepared us for what we were confronted with. My brother picked us up at the airport in our father's small car, his face sad and drawn. He told us that our father had almost died the night before but when he found out that we were coming, he had decided to wait. The doctors had taken this chance to try saving his life once more, hooking him to a machine.

Bewildered, I felt as if words had lost their meaning, not understanding how any of this was possible, deciding not to ask questions while dragging my luggage behind me.

The long walk down the hall of terminal illnesses in which we could see people in small rooms left and right, panting, crying, moaning, screaming, alone with white glaring walls, bright glittering metal, loudly clanking machines, pumping air and blood devices, with a sharp pungent odor of detergents and chloroform embalming all, made Dante's *inferno* seem pleasant in comparsion.

So easy to forget when you're healthy, so horrifying when finally confronted with this carefully avoided place of pain. Doctors explain the rooms have to be hygienic, nurses snap they don't have time, relatives whisper, "Well I guess there's nothing we can do," and friends have flowers sent.

Why is death only dealt with nowadays in splatter movies or police thrillers? Why does our society ignore the one thing we all must go through instead of preparing each other positively? When we got to my father's room I couldn't believe my eyes. They had chained him to the bed.

Incredulously I stared at my brother, unable to speak. "He tried to pull out the plastic breathing device pushed down his throat."

"What?"

"He doesn't want to be hooked onto any life keeping devices."

"Why?"

"He had written it into his will, which they ignored, so he tried pulling it out with his hands. They chained him to the bed and he spent the whole night choking up the tube piece by piece."

"What?"

"He actually managed to choke up the whole tube."

"But isn't he in pain?"

"Terrible pain, but he refuses to let them give him anything. He's had a small heart attack and his one kidney collapsed. His feet hurt because they are so swollen, but he refuses any painkiller. He wants to die naturally."

At that moment my father, who had been sleeping, woke up. He saw me and started speaking in a high, unnatural voice. I couldn't understand him at first, the words poured out of his throat in such a fast and jabbering way. After a while I realized that he was saying, "I want to die Danielle. Help me. My time has come and I don't want to postpone it. I've lived my life. I've had enough and I'm not scared. I want to die now. Don't let them force me to stay."

Tears blurred my eyes and not knowing what to say or do I bent down and kissed his chained hands.

"But Daddy, I love you."

"I know Danielle, that's why I stayed to say goodbye, but now it's time to go on and they don't want to let me. Help me die. I want to die in dignity. Not chained to machines, a helpless, immobile vegetable."

"But you'll be in pain, Daddy. You can do chemotherapy and then if it works we can take you to Europe and you can live with us..."

"Thank you, but no. I don't want to force my life to go on. If I am to die now I want to die now. Do you understand me? This is not your decision. It's God's and mine. It's my life. Help me. The doctors can't and won't unless you do."

Charles, Simone, and I met in the hallway, overwhelmed. The night doctor had disappeared quickly, not wanting to be confronted with the situation. He had told us that my father had a fifteen percent chance of living if hooked up onto machines and put on chemotherapy. He explained that it was his responsibility to preserve life; legally he was not allowed to do anything else. Again we showed him our father's will in which he had explicitly written that he did not want to be attached to machines. Legally he had done everything right. The doctor sighed and said it was our decision. We came to the conclusion that it was our father's right to die if he wanted to and spent the night alternatively holding his hands, silently admiring his strength. The pain was unimaginable. Instead of complaining he hummed ancient Arabian chants learned in Egypt during his childhood, comforting us whenever he was lucid. Watching this fierce old man face his end with such dignity and courage is a lesson I have never forgotten, the last, most precious present he could have given us. After despairing over injustice all his life he proved that one does always have a choice. Even in facing death you have the choice of how to react to the situation.

This death, which I had worried about for years, knowing that he was alone and had no contact with anybody, was not as unexpected as Roland's, but sitting in the dark living room with his urn in front of me, trying to decide what to do about his belongings and house together with my brother and sister, was surreal and ungraspable. We decided to sell most of it, knowing that none of us could afford to take care of a building in the USA while living in Germany. It took us six weeks to put the furniture up for sale and pack a container with the objects we wanted to keep, mainly consisting of his paintings and art books. Going through the objects we knew so well, sifting through photographs of his childhood, packing old army uniforms and boots, paintbrushes, collected newspaper clippings on art shows, drawing techniques, hundreds of slides on deformed skulls, jaws, cavities, and other oral-surgical techniques, watching gilded Super-8 films of his voyages to Paris or Asia, arranging his favorite handwritten recipes and healthy cooking recommendations, folding countless Arabian hand-stitched tablecloths, blankets, and pillows, his life once more was spread out in front of our eyes and we sadly said goodbye.

Having decided to hire a small company to take care of the things we couldn't keep, we specifically chose one that seemed poor, agreeing to their first bid despite knowing that the things were worth a lot more. When the owner arrived and saw what a great deal he had made, he immediately called his whole family to rent another truck and help him load up everything quickly before we would change our minds. Far from doing that, we quietly watched the group packing all the items we knew by heart, knowing that the bulk of my father's belongings created much more joy for this family than for a large company that would have sent a noncommittal employee to pick up the "stuff."

Back in Berlin I sat speechlessly in my apartment, this second loss leaving me immobile, empty, and without the slightest idea of what to do in a future that seemed completely superfluous. At the same time I felt compelled to be as strong and courageous as my father had been until the end.

It turned out that he had diligently saved money for his children, putting away every penny possible from his meager veteran's fee, so when he died we inherited not only his house but full bank accounts, something I could live off for the next couple of years, making possible a freedom to work on my art that he had never allowed himself, caring for me even after his death.

In spite of this unexpected financial relief I was slow in finding the incentive to start working on anything and once again it was a handful of loyal friends who showed up in time to save me. From out of nowhere Blixa called, speaking about the new office his band was moving into and inviting me to share the spacious loft, a real studio to work in. The space was on Chausseestrasse, in former East Berlin and with my newly replenished bank account I decided to take the risk and transfer my career as an artist to a new level. The task of renovating rooms, painting them, tearing down drop tiles to reveal a high old-fashioned ceiling with stucco, and moving all of my working utensils into the new space took my mind off of things. Being in the unfamiliar area, surrounded by the band members and Johannes Beck, inspired me, and a small bubble of creativity appeared on the horizon.

After a couple of months, my studio was set up. The two small rooms were neatly filled with bags of cement, wood, nails, glue guns, hammers, screws, and bolts, boxes with tubes of oil paint, rolled canvases, paper sheets in different piles, pencils, coloring pens, frames, paper clips, shelves of art books, and two or three tables that held, among other things, my first glistening black laptop.

Each room had a small window for sunlight and air, a miniature hallway led to the simple bathroom with a tiny sink and cold water. The cement walls and linoleum floor were easy to keep clean, not necessarily beautiful but practical, and the small cot I placed in one corner was just right for sleeping on if I worked late. The atelier was on the same floor as the Neubauten office but separated by a staircase, with the perfect situation of privacy combined with the possibility of companionship. The communal kitchen was one door away, where I could have cozy conversations with the musicians or Johannes whenever I took a break. Exhilarated by my new luxurious studio I decided to have my apartment scoured by a cleaning lady for the first time in my life. The landlord had renovated the windows and left the apartment in a clutter of dirt and dust. Asking her to come over in the morning and giving her my house key, I decided to sleep over in my studio to be out of her way. Ready to try and start anew, supported by friends, with enough money to survive for a couple of years, with the promise of concentrating on my art and run Dimitri's gallery I went to bed feeling slightly more confident than I had for a long time. But again my turbulent life had more in store than anticipated and I was woken up at 9 a.m. by my frantic landlord, desperately relieved to hear my voice, telling me that my apartment had burned down overnight, due to a hot water tank that had been wrongly connected by the technicians after the renovation, and that everything I owned was now a pile of ashes.

1996

"Here, you should wear this." He handed her a cotton mask to put over her nose and mouth. "The apartment is full of toxic ashes, the boiler took a long time to melt and the smell is really unhealthy."

Silently she snapped the elastic band behind her ponytail and entered the hallway.

The walls were black, with large holes. The remains of her kitchen could be seen, shattered pottery strewn on the black-and-white checkered floor, still-life paintings by her father smudged and burned, the remains sadly strewn into the relics of a metal sink, filled with glass, cutlery, and shredded cookbook pages. The smell was bad even through her mask.

"We are really sorry this happened. K. must have mixed up the wires, and we didn't notice what was going on until the crash, that was when the windows exploded. The boiler just got hotter and hotter until the whole apartment was smoldering, the new windows didn't let in any air and then they just burst, the oxygen igniting the fire. We were so relieved that you weren't there, the smoke usually suffocates people when they are sleeping so when it really starts burning they've already died from the fumes. The door was hard to break into, the metal being so thick."

Silently she went into her former living room, the green sleeping sofa, a present of her father's, a black pile of burned wood and leather, the mattress, now a cloud of melted metal, the shelves with their now fossilized books rearranged into puzzle pieces that barely resembled their former shapes.

Her eyes fell upon the dark portrait of an Asian women, one of her favorites. Her father painted it during his stay in Korea, and the delicate rendering of the woman's face had fascinated her even as a small child, when she had insisted that it be in her room after every army move. To her surprise, the frame remained in one piece but the canvas was burnt black, paint chipping off in small pieces, the silhouette of one breast still faintly to be seen. Swallowing her rising anguish she turned sharply and went into the bathroom, a huge hole in the space where her shower had been.

"That was a toughie, the plastic just wouldn't stop burning so the firemen had to tear it out of the wall."

The new washing machine was unrecognizable, the twenty carefully placed wigs, which were usually hidden behind it, had completely disappeared. So had her shoe rack.

"Oh my god, my clothes!" Running into her bedroom she slammed to a stop— everything was gone.

"We had to start cleaning up the stuff, there was nothing wearable left anyway."

She stood motionless, gazing past the rubble, through the broken window, into the clear blue sky, remembering the watchtowers, the wall, having breakfast with M. in the kitchen after a late-night work shift, working on lyrics in the bedroom with her band, the cats lazing around on the floor on hot summer nights, TV interviewers excitedly exclaiming how picturesque her apartment was with its painted green floors and pink walls, pointed straw-hat lampshades and bouquets of fabric flowers strewn about, her industrial sewing machine, her first large career investment, proudly installed in the corner and lovingly cared for, hand-stitched ball gowns, racks of costumes in the hallway, hand-hammered silver moon masks lined up in the kitchen due to lack of space anywhere else, leftover colorful balloon hats displayed in the bathroom, the remains of her former fashion shows which were sometimes used as PR for her concerts, R. lying in her arms, shyly revealing his innermost yearning to compose music for an orchestra, her father visiting, complaining of missing towels, replacing her torn shower curtain, proudly handing over a new oil portrait of her that he had just finished and painstakingly transported from New York for her to hang in a particular corner next to her sofa, ignoring her softly whispered "but Daddy, I don't want a portrait of myself there..."

"Look, we'll pay you compensation for the things you've lost, and we'll renovate the apartment as quickly as possible so that you can move back into it."

"NO!" Jerking away from her sudden reaction the man looked at the woman questioningly. "I'm not moving back."

BERLIN MITTE

By the mid 1990s many of the neglected, rusted, and pollution-covered buildings in the former Eastern part of town had been renovated. Berlin Mitte, a new and thriving commercial district, was starting to emerge, with shoe, designer, sunglasses, and office-supply stores popping up amid new building sites, offering expensive luxuries and symbols of wealth. The hum of renewal could be heard and felt everywhere.

I enjoyed having lunch in novel eateries like Obst and Gemüse, across the street from the ruins of former Passage Kaufhaus, a department store built in 1909 connecting the two main streets Friedrichstrasse and Unter den Linden to each other; it had now been renamed Tacheles, and was being turned into a underground center point. While munching on spicy tapas or quiche, I watched artists busily renovating the massive, architectural carcass, turning it into a rejuvenated site that attracted curious tourists in high heels and expensive leather shoes who inched around the thick stone walls into dark caverns filled with steel art. I drank the strong tea sold in the studios, and felt the pulse of the city as it shed its old skin and slowly exposed a new one. During this construction era the city's inhabitants usually wore practical clothing, such as sneakers to bypass uneven roadblocks, skull scarves and caps to keep dust out of their hair, combat and military overalls with belts hung with tools, a workmanlike style enhanced by audacious pirate accessories. Everyone gamely adapted to the mud-riddled, broken sidewalks and dusty construction sites.

Dimitri had found a space for my gallery on the corner of Alte Schönhauser and Münzstrasse. On the Alte Schönhauser Strasse he had also rented a huge space in which to open another restaurant. Always intrigued by historical architecture and the photography of it, he bought large art books documenting Berlin's structural design, and we spent many an afternoon in a newly discovered café, eating cake, sipping tea, and reading about the street we were going to become inhabitants of. It had quite an intriguing story. In the 1920s Mitte had been an area inhabited by the poor working class, Schönhauser Strasse offering cheap food and drinks for all. Next to my gallery there was a small triangular alcove which was included in our rent. It turned out to be a former soup kitchen, and had not been renovated since it was built seventy years ago. A thin wooden wall separated one half of the room from the other, with a small square window in the middle from which one could buy a cup of soup for a couple of pfennigs. Narrow wooden benches along the wall provided a place to sit and dunk a thick slice of bread into the broth. My location next door had been one of the first cinemas, and was made up of two large rooms and a small projection space hidden underneath the high ceiling. The back quarters looked out into a large backyard filled with ancient oak trees and shrubbery. During the Cold War occupation it had been a flower store, as I learned from the little old ladies who came into my gallery saying, "I remember this place from when I was very, very small. I saw a Marlene Dietrich movie here for the first time."

When we entered the projection room on the day we signed the lease we were surprised to find it filled with hundreds of faded GDR plastic ice cream holders and spoons, old-fashioned cardboard advertisements, and odd paper cutlery. No one knew why the flower shop had stored these objects, but they were wonderful to mix oil paints in and have proved to be very useful over the years.

After the political upheaval, both storefronts stood empty for a long time. They were too large to be renovated by an artist, and too remote from the first commercial hangouts to be interesting to developers. Dimitri, with his usual foresight, believed that this street was going to become central to Berlin's cultural and tourist scene and rented the spaces immediately, realizing their worth after inspecting them. He was soon proven right.

The café on Schönhauser Strasse 13, an enormous space with stone vaults, had also been one of the first to serve cheap food and coffee in the 1920s. The male and female blue-collar patrons were carefully separated and placed on one side of the room or the other. In the 1970s, after communism took over, most of the high ceilings were lowered with cheap silicon tiles and covered with musty faded wallpaper and fake walls to save on heating, as was true of most of the buildings in the GDR, and all of this now had to be taken down and renovated.

Dimitri asked David Boysen, an artist he had supported over the years, to cover the walls with light brown clay, which was known for its natural insulation, providing warmth in the winter and freshness in the summer, not to mention being an unusual background for future exhibitions. Both the gallery and restaurant were layered with this element, giving them a fresh, earthy feeling reminiscent of Ibiza, which was where the clay had been acquired.

During the restoration I spent my time getting used to living in the small rooms of my studio and reading Alfred Döblin's classic *Berlin Alexanderplatz*, which was particularly known for its film adaptation by the legendary German filmmaker Rainer Werner Fassbinder. It was a perfect introduction to Berlin's new center, my home for the next seven years. I discovered with growing anticipation that Franz Biberkopf, the main character, had lived on the same street that my new studio was situated on and usually went to work by taking the same route as I did to get to my gallery. The description of flower stores, bakeries, schools, and location plans of the 1920s meshed perfectly with the structures I passed, the original signs still shimmering faintly beneath the peeling paint of not-yet-renovated buildings. This area was slow to be modernized and emanated a golden glow of timelessness, clearly disclosing the different layers of generations who had lived before the war, after the war, and during the communist regime. Sitting on green, moldy benches within the many small parks throughout the area, I felt as though I were in a fragile time capsule, dreamily frozen in the past, present, and future simultaneously.

In spite of the nightmarish events that had befallen me over the past two years, this city still possessed a magic that made it unlike any other I had experienced, offering comfort with its bullet-riddled house walls and downtrodden sidewalks. It seemed to have a mind of its own, proudly watching its inhabitants trying to erase the scars of time, knowing they would always remain. The city grew stronger and more persistently individual with the passing of each war, fascist leader, and influx of communist propaganda that tried to overtake it. Berlin was an entity nothing could destroy. This was a fact the new investors were not quite willing to accept, having decided that it was time for the city to get rid of its uncomfortable past.

During the period that my studio and the gallery were being refined, Berlin was so loaded with construction sites that it could merely offer bus tours to entertain tourists, presenting bustling cavities with cranes lining the evening sky, decorated with colorful lamps, trying to augment the city's profile, everything else covered up by scaffolding or huge sheets of plastic advertisement. Especially around Potsdamer Platz, which had been entirely devastated during the war, an ambitious project of international architects had emerged to build a futuristic "Gotham" fantasy onto the existing city, each designer planning a spectacular construction, competing for fame, replacing the former Wall and filling the vacant plaza with an avant-garde assemblage of offices, hotels, or media headquarters. Anything remotely communistic was torn down, or, if preserved for historic reasons, was cleaned up, renovated, and improved by the addition of trendy details.

In the meantime Dimitri had decided the gallery's renovation would be done in about three months, leaving me enough time to turn my quarters into a workable living and studio space before concentrating on my new job.

Originally I had planned on being the first artist to debut the space, and had started to prepare a new body of work for the opening and then concentrate on representing artists, but Dimitri asked me to let David exhibit first as a thank-you for decorating the walls.

David was a typical Berlin artist, complicated, unreliable, prone to excessive behavior, extremely blunt in his uncompromising comments, awfully shy, and very talented. His thickly layered paintings incorporated a palette of beautiful matted blues and browns to portray triangular, abstract figures shadowed by bizarre Viking silhouettes or peculiar spaceship abodes.

He insisted on living in the gallery during its renovation, saying that he wanted to create an exhibition influenced by the space, so we set up a small cot for him to sleep on, along with a water boiler and a couple of chairs, and hoped for the best. While painting the walls and sketching in a small drawing book he invited friends to come and keep him company, some of whom actually moved in with him, and within a couple of days the place was the home of drunk, loudly arguing artists or handymen, who drank vodka at ten in the morning and discussed the different techniques of whomever had drunk the last beer.

I found the situation a bit worrisome. Dimitri, always fascinated by eccentric characters, told me to let him take care of this first exhibition, David being an old friend of his and both of them used to each other's idiosyncrasies. I was happy to be relieved of the responsibility and concentrated on my studio, hanging out with Johannes on his large red office sofa in the evenings or preparing my own exhibition, pouring cement into small doll-head forms and hammering away at brown wooden frames for my photography.

Two days prior to the opening, Dimitri called, sounding worried, and asked me to come to the gallery immediately. When I arrived I was shocked to find that aside from one finished painting there was nothing else to be seen. Dimitri stood in the empty rooms holding a pile of frames and photocopies. He told me that David had been overcome by the responsibility of exhibiting in such large rooms, and had disappeared, leaving his small sketchbook of drawings behind. They were beautiful but tiny, so Dimitri had spontaneously decided to make enlarged photocopies of each and bought thirty medium-size frames to place them into. Impressed by the matter-of-fact way he had set about saving the situation, I helped him place the pictures under the glass, mentioning that I would have been furious after being let down in such a manner. But all he said was, "I've always respected him for his talent and his quirks so I can't really complain. I knew what I was getting into."

We framed the prints carefully, hung them, arranged the new sofas and small desk, unpacked glasses and bottles of red and white wine, swept the floors and scrubbed the bathrooms until all signs of boozing artists had been cleaned away.

The renovated gallery was beautiful. The large front room had lacquered floors and spacious windows that opened out on the main street, inviting passersby to enter and have a coffee at the counter installed next to a cognac-colored leather sofa that Dimitri had found in a secondhand store. While looking at the art, visitors could also enjoy the reflective light of ivy-covered windows illuminating the pictures in the back room, in which my small office desk stood with a view of both one-hundred-meter large spaces. Large paintings and objects could be shown in the lofty space. We had included one more special feature, which would attract yet another, completely different crowd of visitors. Dividing the two main rooms, a small alcove had been included to exhibit "cheap art," a movement initiated by the artist Jim Avignon, based on the belief that everybody should be able to afford art and that objects produced at a low cost could nonetheless offer a high quality experience.

Jim Avignon and the Cheap Art Movement

I met Jim Avignon around 1991 shortly after he moved to Berlin. It was at one of my last fashion shows for a fair, where I was presenting hip-hop tracksuits appliquéd with mock symbols of luxury. Having arrived late for dress rehearsal and rushing backstage, I saw a man painting a huge sheet of cheap paper at breakneck speed next to the entrance. The artwork was about ten meters square, and covered with black and white sketches that he was coloring in. The size of the backdrop and the concentration with which he painted amid two-dozen chattering, giggling, dressing, and undressing models was astounding. By evening the work was finished and hung over the catwalk, an ironic pop portrait of the fashion world and its participants.

Despite being a newcomer to Berlin, Jim's name was soon mentioned regularly in numerous newspapers, his pace at finishing projects and attracting admirers as rapid as his drawing technique. From afar I watched his fan base growing larger with every new exhibition or performance.

Jim called his art U-Kunst (Underground art) or Cheap Art, encouraging young artists to ignore the standard regulations of where, how, and what to paint, and to create their own rules. Made with cheap material, such as cardboard, wrapping paper, beer holders, wooden fruit crates, old boxes, and cheese cartons, this art was possible to make without needing money to finance expensive art supplies. Combined with projections of odd photography and lustrous lamps, the works transformed their surroundings into glowing, fantastic environments, with young, unknown DJs or Jim himself spinning an eclectic mix of easy-listening records. As a result of these parties, Jim became more interested in music and started composing his own songs, performing them live. His shows were a humorous mixture of painstakingly painted and cut-out cardboard masks, stage backdrops, costumes, ironic English texts including a charming German accent, impromptu dance steps and audience interaction—all contributed to an expanded Avignon universe. His figures, an eclectic mix of half-human, half-robot, were often portrayed as dealing with a confusing world of commerce and mass production.

Works such as *The Press Conference, Communication Disaster,* or *Interview Disaster* were tongue-in-cheek, composed of comic shapes, thick black outlines, and geometric, pixeled landscapes, accessible simultaneously to both highbrow art critics and clubgoers. He became the admired teacher of a group of young artists, who initiated numerous happenings, drawing in parks, on sidewalks, second-hand markets, or neighboring lots, setting up tables laden with magic markers and beer bottles, sketching portraits of each other and curious bystanders, performing in front of the Documenta X in Kassel as uninvited guests, painting comic strips, pasting collages of ridiculous newspaper ads and forgotten photos, gluing catalogues, cutting furniture from cardboard and old fruit crates, designing crayon postcards, and knitting plants or flowers. Thanks to his amazing productivity Jim not only became known in the underground club scene, he was also asked to decorate a British Airway plane, design Swatch watches and Rover cars, illustrate a cookbook, decorate a Berlin bear statue for an international buddy bear Berlin project, and, when the Olympic stadium reopened after extensive renovation in 2004, his painting, which was 2,800 square meters large, was carried into the stadium by 132 athletes and applauded by all who saw it.

Busy working on my own projects, I witnessed Jim's progress from afar, enjoying my brief encounters with this intelligent and friendly artist, until one memorable summer day, when I chanced to walk into one of his gatherings. About twenty artists were sitting at a low picnic table in front of their favorite gallery, drawing and drinking juice. Jim invited me to join in the fun—they were decorating beer coasters. Hesitantly I sat down, not sure what to draw, my art usually consisting of installations of objects, collages, or photography. I had always enjoyed sketching but a severe, uncompromising art schoolteacher had managed to convince me that my instincts were lopsided, resulting in my concentrating on other techniques instead.

Jim handed me oil pastels, magic markers, and simple crayons. As I sat looking at the small cardboard squares, which my neighbors were covering with funny scribbles, cartoons, quirky comic strips or beautiful intricate designs, I felt inhibited. Jim looked over at me quizzically, noticing that I hadn't started, and winked at me, saying, "Beauty is in the eye of the beholder, nobody has the right to really decide on what is good and bad. In the end it should just be fun and make you happy. A tiny scribble can make that happen. Just start!"

After spending the afternoon and evening with the cheerful artists I had discovered a new realm in which to articulate myself, deciding not only to exhibit in their gallery, as they had invited me, but also to represent their work in mine, installing a space in between my two large exhibition rooms for about two hundred of the "Cheap Art artists."

Dimitri had wanted to have a small shop for unusual artifacts for years and enthusiastically agreed to cover the extra salary of an assistant solely in charge of this niche. The small Cheap Art shop became a complete success, attracting visitors from all over, some of them dropping in to buy a last minute birthday, Christmas, or wedding present, happy to be able to find something with more meaning than chocolate and nonetheless costing less than one hundred Deutschmarks.

Knocking on the glass door she tried peering into the dark room. *Nothing moved. Knocking again, she shook the metal frame impatiently, wondering if it had been a good idea to give away the key. A shadow could be seen moving slightly. Relieved, she heard the key turning awkwardly.*

"Don't tell him anything, he's a spy."

Baffled she looked at the small figure, peering at her with unbrushed curly hair and large, tired eyes.

"I thought he was your new lover?"

"Yes, he is but he's a spy."

"Hmmm, well why don't you let me in first and then we can speak about it. Is he here?"

"No, he left an hour ago 'cause he's got a job at the moment—otherwise he couldn't finance my stay."

"That sounds kind of nice... Why do you think he's a spy?"

Entering the large, cool gallery she noticed that nothing much had changed from the night before.

"He always wants to know what I am planning and calls my contacts. I am sure he's telling people my secrets."

"Oh, come on now, he's been helping you with everything, giving you a place to sleep, transporting your work, and obviously adoring you, maybe you should give him some slack."

"NO! You don't understand—he is a spy. And I need you not to tell him anything we speak about."

"OK, OK, no problem, I won't."

Looking around at the artwork she noticed that it had been distributed evenly around the rooms, leaning against the walls in different sizes.

"So I guess you've decided on where to place the pictures? Do you want me to hang them now?"

"They already are."

"What do you mean? They're propped on the floor."

"No, I stapled them."

"You mean you stapled the pictures onto the wall?" *Shocked, she walked toward a painting and saw that it had been pierced directly through the middle of the canvas.*

With an effort to be diplomatic, she slowly turned and sat down, looking at the art that she had paid to have transported to Berlin on the small budget she received, and asked in a friendly tone: "Don't you think it would look better if they were hanging a little higher and not just standing on the floor? I'm sure we can get a lighter, more enchanting look if they are all about the same height. The way they are now, the small ones seem very insignificant, and if you really want to sell them for twenty thousand Deutschmarks it could be difficult..."

"Oh, you think so?" The tiny artist pensively looked at a piece in front of her feet. "Maybe you're right," and bending over she tore the picture off the wall. A large piece of canvas remained stuck under the metal staple.

"What are you doing!!!"

The horrified curator ran over to the decisive artist who was about to tear a second picture down.

"I'm taking them down so that you can hang them higher."

"But you're destroying the art, can't you see the hole?"

"Oh, that's no problem, I can cover everything with fabric—see..." pulling some flowery cotton from a bag she gracefully draped it over the hole. "That's what people expect you know."

"To be honest, I think it really would be better if we carefully take out the staples and try not to tear them. I doubt I will get the prices you are asking for otherwise..."

"Whatever... I have to leave now. B. has invited me to breakfast. He's picking me up in five minutes so I have to get ready. See you later." Taking her handbag she closed the buttons on her jacket and slipped through the door, waving cheerfully.

In shock, the curator slowly went to her toolbox and picked a small wrench with which she could grasp the tiny staples. After ten minutes of futile struggle she went to the phone.

"Hi honey, could you come in today? I have a problem I can't fix on my own, and the catalogue and invitations have to be sent out too, and I spent all night preparing the flyers... I'll pay you from my fee, its no prob..." While listening she leaned down to pick up a piece of fabric, twiddling it aimlessly in her fingers, looking through the window and watching tourists walk by.

"Oh wonderful, thank you so much! You're a lifesaver! I'll be here taking care of the damage..."

Dialing the next number she started her day's work of calling the press, promoting the upcoming exhibition, and thanking the gods that she had a couple of assistants she could rely on.

"Das Institut"

After we launched the gallery, successfully pulled off David's exhibition and set up two hundred Cheap Art artists in their designated space, I started mounting my first large solo exhibition, "Heroines," an installation I had been working on ever since the Angry Women Festival in 1993. Working with Gudrun Gut had woken in me an unfaltering interest in women, their work, issues, themes, and biographies, recognizing how even in 1996 they were still being confronted with obstacles that their male counterparts did not have to face. I found out that the accepting attitude of Berlin's artists in the 1980s was not the norm in the international music industry, in which females were usually categorized as chicks or bitches, and Gudrun's persistence in focusing on these performers had demonstrated a rare approach, rarely found outside of lesbian communities.

After Roland's death, when everything seemed meaningless and I struggled to find comfort in basic realities, I started searching for biographies of people who had experienced similar tragedies, and decided that these people would have to be women in order for me to be able to identify with them. Previously I had devoured books about William Burroughs, Jackson Pollock, Vincent Van Gogh, Degas, Gauguin, Hemingway, Fitzgerald, Beckett, or Toulouse Lautrec, enjoying the descriptions of their technical work, experimentation, choice of themes, love affairs, and friendships, but their objectives and conflicts were that of male artists, concerned with a different universe of themes, confronting fewer barricades and having greater possibilities than most women. When I saw a movie on Camille Claudel, with Isabella Adjani playing the role of the depressed sculptor, ending up in an insane asylum, dejected, exhausted, and defeated in art and life, the contrast to her husband's success was astounding. Rodin became a legendary figure in the art world, famous and admired with a museum of his own in Paris. It was not the fact that her work had not been considered good, it had just not been taken as seriously. This of course meant no collectors, no support, no recognition, and no success. Today, although her work has been acknowledged as outstanding, her madness, hysteria, and despair are the attributes emphasized in the movie, instead of her work. This distinguished her from artists such as Van Gogh, who was clinically mad but internationally recognized for his work.

Roaming Berlin on a search for more uplifting information, I was appalled at how little one could find, discovering only one lesbian bookstore in Charlottenburg that had quite a large collection of female biographies, and I began reading them ravenously, discovering Gabriele Münter, Romaine Brooks, Leonora Carrington, Carson McCullers, Edna O'Brien, Flannery O'Connor, Simone de Beauvoir, Gertrude Stein, Peggy Guggenheim, Colette, Virginia Woolf, Meret

Oppenheim, Louise Bourgeois, Djuna Barnes, Sylvia Plath, Anne Sexton, Lotte Lenya, Anita Berber, Nancy Cunard.

None of them had an easy life and even though every one of them is today an acknowledged and respected artist in her field, they are less known than their male counterparts.

All experienced discrimination; Collette's earliest books, the first French best-sellers, were signed and sold by her husband Henri, Lotte Lenya's performance was not even mentioned in the program notes of the premiere of the *Dreigroschenoper* in 1928, and Louise Bourgeois was internationally recognized only after reaching old age, ironically outliving many of her more successful male colleagues. Illness and solitude predominated in many of the stories, both Carson McCullers and Flannery O'Conner battling wheelchair confinement, and Sylvia Plath, Virginia Woolf, and Anne Sexton living in institutions for long periods of their life. Even millionairess Nancy Cunard, who worked fearlessly as a journalist during the Spanish Civil War, battled racism in New York, printed and published Samuel Beckett's first books with her own publishing company, an admired muse and lover of many artists of her time, died alone and forsaken, ridiculed and avoided for the same traits that made Ernest Hemingway a legend, namely stubbornness, individuality, a profound sense of justice, and active defense of refugees during a war.

Realizing these facts was disheartening, and opened my eyes to incidents in daily life where discrimination prevailed, making women feel bad if they were as ambitious, tough, or goal-oriented as men. Most accounts highlight the fashionable aspects of what they wear rather than their actual work, and insultingly describe them as control-freak monsters. Yoko Ono, Madonna, Angelina Jolie are but a few contemporary examples. Does anybody seriously think that John Lennon, Guy Ritchie, and Brad Pitt are any less ambitious?

Why are they described as good-natured, supportive, and slightly naïve?

I found it hard to believe that all of this could be happening in my generation. Coming from New York, where feminism was taken seriously, and growing up in a liberal household had made me believe equality was a given. To realize that this was not the case, not even in Central Europe or Berlin, the city I considered a stronghold of independent women, was shocking. I decided to dedicate my first spacious exhibition entirely to this theme and artistically observe how these issues had developed over time and what my contemporaries had experienced on their path to implementation.

I divided the exhibition into three parts, the past, present, and future, investigating the history, examining current situations, and evaluating a possible future.

I did not consider this an act of feminist art; it was not done to prove a point against men. I was just trying to understand an aspect of life that had previously been hidden to me.

For the "past" I continued reading as much as possible, finding artists I could identify with, women dealing with themes, tastes, and questions similar to mine, tapping into a inspirational well of creativity that has stayed with me ever since. I printed out ten three-meter-high lists of women artists I admired from the past. From these lists I chose ten to depict more closely, putting together paper collages of photocopied portraits, making bold acrylic comic "cover-versions" of their features, an attempt to portray the rough and imperfect picture of their lives that has remained for us to discover.

Each accompanying golden frame had small loudspeakers attached to it, from which one could hear whispers of texts, music, or sound collages that I had recorded on endless tape loops, thus installing a gallery of whispers from the past.

Additionally the gilded frames, which were bought in a Turkish store in Kreuzberg, were covered with objects inspired by the women's personalities, giving them an appropriate household of objects to live in. All of the biographies I read put great importance on the fact that each woman endeavored to construct a personal universe, a fortress as protection from the indifferent world outside. Virginia Woolf, with her room of her own, Carson McCullers, who filled her garden with peacocks, watchdogs, and beautiful friends, Colette acquiring retreat cottages in her beloved French countryside over the years, and Nancy Cunard surrounding herself with hundreds of African masks and bracelets.

In spite of the bold and courageous accomplishments achieved by these pioneers, "sacrifice" was a strong element I felt while reading the diverse biographies, crucifixions seemingly without resurrection. Trying to express the contradiction of "optimistic-sacrifice" I constructed five large wooden objects depicting clay females fastened to a cross, with colorful, small plastic objects collected or found, glued on top, expressing the fact that in spite of living as an artist, giving up on health, security, children, families or common female commodities, confronting prejudice and poverty, none of them wanted to be seen as victims, even at old age, in spite of living alone and in poverty, they were always adamant about being portrayed in a proud, independent, and confident manner. Sylvia Plath smiling happily shortly before her suicide, Dorothy Parker preferring a bad temper to helplessness, making an art of it in her books, Anne Sexton as the beautiful, cultured superwoman, Luisa Casati as an eccentric, living art installation. Each woman hid the cross she had been nailed to with a large number of colorful crutches, creating an image of the bold Amazon as an alternative to the crucified dependent. Interestingly one of these large crucifixion objects was the first major art sale I made in my life.

After having finished constructing the "past" section of the exhibition, I set about interviewing twenty colleagues living in Berlin, artists, musicians, DJanes, businesswomen, actresses, writers, and teachers. I interviewed women of all ages, mostly freelancers, self-taught, and very individual, the legendary "Berliner Gören" (Berlin brats).

After constructing simple frames, sawing and hammering the rough, dark wood in my studio until everything was covered with a thin layer of sawdust, I built tryphticon altars, using the old-fashioned Western "Wanted" composition style, with three photos, one straight-on and two profiles, and fastening them centrally in the wooden constructions with fake identification numbers under their heads. The unified look and stereotype number had the effect of individualizing the depicted woman, making her look even more alive, accentuating eyeglasses, hair color, nostrils, or jewelry, an allegory on how putting people in uniform actually highlights their uniqueness, accentuating details that might go unnoticed if the restriction wasn't there. By keeping women at bay and turning them into a mass of placid housewives, teaching them to read manipulative women's magazines dictating fashion trends, just the fact of not wanting children, preferring a career or reacting hysterically to injustice or discrimination, something that was considered heroic for men, stood in such huge contrast to the female norm that for centuries it seemed perfectly justifiable to lock them away, calling them criminally insane or simply "difficult."

To additionally accentuate the complex situation of emerging from such a history I placed interview sheets next to each wooden object, handwritten and filled out by my interviewees, speaking about their curriculum and accomplishments.

The matter-of-fact, down-to-earth questions again had a leveling effect on all participitants, but this time by accepting their individuality as a given fact. The stylized objects that society wanted to domesticate, reminiscent of Shakespeare's *The Taming of the Shrew,* had been transformed into subjects, the details of their development taken seriously in the interview sheets.

Art experimentation has always been a means of learning and comprehending for me, a way of understanding social structures, human interaction, and unmentioned connections. Discovering how even the setting of an interview can change the perception of a personality was one of the things I realized through this research, and suddenly I understood global manipulation in greater depth and how it has conditioned every aspect of our lives. Simply by altering a word in an article, a person can be made to look ridiculous, interesting, dangerous, or impressive, no matter what she has actually said or done. From that day on I have always tried to be observant of language and what it is really trying to say.

It always comes down to basics when one is looking for truth.

The next phase of the exhibition, the "present" section, involved my filming a three-minute Super-8 clip of each of my Berlin heroines standing in front of their favorite habitat, coming alive, presenting their world and surroundings, voicing opinions.

The interview sheets were hung next to the "wanted" photos, the Super-8 clips edited into a movie and exhibited between the portraits. The immobility on the one hand mixed with the sparkling charisma on the other, created an intense, personal atmosphere of uniqueness.

During the opening the room was packed with captivated visitors going from one interview to another, fascinated by the colorful and unexpected cosmos displaying actress Sophie Rois, known for her performances at the Volksbühne, cabaret performer Andrea Schneider, writer Thea Dorn, young DJ-producer Ellen Alien, powerful businesswoman Chris Häberlein, painters Betty Stürmer and Beth Moore Love, top-notch lawyer Angie Strittmatter, and journalist Martina Wimmer.

All of the interviews portrayed lives in which decisions were based on instinct, taste, and common sense, ignoring the fact of being constricted in a man's world. Many admitted never even to have consciously thought about discrimination, taking equality as self-evident, and considering women's liberation achieved.

The oldest protagonist, sixty-five-year-old musician Dorothy Carter, an expat from New Orleans, was the audience's darling, producing exclamations of disbelief over her anarchic life, while she herself laughed at their surprised exclamations.

Dorothy Carter

Tiny, frail, with blond hair and green eyes, invariably wearing black dresses, floral patterns, and heavy boots, she seemed so delicate that most people were taken aback when she mentioned adventures with drug-crazed hippies in Mexico or an upcoming tour with her all-girl band the Mediaeval Babes.

Dorothy specialized in antique instruments.

The dulcimer and hurdy gurdy were her favorites among the immense collection of zithers and flutes inherited from a grateful student who had died of AIDS years ago. Her solo concerts were conjoined with these delicate, beautifully carved historical pieces, creating a seductive atmosphere of bygone sounds. Born in 1935 in New York, she grew up in her grandparent's Victorian mansion in Boston, living a lonely childhood, hidden away in the huge library, playing piano and listening to her grandmother belching. By eight she was an expert pianist and knew music would be her life, so she enrolled at Bard College in New York as early as possible.

Her adventurous life thereafter included runaway trips to Europe, bicycling from London to Paris, enrolling in and escaping from the London Royal Music Academy, initiating concerts, exhibitions, and psychedelic experimentation, performing with underground, avant-garde musicians in Maine and falling in love with wild, uncontrollable men, one of whom she moved to Mexico with. This relationship was as rocky as the others, and after being abandoned she joined a convent in Northern Mexico, experiencing religious visions and working with a reputable, anarchic monk. She stayed for a year until the monk was arrested and her broken heart had mended.

Moving back to the East Coast of the United States, she bore two children, Justin and Celeste, moved into a hippie commune in Maine, and earned money by weaving baskets, selling cakes, and performing. During these years she also discovered herbal science, and became fascinated by the ancient remedies and secret recipes she would continue experimenting with for the rest of her life. Being a single mother was not customary during those times and the tight-knit support of an alternative community made survival more possible. This phase was later often mentioned as having been the quiet haven in her otherwise restless life. Nonetheless Dorothy wanted more than to just be a mother, and she quickly integrated within a colorful crowd in New York City, where she co-founded the avant-garde music and art gallery, A Bird Can Fly But a Fly Can't Bird, with interdisciplinary artist Bob Rutman in 1966.

Their friendship would last a lifetime, but after having a disappointing affair with yet another man, she decided to enlist as a deckhand on a Mississippi steamboat, scouring the ship and living the life of a sailor for over fifteen years.

Bob finally told her to come to Berlin in the early 1990s, inviting her to move into his huge factory loft and perform with him, describing Berlin's anarchic spirit in bright colors and succeeding in awakening her interest after the steamboat had sunk. Deciding to follow his advice and discover a new continent she arrived with nothing more than her instruments, two or three light dresses, and her one luxury: a small collection of embroidered shawls. She was content sleeping on Bob's studio floor, arranging a small nook in one of his storage rooms with nothing but a thin cotton blanket spread out on the cement, tucked in between the piano and small organ, entirely disinterested in comfort.

The underground music scene immediately took notice of her after Alexander Hacke met the tiny lady who could drink like a sailor, protecting her under his broad shoulders and enthusiastically announcing her concerts to everybody he knew. In this way Katharine Blake, the singer of an English band Miranda Sex Garden, with whom Alexander had collaborated frequently, was introduced to Dorothy while visiting Berlin, and soon both of them were giggling over bottles of red wine and loudly dreaming of a band that played medieval music. Katharine had been singing madrigals for some time and had been thinking of starting a new enterprise. After meeting Dorothy she made this goal come true and soon after an all-girl group of untrained musicians had been formed, signed by Virgin as a classical alternative to the Spice Girls: they called themselves the Mediaeval Baebes. In 1996 they went on tour with Salva Nos and their record became Virgin Classic's fastest selling debut album, catapulting Dorothy into worldwide fame and raucous after-show parties. The beautiful girl group was wild, destroying hotel bars and band buses as quickly as their male counterparts, giving scandalous press conferences, having wild affairs, and recovering from their hangovers in train stations or hotel lobbies. Dorothy's dream had finally come true, living the adventurous life of a traveling gypsy with an admired band, and being respected for her musical handicraft of antique instruments. Thanks to earning more money she could even afford to rent a room of her own in friends' apartments, returning on tour breaks, happily telling us stories of stripping girls, falling off of bar stools, and successful concerts, ignoring her age or the hard knocks of tough tour life. When her back would hurt or a nasty cough emerged, she would say things like, "When I'm old I'm gonna get myself a little house back in New Orleans, it's warmer there than it is here and I can parade on Mardi Gras and throw my bra into the crowd, but until then I'm going to stay in Berlin."

I met her on one of my many drinking bouts after Roland's death. I had been sitting at the Ex 'n' Pop downing whiskey with friends when Hacke came storming in during one of his weekend bouts, his entourage of fans, lovers, and friends following as usual. It was only after a while that I noticed the fragile woman quietly standing next to him, watching a band performing and sipping the red wine

Alexander would carefully hand her at regular intervals. Immediately attracted to the perky look in her eyes I introduced myself and went to see her concert a couple of weeks later, on the same stage.

The ruckus in the overflowing club turned down for a surprising moment as the small woman began plucking her ancient instruments and singing in a high, sweet voice.

Some musicians possess magic on stage that cannot be explained by technique or talent, they enter a sphere that can best be described as the space "in between," something that has been beautifully expressed by T.S. Eliot or painted by Edward Hopper, the time span between inhaling and exhaling, as if the heart stopped beating and breathing became superfluous, a pressure comparable to being underwater or flying in a dream. The style of music and the age or gender of the musician are irrelevant to achieving this effect; it is not something one can learn, and those that possess this magic always look like their hair is flying in the wind.

Dorothy had this gift and everybody in the club that night experienced the enchantment. In spite of her bashful bows at the end of her set, the crowd clapped and screamed for encores, forcing her to go back on stage again and again, hungry to hear more and more. The fact that she was almost sixty was not noticed by most, since her personality outshone many younger colleagues who came to her performances.

Dorothy was invited to play in Berlin's cafés, clubs, galleries, birthday and wedding parties, everybody mesmerized by her incomparable presence, wanting to experience, speak to, or support her in any way possible.

I enjoyed seeing the tiny figure at these various festivities, her laconic humor and slight cynicism intelligent and entertaining. Having remained a bookworm throughout the years Dorothy was well informed on many different subjects: *A Hundred Years of Solitude* by Gabriel Garcia Márquez was her favorite book, and Ali G. her favorite entertainer—she discovered Sacha Noam Baron Cohen long before anybody else in my proximity had heard of his wit. Traveling, magic potions, herbal remedies, BBC news reports, Russian politics, Italian history and how to clean a kefir were but a few of her pastimes. She had no understanding of ownership or luxury. She often asked why I kept my father's paintings and Roland's hundreds of books, and prefered a blanket on the ground to a soft bed, always afraid of growing pampered or lazy. When her enthusiasm for her surroundings and their accoutrements became too much, she would pack her huge blue suitcase, which was covered with patches of duct tape to keep the thin material together, fill it with as many instruments as possible, and strap it to a small trolley. Then she would hike off to Italy and go busking, her method of warding off vanity and corruption.

Despite the many projects Dorothy participated in, she remained poor, usually too humble to ask to be appropriately paid, preferring to drink a glass of wine at the free buffet rather than ask for a meal before the show. Although she now earned more money thanks to the Mediaeval Baebes, the checks did not come regularly and she moved from one friend's guest room to another, unable to afford her own apartment. I transported her few belongings into new abodes often, always worried she would trip or sprain an ankle trying to do it on her own, since she was too proud to ask for help.

After residing in my studio for two years I finally decided to move into an apartment again, tired of cold water and no shower. To my surprise I quickly found one around the corner from my working space, in a vacant building that had not been claimed after the war. Therefore it was rented out by the official company in charge of Berlin's abandoned buildings, the BEWOGE. The three-bedroom flat with stucco ceilings and wooden floors was amazingly cheap and central in Berlin's trendy Mitte area. When I moved in my father's inheritance was still abundant, making the luxury of having an apartment and a studio possible. A couple of years later, after having thrown out a brutal drummer who had fed off of me for months during a regrettable affair, I decided that it was too large for one person and invited Dorothy to move in, offering her the back room which was cool and quiet. After quickly adapting to the area, Dorothy discovered a couple of corner bars, and often came home with friends in the early morning hours, drunk and giggly, usually forgetting her key in the outside lock and continuing to celebrate long into the day.

During our rare moments at home together we would quietly listen to underground radio stations, Dorothy clicking away on her typewriter, writing stories, lyrics, and jotting down Cajun recipes for a book she was writing or working on a CD compilation of country songs she was composing, while I painted or practiced singing.

A typical morning would involve us meeting in the kitchen, me brewing coffee, her making green tea, chatting about what we had done the night before. We told each other stories of tours, concerts, odd love affairs, destructive relationships. We also spoke of more serious subjects, such as death, and Dorothy told me about her experiences in Mexico, and what it was like to grow up in the 1960s. After our friend Ed Csupkay, a talented mandolin player and singer who funded his music by working as a bouncer and bartender, moved in next door, we became a trio, a fun community who laughed about the loud sex or snores emanating from around the neighborhood and celebrating with excessive parties during which one of us always got into trouble. The most memorable of these incidents was when Ed came home at ten in the morning, ringing our doorbell and whispering with agitated backward glances towards the staircase, "In case a gang of very angry Lebanese men suddenly storm your apartment with machine guns just tell them it's the wrong apartment and tell them to try the door across the hallway, but be sure to thump on my wall beforehand," leaving Dorothy and me scared out of our wits and using candles for days, pretending we weren't at home.

Dorothy's fervent dream was to produce her record and release the book she was writing. After asking institutions around the city for help, she was rewarded when the Berlin Academy of Art offered her the use of their recording studio free for three days, including a sound engineer. Excitedly we transported her instruments into the aseptic rooms and started recording the numerous songs she had been working on for years. Asking friends and acquaintances to participate, we stood around in the studio with huge headphones chanting "oohs" and "ahs" to her flute solos, humming along to the dulcimer or clapping rhythmically.

Dorothy managed to record all of the songs within the three-day limit. With high hopes and fluttering hands she burned promo CDs in the neighboring "repro shop" and sent them out to record labels with the money earned by playing on the street, hoping to get a deal.

In 1999 it was still difficult to produce, print, or sell a record without a record company, in comparison to today, when anybody can sell their wares over the internet. In Dorothy's case her age was a problem for most companies, as they unmistakably told her. After trying to find a label for over a year she became more and more depressed, atypically complaining of poverty and hardship, losing the exited sparkle in her eye and becoming quarrelsome even with the Mediaeval Baebes, finally asking them for the amount of money she was worth. Her back had become worse, the climate in Berlin exacerbating her rheumatism, and with her grandchildren clamoring for her to come to New Orleans, she finally decided to move back to the USA in anticipation of finding cheaper living quarters, more accommodating record companies, and family support. The bitterness of being forced to admit defeat in the face of bias against her age lingered, and her jaunty soul was not able to understand how wrinkles could make any difference to the quality of a record, or how an adventurous biography could reduce sales. Realizing that this meant that she would probably never really earn enough money to survive, she decided to accept facts.

Everybody was sad to see her go, but we could understand her concern of how to spend her old age, an issue every freelancing artist faces, one that is even more difficult in an uncertain culture, without health insurance and few rights. I myself often worried about what we would do if she became seriously ill.

We bade each other goodbye, hoping that fate would bring us together again sometime. Back in New Orleans she received an old-age pension that she had not expected and which eased her financial burden immensely. Happily feeling supported she regained her enthusiasm and made friends in the young, alternative music scene in that city, initiating small gigs and performances, as well as touring with the Baebes.

We met one more time in London and spent the afternoon drinking ale. Dorothy said she missed Berlin, told me about her plans to rent a warehouse in the French Quarter of New Orleans and establish a cultural center to which she would invite all of her German family to come and perform. We strolled over to Camden market, the feeling of mutual appreciation strong as ever, chatting about life and how her book had proceeded, new friends she had made, and the development of New Orleans. I bought some shoes and Dorothy one of her beloved silken shawls, saying that she had loved them since her childhood.

Then we said goodbye, smiling wistfully, hoping it would not be the last time. In the last image I have of her slight, blond figure, she is wrapped in the hue of light violet silk.

Dorothy Carter died in 2003. She continued touring up to a month before her death.

In 2004 I was finally able to visit New Orleans, discovering it together with Alexander during the Einstürzende Neubauten *Perpetuum Mobile* tour. Ambling slowly through the intense heat, we experienced the city Dorothy had loved so much, her cheerful words still lingering in our ears: "Oh, I'm just a little old lady from New Orleans and I play that plinkety plonk music." After wandering out of the tourist-infected French Quarter, we discovered a small sideshow paraphernalia store, in which a beautiful dark-haired girl sat working behind the counter. She recognized Alexander immediately, having been to his show the day before and invited us to a party in a small juice bar. While speaking about New Orleans we mentioned Dorothy. Immediately her large eyes filled with tears and she excused herself to go to the bathroom. After coming back she explained that they had become very close, playing music and initiating concerts in backyards or flea markets. She described her as being her muse and the most amazing woman she had ever met: "I will never forget Dorothy and think of her every day since her death. She was one in a million."

Alexander and I nodded silently, we could only agree.

The "present" part of my show had managed to answer many of my questions. The carefully filled-out interview sheets demonstrated clearly that many of the women did not consider themselves victims in any way. But by going into depth we were all surprised to discover that there was prejudice even in our independent community. The teachers and lawyers admitted to confronting discrimination in their line of work: lawyers having to deal with cases of professional injustice towards women, teachers in noticing how boys and girls were still being raised very differently.

Interestingly the project had a strong impact on one of the youngest collaborators, Ellen Alien, who had been the only one to hesitate when I had asked her to participate, honestly admitting to prefer working with men rather than collaborating with women, whom she considered complicated and catty. After answering my questions and being intrigued by her reaction to my proposal, Ellen participated in a business course for women entrepreneurs to find out if she was being discriminated in any way. The instructor demonstrated how if she had been a man she would be earning double the amount of money she currently made, and would be far better known. Having worked as a DJane for years, independently starting a record label and merchandise line, she had considered herself a successful entrepreneur. Taken by surprise by this revelation, she changed her strategy, building a stronger universe of support, incorporating women within her enterprises, and used her newfound knowledge to become a respected figure in the international club world, setting an alternative example for young girls to follow, a glowing icon of independence at the DJ pulpit.

After having completed the "present," I was faced with finding a fitting solution for the future section of my exhibition.

Noticing that all the women I admired were united in terms of specific characteristics, such as being noncompliant, rearranging realities according to their own needs, simply ignoring accepted traditions, and, especially, not accepting prejudice or intolerance within themselves, led me to the conclusion that only by changing one's "state of mind" could anything in society be rearranged. In other words, a lot depends on the attitude that women themselves have. Considering that girls still get murdered at birth because of not being a boy, or are killed because of having an affair, or have their clitorises mutilated so they can feel no joy during sex, or are forced to wear veils, or are not allowed to be part of "men's only" social clubs, and are the minority in museums, biographies, curricula, movies, and legends, such a stance could seem odd and unfair, but it was the only one that made sense within my personal surroundings.

I enlarged a photograph I had taken of my friend Beth Moore Love in New Mexico, in which the lighting had gone awry, resulting in an overexposed sun explosion in which only her legs could be seen standing in front of an old-fashioned house. The picture radiated a strange feeling of immobility before preparing to move; it had an ethereal feel of empty space filled with light. In front of the enlarged picture I placed a wooden crib built from old chairs holding a small television set, which portrayed an endless loop of a small girl waking up and laughing. Laughter is a proud, active gesture in comparison to smiling. For centuries women were taught to smile, not to bare their teeth, in other words, to be submissive.

To be able to laugh freely is a process of shaking loose.

The women I chose have influenced countless girls simply by acting as independent individuals, taking it for granted that they should follow their instincts and express their ideas and incomparable opinions. They represent the definition of a heroine: "a heroine (female) came to refer to characters (fictional or historical) that, in the face of danger and adversity or from a position of weakness, display courage for some greater good or excellence." My girls were wide-awake, looking at their situation realistically and pitching in actively. None of them denied realizing their dreams or desires, they took risks, encountering failure and hard knocks to achieve recognition. When I walked past the many portraits I had done, reading their different answers over and over again, looking into their eyes, I felt the long years of work had been worth it. The greatest lesson was one I had not expected: All of these women shared one more attribute, one that made life more bearable and is seldom mentioned in discussions on feminism, since strong women are represented as serious and grim. But, as is true of most clichés, this one also proved to be wrong—the common characteristic among the women that was the greatest influence on me was their humor.

BETH MOORE LOVE

Beth Moore Love was one of the few artists I met in Berlin who never felt comfortable in the German capital, in spite of being one of the eccentric creatures who enriched the city for a couple of years. Coming from Albuquerque, New Mexico, a Wild West paradise of red earth, deep canyons, tumbleweed, Indian culture, and circling eagles, the heavy Prussian buildings made her feel like a mouse trapped in a maze, not able to see endless skies or wander off into her beloved nature. Her connection to wildlife reminded me of something I had forgotten: untamed forests, wild animals, sparkling rivers, and the indigenous culture, things I had identified with strongly as a small girl, telling my brother and sister that I was an adopted Indian child and that I would go back some day.

I had completely forgotten this over the years.

Ghazi found Beth in Albuquerque. He had heard of her impressive art and after meeting the bewitching creature fell in love immediately, taking her to Berlin in a cloud of happiness, presenting her to his good friend Chicken, the curator of the Endart gallery on Oranienstrasse. The Endart had been an icon in the 1980s, specializing in non-academic outsiders painting arguable themes, enjoying havoc and shock, and representing a more or less visual interpretation of the Geniale Dilletanten philosophy. After causing quite a stir with outrageous exhibitions that dealt with politics, sex, and gender, the art world's mood changed and focused on other areas. Unperturbed, Chicken continued curating and representing his artists, convinced of their worth and financing his venture over the years with social work and art sales, his exhibitions loyally supported by a large group of admirers and artists.

In spite of being a musician, Ghazi had always held a fascination for art, writing and editing catalogues, collecting work whenever his financial situation allowed it, and enthusiastically going out of his way to visit outsider-art exhibitions. Beth's fairytale horror paintings of modern society immediately captured his attention. The beautifully rendered drawings of mutilated girls, dwarf throwings, burning buildings, or cannibals fit perfectly into the Endart style and as expected Chicken offered to represent her work. The gallery's atmosphere, with storage rooms filled to the ceiling with odd scraps, leftover or forgotten art pieces, torn comic books, catalogues, remains of former exhibitions and parts of Chicken's household was a perfect replica of the place Beth had left in New Mexico and she felt at home immediately. Our introduction took place shortly after she had arrived in 1995. Ghazi invited me to an Indian meal, eager to show off his new lover and tell me about his US tour. Upon entering the restaurant I saw them sitting in the backroom, tightly entwined, oblivious to the world and happily kissing and holding each other tight. After I loudly pulled up a chair, Ghazi reacted, pulling Beth up and introducing me to the most beautiful woman I had ever seen in my life. She seemed flawless, emitting a strange, old-fashioned 1950s glow, reminiscent of Rita Hayworth or Ginger Rogers in their most glamorous roles, a heavenly apparition—until she started speaking. John Wayne was the first thought that sprang to my mind, "John Wayne is standing in front of me in the form of a lingerie model." Her slow, husky, southern slur, including obscenities, outrageous jokes, psychology, philosophy, and unusual trivia was almost too much to take in, the contradiction making her even more fascinating than if she had been only beautiful. Together with Ghazi I sat for almost an hour breathlessly watching and listening to her, both of us rendered immobile by the amazing creature. After having finished dinner, during which all of us ate very little, Ghazi proposed going back to his place and we ambled through the warm summer evening, chattering and laughing, forming a lasting bond. In their small, modestly furnished apartment in Neukölln, an area known for its low rents and high concentration of Turkish immigrants, Beth immediately pulled out a sheet of paper and started working on a complex drawing for the rest of the evening, letting Ghazi do his usual entertainment of presenting s/m lesbian vampire movies and playing Suicide records as loudly as possible. I left their apartment at around two in the morning, dizzily happy to have met a new, fascinating friend, impressed by her quiet dignity and dry, outrageous humor.

Beth called the next day, saying Ghazi wanted me to show her around town while he was working, and we quickly became friends, visiting each other, cooking dinners, reading books, painting, hunting for good deals in Berlin's main thrift stores and going out at night to listen to DJs at the Sniper bar. The club, a small storage room filled to the brim with forgotten furniture, stuffed animals, faded paintings, chipped glasses, and ripped bar stools, was Beth's favorite hideout and we would spend hours drinking tea or tequila out of jam jars, listening to the owners Rosa and Safi playing an eclectic mix of rare music. Sometimes we would go to performances of Ghazi's band the Golden Showers, an eclectic sleaze rock combo, with which Beth would sometimes perform, walking on stage topless wearing a huge ape mask. In front of the audience's amazed eyes she would then climb on top of the amps or a prepared platform and slowly swing her legs, giving the show a surreal, erotic flavor.

Although she was enthusiastically received in Berlin, with her shows selling out and jobs flying in, fashion shows featuring her as their main model, she was never really happy, missing snow-topped mountains and beautiful sunsets, repeatedly saying, "You can take the girl out of Albuquerque but you can't take Albuquerque out of the girl. I wish I could beam my Berlin friends out there, then I would be perfectly happy."

Finally she convinced Ghazi to move back to the US with her, hoping to be able to shuttle back and forth, living in New Mexico but visiting Berlin in long stretches as many expats do. I was very sorry to see them leave but promised to come and visit a couple of months later. We had met during the renovation of Das Institut and it was due to be done soon. Deciding that it would be good to execute such an extensive journey before entering the world of curating, I booked my flight. I had never flown to the States without going to New York, always feeling that I should spend as much time with my father as possible, but now that he was gone I decided to see some more of my native homeland.

New Mexico was sublime, just as Beth had promised, a true-to-life version of the Ennio Morricone-scored Westerns I watched over and over again as a child.

Experiencing it together with Beth turned the trip into a surreal dream, reality wobbling on the horizon, leaving us in a fairytale country of friendly human beings, animals, and very strange situations reminiscent of bizarre LSD trips.

On one of our regular outings in the red desert, her father's jeep suddenly collapsed in the middle of nowhere. It was a beautiful area of dry earth covered with tumbleweed and thorns, ancient cattle bones decorating the scarlet soil, the very bright blue sky glaring down from its midday peak, silhouetting canyons and snow-covered mountains in the distance. The solitude was a beautiful change from Berlin's mad bustle of creativity. We were miles away from any kind of town or gas station and had no idea what to do. Beth was wearing a light brown cowboy hat covering her now-blond, curly hair, a tiger-striped string top and a pair of light purple Levi's. I was not wearing a cowboy hat, and my dark hair got hotter and hotter every minute the late-August temperature of the West mounted, but I was wearing a pink snakeskin string top that matched my satin pink Levi's and purple snakeskin stilettos. We always had a lot of fun dressing up, a welcome change from the black clothes I had become accustomed to wearing. Beth preferred soft, pastel tops, tight pants and high heels, and encouraged me to buy some frilly pastel tops in the neighboring markets, gently helping me to lighten up and relax. If any guy made the mistake of thinking we'd be easy lays, her dry, sarcastic comments and utter fearlessness quickly steered him in a different direction, and he would usually end up falling in love with her, admiring her every move.

We must have been a colorful sight standing on the dirt road, surrounded by bent, torn wire fences, cow dung and pebbles, not doing anything but admiring the landscape. It almost felt like a Levi's commercial, except that Brad Pitt was nowhere to be seen. I can't imagine how we must have looked to the Navajo Indian who happened by in his pickup right at that moment. He slowed down and leaned out of the window staring at our shoes. Taking this as an invitation, Beth strolled over to his door and shook his hand.

"Hi, my name's Beth and my car seems to have a problem, do you think you could help us out?"

He didn't ask any questions and disappeared under the hood of our car, which emitted a series of clanking noises and muffled bumps until the motor ran smoothly. A connection had come loose and cut off the electrical circuit, he explained. After thanking him, Beth spoke a little about her life as an artist and accompanied him back to the pickup, shaking his hand once more. Without having said a word he climbed in. The guys in the back hadn't moved either, and continued to stare at us.

Before starting the engine he cast another disbelieving glance our way, and then unwillingly asked Beth, "How old is your car?" She told him that the bright yellow jeep belonged to her sixty-year-old father and that he had collected a couple of really nice ones over the years, each one of which she described in detail. She also told him how profoundly she loved the rituals of his people and that her dream was to live in a wagon pulled by a mule, traveling the desert. The man started his car after a pause and left, watching us in his rear mirror. Beth got back into our now-functioning vehicle and commented on how nice he had been, and that Navajos were wizards with cars.

On the road again, we stopped at a Dairy Queen, eager to order a root beer sundae, something Beth had assured me would be delicious. Listening to music and chatting we waited for the order when another Navajo suddenly popped up next to her car window holding an electrical drill, screaming, "If you don't give me all your money I will kill you with this here machine." Beth offered the desperate man our last sandwich, while explaining that we were very poor artists with no money to spare and that we could use some ourselves. The Navajo listened politely while munching the sandwich, finally commenting that he hadn't known how hard it could be to find work as a painter and left, wishing us luck.

I sat listening and watching silently, admiring her ability to respond calmly and with equanimity to any situation.

After leaving Berlin, Beth had moved back in with her old friend and mentor Bo, the gay son of a trapper, and the former owner of a secondhand boutique. She had modeled the clothes frequently in the past and after the store went bankrupt they decorated his house with the remnants, draping ball gowns, fur jackets, turtleneck suit jackets, ballerina flats, and golden high heels inbetween stuffed animals, jewelry, postcards, newspaper clippings, record covers, smiley faced cups and art books. Nailing and gluing everything to the walls, floors, and ceilings, Bo created a labyrinth of found objects, blocking windows and doors with the immense mountain of stuff. I could now understand why Beth had immediately taken to the Sniper bar; the Berlin club was a replica of the desert mansion. Bo's house had about five or six rooms, all very muffled because of the piled objects, creating a rabbit hole atmosphere with no air. Beth would try dusting the objects once in a while but Bo was never happy about anything being rearranged. Although the collection was an unsurpassable treasure chest of unusual objects, the slightly claustrophobic atmosphere was a sedative, turning its inhabitants into part of its decoration, where they sat next to the stuffed animals in a trance.

Beth and Ghazi lived with Bo for about a year, each working on their projects, Beth drawing and applying for exhibitions, Ghazi writing songs or art reviews and visiting neighboring artists. New Mexico has been known as a refuge for reclusive personalities since Georgia O'Keefe moved into the desert in 1949, painting bones and skulls instead of flowers. Joel-Peter Witken, an already legendary contemporary photographer, known for his depictions of freaks, skulls, and oddities, and for whom Beth had painted backdrops and modeled, lived around the corner; the "noir cult figure" John Gilmore, friend of James Dean, Marilyn Monroe, and Brigitte Bardot, was working on his first book of memoirs, *Laid Bare*, and I was introduced to countless unusual folks that had built their own, alternative universe in the desert, constructing houses according to astrological charts and energy routings, concerned with medicine and magic, growing their own vegetables and creatively designing their lives. Astonishingly the people I met there were very similar to my friends in Berlin, both places attracting nonconformists, and I felt I had found a Wild West parallel universe to my Prussian home town.

The problem with surviving in this heavenly natural landscape was that there was no real way to earn money through making art. Santa Fe was close enough to visit but the galleries were too dependent on tourists' income to appreciate Beth's art. Ghazi made an effort to manage Beth's exhibitions, contacting galleries in Los Angeles and New York, coordinating the career of his band from his remote dwelling, but the experiment resulted in both of them going broke. To create a cash flow Ghazi finally called his bandmates in Berlin and organized another US tour with the Golden Showers, generating enough money for a return ticket to Europe but the burden of poverty, disappointed hopes, and desperate career ventures had destroyed their comradeship and after arriving in Berlin they separated, leaving Beth stranded in a foreign country with no money or close relatives. After sleeping in various friends' guest rooms she moved into Chicken's tiny storage space behind the gallery and became a part of the shop window. Occupying a rickety old rocking chair, she would sit, inviting friends over for coffee and cake, initiating wild and turbulent discussions on art, German politics, and philosophy in general, making the best of her "Robinson Crusoe" situation and turning the Endart into a popular hangout for her friends.

She sat in the gallery for about half a year, rocking patiently until Alec Empire, the founder of the band Atari Teenage Riot, bought her most expensive painting, enabling her to purchase a plane ticket and fly back home.

I miss her laconic, down-to-earth comments and hilarious wit, and wish she would email more. But Beth long ago decided that she was not interested in the mad race of the modern art industry or for that matter any commercial enterprise, and now calls herself a Sunday painter who enjoys nature and native culture at her own pace. She decided to do what was best for her, despite the art curators wailing about lost talent and throwing away possibilities. She is a woman who doesn't want to conform to anyone else's expectations and actively chose to stay in the place in which she felt happiest.

The last time we spoke, she had moved into an adobe hut, did odd jobs sporadically to make money, and sounded very happy.

1998

The vast hall steamed with murky clouds. A fire glowed in the innermost round cubicle which had been inflated by old wooden boards, swelling into a monster of heat and flames, the smoke resisting the funnel overhead and instead pouring into the dusty venue, darkening the already blackened nooks and corners of the industrial ruin.

R. had called, inviting friends and fans to partake in an extensive happening, chuckling evilly into his white beard, mentioning that he wouldn't mind a good fuck after the concert.

She had been asked to film the performance, for free of course, and had consented.

The stage stood in a corner of the room, enhancing the frostily shining metal of handmade instruments glimmering dimly among monitors and microphones, set up to accommodate guest musicians. It was an honor to participate in this event series, most of the guests were in awe of the unfaltering, tirelessly working master who had ignored commercial markets and financial success for most of his life. He had decided to arrange a three-day concert sequence and invite every successful musician he knew to join in his endeavors, proudly demonstrating his independence in spite of his age.

Moving to the front of the platform, trying to catch the dimly lit performers, her camera's eye stumbled into huddled hipsters, barely concealed, sniffing huge amounts of cocaine from CD covers, and she filmed their dirty nostrils, grinding teeth, and rolling eyes, speeding, snorting, sneezing, and grimacing without cease.

After the master had performed his favorite Styrofoam ode "Dry Fuck," and retired, she continued capturing the evening as agreed, a silent visitor backstage, which was now full of celebrating friends and guest musicians ordering drugs, drugs, and more drugs, and drinking vast quantities of beer and whiskey, telling each other stories of other parties during which they had taken drugs and drunk bottles of whiskey.

Bored with the repetition she gradually filmed herself out into the mass of dancing bodies moving around the fire, their eerie, skeletal shadows enlarged by the flames and covering the walls.

The club was roaring, boisterous orders were placed at the bar, studiously "cool" figures hung out in corners, wearing seedy leather jackets and selling magic cookies and small white tabs with funny faces marked on them. Trying to escape the mass of bodies she wandered into the next hall and stumbled against hooded shapes having sex on the cold cement floor. "Oops, sorry didn't

*see you," she whispered, annoyed that her camera was not able to focus in the
dark and went back into the main room.*

*Turning, a friend smashed into her violently, causing the camera to unfocus
once more and snarling she lashed out, losing her patience, "For God's sake,
watch where you're going!"*

*Grinning, H. caught her arm and good-naturedly said: "Hey, stop working,
let's have some fun and go backstage."*

"Ok, I think I have enough material for a short documentary."

*Carefully placing her Super-8 camera into its small case she started walking
backstage. H. recounted a detailed story of taking drugs at the last concert, his
voice fuzzy among the drum-and-bass noise.*

"Hey-ho."

*Another acquaintance appeared, asking her companion for some drugs. Silent-
ly following their conversation she increasingly felt worn-out and estranged.
Taking the chance of flitting behind a pillar as their heads bent down over
the plastic bag she quickly veered towards the entrance door, slipping out
quietly.*

*The bouncer, an acquaintance, grabbed her sleeve, "Hey, why are you leaving,
isn't the party any good? Need some ammunition?"*

*Looking at his tired face, lined forehead, large pupils, and red hands she
hesitated:*

"No, it's fine, I just have to get back to work, my opening is in two days."

And with that she quickly disappeared out of the front door's spotlight.

Setting up a gallery

After my exhibition was installed, the opening come and gone, interviews dispatched with, and my small catalogue distributed, I set about learning how to represent other artists, setting aside any creative output for a year to see how I would enjoy dealing with the commercial aspect of my trade.

Dimitri had decided that the gallery should feature a mixture of local and international artists, so after taking a good look at the current art styles, I determined the safest route would be to represent art I personally liked the best, and rely on my instincts. After looking at countless portfolios I became aware that I was always instinctively drawn to a combination of surrealism, dada, pop art, and expressionism, a combination that, unbeknownst to me, was developing into an art form in LA known as "lowbrow" art or pop surrealism.

I decided to stick with these parameters. My guidelines had been found. While finishing building the gallery, artists had already started walking in, courageously presenting large portfolios in various shapes, hastily stuttering their biographies, trying to sound as self-assured as possible and nervously waiting for my verdict. Thrust into the unaccustomed position of having to evaluate their vision, I initially felt overwhelmed, but soon learned that it was best to be honest, to just explain to the artist whether or not they were in line with what I was looking for. This kept me from being judgmental. Another direction I had always been very interested in was the Gesamtkunstwerk, artists creating a universe of interactive expression. Edward Kienholz was one of my favorites in this regard, so the first on my list was Bob Rutman, the American/German musician, painter, drawer, instrument maker, sculptor, sound inventor, curator, mentor to many and Berlin icon. I invited him to do a large solo show.

ROBERT RUTMAN

Born in Berlin, Bob Rutman fled Nazi Germany in the 1930s, traveling through Poland, Finland, and Sweden and eventually landing in the US. He studied art in the 1960s, and his adventurous spirit led him to Mexico where he developed an intense friendship with the beat poet Philip Lamanzia, a member of the San Francisco beat generation and the surrealist movement.

In the gallery A Bird Can Fly But a Fly Can't Bird that he co-founded with Dorothy Carter in 1966, he began developing prototypes for the instruments he would later become known for: the steel cello and bow chime. The sail-like pieces of gleaming metal supported by metal frames wrapped around steel rods produced an eerie, diaphanous ambience, reminiscent of melancholic whale cries and shifting universes. Playable objects have a long history within the disciplines of music and performance art, used to challenge Western musical traditions.

After founding the Steel Cello Ensemble, Bob toured the United States and Europe during the 1970s. Alternating between music and art, this multitalented figure executed many of his paintings, sculptures, and mixed media installations in Boston, finishing a beautiful collection of religious themes and *Nudes Sitting on Chairs*. The *Nudes Sitting on Chairs* collection sold very badly so he decided to discard the nudes and only painted the chairs and these immediately sold much better. Happy to find a theme that was abstract, humorous, and commercially successful he continued working on the chair theme for many years. In 1990 he returned to Berlin to collaborate with Peter Sellars, Merce Cunningham, Einstürzende Neubauten, Robert Wilson, and Wim Wenders, permanently etching his name in the annals of experimental music.

Bob became an institution one could find at the Ex 'n' Pop most evenings, enjoying the music and wild bunch of guests, his cynical humor and deep dedication to controversy always alive and kicking. Visiting him in his huge studio behind the Ex 'n' Pop, especially after Dorothy moved in, became a popular pastime for my circle of friends. We celebrated birthdays, Thanksgiving, or Christmas in the bare cement rooms, with their putrid odor of chemicals and oil paint, the walls covered with smudges, and the space filled to the brim with steel cellos, metal sculptures, and Dorothy's string instruments. Although Bob was an acknowledged artist, he had remained quirky and stubborn, rejecting mainstream success, so despite or because of his ripe age in the 1990s, he was always on the lookout for exhibition possibilities or other ways of earning money. It had become a common mission for his friends to try and support him in this endeavor, realizing that we would all be in the same position one day.

Dimitri agreed to publish a CD of Rutman's newest composition in conjunction with his solo exhibition, thereby giving an added oomph to the hype surrounding the show, and enabling the promotion of all aspects of Rutman's work. We set about preparing the press kit.

Unexpectedly, Bob had a stroke, scaring all of us dreadfully. Multitudes of musicians visited him in the hospital, bringing him books, wine, and music to pass the time, shocked at seeing this dauntless bastion suddenly bowing to a strike of lightning. After he recovered and had moved back home it was obvious he would not have the time or strength to paint a new body of work so we decided to mount a retrospective instead. Luckily there was plenty of work to choose from, and we hung the gallery with examples from the different stages of his career, impressing the numerous admirers, friends, and collectors who flew in to support his show. A number of prints and etchings were sold. During the run of the show we organized small concerts within the gallery to continue attracting potential buyers for his larger editions, asking friends to participate.

The CD titled *Music To Sleep By* had also been finished, with Johannes Beck designing the cover and Alexander Hacke producing it. The disc was timed to be released during the exhibition, insuring further income for Bob.

In spite of the support, Bob became very depressed during the recovery from his stroke. The feeling of unjust punishment prevailed. He could not understand why the success he deserved was not rolling in after a life of unwavering dedication to valuable, serious music experimentation, particularly since he had watched others in his field become legendary and rich. He was consumed by cynicism and would suddenly start raging, throwing black tantrums or slinging furious, poisonous barbs at anybody who came close. He entered a dark phase of his life. In spite of everyone's discomfort, his friends understood the frustration of not receiving well-deserved acclaim, and deeply respected his stamina and continued organizing performances and concerts, telling promoters about him, helping him receive social security and grants.

Bob experienced a second stroke about a year later, throwing the large group of supporters into utter despondency, wondering how to help him recover from the stronger and more damaging attack. But, impressively, Bob did not succumb. Instead he started working hard at rehab, relearning how to speak and move, stubbornly getting up and asking for concerts and support everywhere he went, and though he wobbled a bit more than before he was just as resolute as ever. By 1999 a secure net of assistance had been built around him through loyal friends such as Pepi Streich and Miguel Ibanez, who took turns living with the grouchy eccentric, shopping for food, taking care of his taxes, and cleaning his apartment. Others organized concerts or, as did Einstürzende Neubauten, invited him to go on tour in order to garner international recognition. Thanks to all of these supportive initiatives, Bob's life became more stable and financially secure, with social security coming in alongside a steady flow of concerts.

The many facets of old age—such as social security, illness, failing eyesight, cancer scares, pension, retirement, and the discrimination against the elderly—are ignored during youth, disregarded by our society, and pushed aside as long as possible with everybody secretly hoping to live forever. Bob Rutman and Dorothy Carter's interaction among us younger artists was an invaluable lesson, since they demonstrated how old age does not mean the end of creativity, social interaction, resistance, intelligence, dignity, or beauty. They gave us a different vision of how fulfilling it can be to continue one's quest after middle age, in spite of difficulties, instead of considering one's life as being over.

Their experiences also demonstrated how demanding it is to achieve recognition due to our civilization's fear of growing old, going so far as preventing it from being exhibited on stage or depicted on magazine covers. Being with them taught us how important it is to include all ages during social interaction with others, and how vital families, friends, and support are for anyone to survive and achieve a fulfilled life, even at seventy. It has been proven that having responsibility, feeling needed, and being integrated within a functioning social structure is integral to longevity and instead of trying to ignore this fact, it is wise to include seniors in our lives from the start. Many of the problems in our society stem from loneliness and inflexibility, issues to which depression or health problems have been directly related. If there were a greater effort to integrate our elders into useful, fulfilling jobs, supporting single mothers, helping teenagers, organizing charitable functions, and of course also supporting their ongoing projects, promoting subjects that do not solely deal with teenage ideology, we would have a better off culture in which all could profit from the wisdom and knowledge acquired through such interaction. It is obvious that greed and commercial gain are not the answer to happiness, so why not try something new?

Ten years after his two attacks Bob still performs regularly, goes out, bums cigarettes, drinks wine, and insults his friends. He is an unshakably talented musician and critic, an impressive, proud figure who lives his life to the hilt and dismisses even the slightest suggestion of compromise with an impatient gesture. I wish there were more like him.

The Life of a Curator

I spent the following year busily promoting artists.

Sitting in my gallery from 10 in the morning until 2 AM the following day, I would look at portfolios, art books, and applications, and prepare exhibitions, invitations, and mailing lists. Although the neighborhood was not on the usual tourist's track, at least one artist a day would show me his portfolio.

I began to understand how much nondescript art there is, and how many good and talented artists are unable to market themselves. Picasso's quote that success is only possible through the combination of talent, charisma, and a good manager started to make sense, and my new job made it clear that none of these attributes are easily found, and therefore not to be taken for granted.

I had promised Dimitri that each exhibition would have a small accompanying catalogue, discussing the paintings and drawings with the artist, and would have them printed and ready for distribution at the opening. This in addition to organizing bartenders, cleaning staff, and bouncers for the openings, and ordering wine or beer while preparing small buffets of cheese sandwiches, chocolate desserts, and pretzels.

I had also promised to keep costs at bay, since Dimitri was willing to pay for the rent and my tiny salary, but expected money to be generated from the start. So I decided to organize at least one small event per week to promote the space, such as readings, concerts, and film screenings, on top of my other responsibilities, and made a little extra money by selling drinks and small inexpensive art objects on the side.

Apart from the main exhibitions in the two large rooms I also organized small openings every two weeks for one of the "cheap art" artists in the shop. That meant distributing and sending out about three thousand invitations per month.

To be able to do all of these tasks and still have time to reach out to collectors and other art lovers, I needed assistants. So I discovered the world of "management." I expected assistants to be similar to freelance organizers, bearing responsibility, making decisions independently, aware of their assignment, correcting mistakes, learning how to do things better, willing to work hard for small pay. The concept of telling people what to do seemed very strange, almost surreal, but I dealt with that by not taking this seriously, so assistants either became extremely lazy or frighteningly overbearing. I had aides that would stop doing a chore in the middle of the job if time was up, leaving me to clean up their mess or finish it on my own, while others pretended to be the boss in my absence, making decisions or agreements they had no authority to make, and turning insolent when caught in the act.

In the end I was lucky to find an honest and serious helper, Maxi Neugebauer, an aspiring architect looking for a job to finance her studies. She saved the day by pitching in as hard as I did, a gem of support and understanding. Without her assistance I would not have been able to accomplish the huge load of work necessary to promote the artists. Over time I realized that the search for collectors, grants, financial support, and press contacts was the main, never ending, draining pastime curators are faced with, exhibitions only being the fun part, and although I had always enjoyed organizing projects, I found that asking for support, money, or sponsorship was not my forte. Obviously I had to learn this aspect of the job if I wanted to represent the artists professionally, and bit by bit I began learning how to orchestrate dealings more effectively, seducing art lovers into becoming collectors, showing them details, revealing connections to historical precedents, and explaining unusual approaches.

In the mid 1990s Berlin was still recovering from the financial aftermath of the turmoil that came with reuniting Germany, and the city known for its many galleries and artists was dependent on collectors coming in from the outside. Finding investors was very difficult in general, but especially so for a small underground establishment.

Thanks to my long history of working in different areas I had a list of favorite artists, whom I selected from the hundreds I knew or who contacted me: it included Ralph Meiling, a multimedia artist, who made strangely shadowed, old-fashioned horror-fairytale photos of indistinct faces warped by flashlight movements or long exposure. He agreed to show with Hanayo, a beautiful Japanese geisha turned photographer, who had been celebrated as a nationally known pop singer in Japan, but had moved to Berlin to participate in punk concerts, Schlingensief performances and outrageous happenings, and offered to exhibit a collage of five hundred small photo scraps taken in Japan, depicting gaily costumed babies in dreamlike bright blue and pink settings, with masks, flowers, and cute animals surrounding them. The combination of these two opposing cultures, styles, and characters turned the joint show into a sensory feast, flinging the observer into a melting pot of impressions and reactions. At the end Dimitri invited Ralph to fill his spacious Schwarzenraben restaurant with large prints of the impressive photography in order to promote and finance his art simultaneously, once more taking the role of patron. The next artist, Gary Griffith, a filmmaker and painter from England, exhibited beautiful oil paintings with an Edward Goreyesque, nightmare atmosphere, depicting small children in sailor suits digging their own graves or floating above indiscernible objects to symbolize decay and progress. He also installed a group of jelly rabbits in the window, which slowly decomposed throughout the exhibition, growing an impressive green fur in front of surprised tourists.

In general most of the artists I invited to show with us worked in multiple areas, due to my affinity for multitasking and curiosity about how others use different techniques. Kai Teichert, my favorite Berlin painter, who had introduced himself to me at one of my Tresor events, slipping a small photo into my hands and disappearing immediately, agreed to show apocalyptic oils of sinking civilizations with green skies and fantastic landscapes reminiscent of Bosch or Breughel next to his carefully formed clay busts of eccentric Berlin characters; these pastel figures silently looking at each other filled the room. Kai's statues became very successful, bought by museums and commissioned by politicians in later years; the old-fashioned bust revolutionized by being painted with oil instead of enamel and not being fired in an oven. This way they remained covered with a powdery pastel sheet of delicate color, giving the faces an unusual innocence.

I enjoyed being at the center of a lively group of artists, speaking to newspapers, writing art reviews, finding creative jobs for my flock, experiencing what it's like to go to work every morning, nodding hello to the neighboring secondhand store, getting a coffee at the newly opened coffee shop around the corner, stopping to gossip with the waiters of the Schwarzenraben Dimitri's now thriving restaurant, and then unlocking the door of my gallery, sifting through the mail or news articles and making my first phone calls. It was an inspiring adventure in discovering art in a new way.

By 10 a.m. the first artist would drop by, casually asking how many paintings I had sold, a stray tourist would wander in, inquiring how to get to the closest subway station, only to be lured into buying a small cheap art object, then the wine was delivered, with journalists arriving for an interview, more artists slinking in with heavy portfolios, girlfriends calling up to catch up on news, or a whole group of art lovers rushing in to look at an exhibition because they had missed the opening.

In contrast to the lonely hours spent in my studio, it was an easygoing, entertaining life and Dimitri's conviction that I had a knack for representing art proved to be true. The gallery speedily became a sought-after space, attracting crowds to the openings and generating a small but steady flow of money. The success of my endeavor encouraged me to try larger exhibition strategies and I decided to look around for spaces in which I could exhibit all of my artists at once in order to expand their recognition and create even more media coverage to attract collectors.

1999

She had formed small, nude figures out of clay, putting them together in the shape of a woman's skeleton, her interpretation of the earthy brown landscape of the Havelland countryside outside Berlin.

It was fun being creative again and the invitation to exhibit in the castle was intriguing. Collecting tree branches and shrubbery, she decorated the walls of her room, the earth on the floor mirroring the projected slides of breasts and hips.

A friend had come along to help install the objects. For two days they had carried the heavy, rain-sodden pails of soil from the forest, through the window into the ballroom, since the main door of the patio was stuck, up the monumental marble stairs and into a medium-size room on the second floor.

The downpour of rain increased steadily, transforming the neglected park into a muddy puddle of weeds and happy worms. While scurrying back and forth, reduced to wet, shivering animals, yelping for shelter and wiping the water from their faces in the dry interior, they were confronted with a group of dour, red-eyed locals whitewashing the corridor walls. R. had hired them with the idea of creating positive neighborly interaction and job possibilities for all, oblivious to the barely restrained exasperation provoked by his friendly offer.

Annoyed by their sudden predicament of working for money instead of receiving welfare the dawdling men muttered insults through their teeth, burping and spitting loudly each time she passed, cursing eager Westerners and newfangled socialization ideas.

Deciding not to react while trying to get her job done as quickly as possible, she ran faster and faster, hoping to finish by sunset, rushing up and down the stairs and through the forest as if demons were pursuing her.

Realizing that their obscenities were being ignored, the handymen decided to lock the window each time the artists went into the forest, making them stand in thunder and lightning with pails of soaking earth begging for entrance.

"This is bullshit!" Her friend's brow curled in anger, thunderously similar to the black clouds above.

"I know, but what can we do, there's nobody here to help us, let's just get it done as quickly as possible and then come back when all the others are here."

Stumbling up the second floor for the hundredth time she furiously contemplated their helplessness when a loud bang and frantic shouts could be heard. Dropping her pail she ran down the stairs just in time to see her partner covered in blood, his T-shirt torn, pushing one of the smirking aggressors, who was twice his size, against the wall with an enraged look on his face.

The room was covered with glass and broken wood. Together with R., who had just arrived, they managed to pull the incensed men apart, trying to calm them and clean away blood and splinters until the police arrived.

The uniformed officials turned up quickly. They knew most of the workers personally and greeted them jovially by their names.

Her helper had thrown a garden chair into their smirking faces through the locked window, then leaped through the broken glass immediately after, covering himself with blood and splinters of wood and hurling insults while charging towards them. He was charged with attacking innocent employees without cause. The men testified that they had been assaulted out of the blue after they told him that he should use the door on the other side of the castle. They seemed happy to condemn the arrogant city slickers and hoped to get rid of them quickly before more harm could be done.

Senzke

Senzke was a small village about an hour's drive from Berlin on the way to Hamburg, and had formerly belonged to East Germany. The community consisted of about 230 inhabitants, and had no stores, no cafés, and no school. The small farmhouses and cottages clustered anxiously along the main street, guarded by snarling dogs and high gates.

As with most European villages, there was one reminder of past luxury, a desolate mansion sheltered by a colossal park, overflowing with gnarled oak trees and sunken hedges, proudly called "The Castle."

The building had been used by the communal school until 1997, but due to financial issues and ensuing bankruptcy it had been abandoned. The children were shipped off to neighboring districts, leaving classroom tables and blackboards behind, sadly collecting dust in the now silent rooms. In spite of escalating mildew and outrageous rust, the center point of the town sustained an aura of past splendor, which was immediately perceivable upon driving into the village.

Anno Dittmer, a photographer with whom I worked occasionally, introduced me to the community. He drove out to the countryside regularly to visit his friend Antje Fels, one of the original Endart artists, who had moved out to the countryside years ago to found a small artists' colony.

The journey to Senzke, through bright green meadows, oceans of sunflowers, and snow-covered pine trees in the winter, was picturesque and inspiring. Arriving with Anno, I was immediately captivated by the rural paradise, Antje serving cookies and food flavored with herbs from her garden, arranging them on handmade ceramic dishes and mosaic-covered tables, with roses and marigolds peeping through her large windows and countless cats slinking in and out of the sunlit doorways.

Antje had invited a few friends to visit and when the sun set a small fire was ignited, around which we grouped comfortably, roasting chestnuts and telling stories.

I had forgotten about rural life, having lived in the city for such a long time. Now I suddenly remembered the suburbs of Washington DC and skipping along small creeks, discovering a raccoon family and spending afternoons watching ants crawl over my fingers, with the smell of freshly mowed grass lingering in the hot summer air. After spending the night in Antje's attic, encased in a wool sleeping bag and waking to silence with only birds singing and horses neighing in the distance, I lay stretched out for a long time enjoying the unexpected peace. The remaining guests were served fresh honey and milk with homemade blueberry muffins and then invited to explore the forest. We passed deer and rabbits softly eating in the shadows, a deserted chapel covered with spider webs, and peeked into the splintered windows of the deserted castle. During this walk

Antje told us that she was looking for a new tenant and asked us to inform anyone that might be interested.

Back in Berlin I contacted Motte immediately. During one of our regular cake and coffee afternoons he had mentioned being bored of city life. After having converted to Buddhism and studying natural ways of living, he was interested in finding alternative lifestyles. The description of the idyllic country art space was exactly what he had been visualizing and he immediately called Antje to make an appointment. When I met him a couple of weeks later he told me that he was packing his furniture for the move.

Motte and I had spent a great deal of time together after Roland's demise. In spite of having separated, our friendship remained my strongest support—I felt protected by the warmhearted generosity of my loyal friend.

The Institut had become my main occupation, and everything else was pushed aside by the many tasks I was confronted with. I spent a great deal of time discovering the financial chess game within the world of art, and since Motte had been interested in this from the start, he came by to visit regularly, looking at the exhibitions, cracking jokes with the artists, and helping with chores or filming openings. We very suddenly fell in love again at one point. Both of us were taken by surprise by the resurgence of our feelings, but as we had never lost sight of each other and remained true friends, we quickly fell into a very natural, relaxed symbiosis of togetherness. After the move to Senzke we began spending weekends in the countryside and the weekdays in my renovated studio, enjoying an exciting, entirely new way of living, since we were used to old-fashioned coal stoves, noisy train tracks, honking traffic, gray pollution, and clamoring radios.

In Senzke you had to drive at least half an hour to the next mall to be able to go shopping. Huge conglomerations containing the likes of Ikea, with its endless household items, Bauhaus, which had mountains of tools, and Kaiser's multiple rows of food could be found every fifty kilometers, which was very different from the small, specialized stores in Berlin. In addition to these faceless, mass-market merchants of trade we were happy to discover small food vendors on the sides of byways selling typical East German sauerkraut, sausages, and jam. We chatted with the friendly grandmothers sitting with a blanket on their laps, knitting little dollies or catching up with a friend who had stopped by. Depending on the season, famous Beelitzer asparagus or special hams, tiny strawberries, and homemade ice creams were added to the variety.

East Germany had remained disadvantaged after the political upheaval, abruptly being placed in the position of the poor relative adopted by a wealthy family, without having the financial means of assimilating or easily becoming part of the landscape. This resulted in a whole population feeling neglected and insecure, with a rising sentiment of great injustice becoming apparent, making Berlin the clashing mid-point of East and West interaction. Because of the steady interaction which already existed during the Cold War, with people smuggling wares to each other, meeting secretly, helping each other survive and perceiving life behind the other side of the Wall firsthand, a relatively natural interaction had been possible in many districts after the curtain fell. Prenzlauer Berg was now turning into a trendy neighborhood, with yuppies and artists crossing paths. Pankow or Weissensee, working-class areas with very low rents and numerous children's daycare facilities for working mothers, on the other hand remained largely populated by former their residents. Friedrichshain, a district that had been divided by the Wall, with Warschauer Strasse and the Oberbaumbrücke marking former border checkpoints, now became the new "Kreuzberg," a haven for youngsters, where opposing cultures blended into an adventurous mix of secondhand clothes, punk concerts, and underground events. Those working in the arts especially appreciated diversity. People moved into deserted apartments in the East, befriended new shopkeepers and neighbors, decorating local stores or selling comic books in deserted hair salons, putting a positive, creative perspective on integration within the community, focusing on parties, events, and exhibitions in contrast to the discrepancies growing outside of the city.

Here an entirely different atmosphere reigned. The neglected, disenchanted inhabitants, simultaneously betrayed by their former and current governments, switched from their customary passive resistance to actively aggressive outbursts of revenge.

Stories of Nazi raids, right-wing meetings, and acts of discrimination towards foreigners increased, although they were considered distant thunder claps by politicians, who ignored or trivialized such events, describing them as the outbursts of a few numbskulls.

Thus Motte and I were quite innocent about the depth of the political situation when we moved to Senzke. Thanks to his fame within the techno scene, a music style hugely popular among East Germans because of its communal principals declaring "no more heroes," with hundreds dancing to repetitive samples at vast, low-priced raves, we were initially met with enthusiasm. The villagers were excited to have this celebrity move into their tiny, unassuming village, and lined up in front of our fence to ask for autographs.

Born with a sense of fun-loving justice, Motte enjoyed the attention, speaking about Buddha and the necessity of compassion while signing their postcards. The young villagers responded warmly, happily offering homemade bread, party locations, and further records to be signed, feeling flattered by his arrival. Our lodgings were surrounded by an ancient, lofty stone wall, protecting us from unwanted observation and barring any menace, so for a long time the bright side of country life was dominant, and the darker aspects exposed themselves only after a couple of months.

It was during the annual summer fête in the castle's park, as we stood speaking to a couple of fans, eating delicious apple pie with fresh cream, that we noticed a slight, almost imperceptible change. Having become accustomed to our presence the fans had opened up and suddenly their stories became increasingly sprinkled with descriptions of weapons, battles, youngsters dying, sexual abuse, drug dealers, and alcoholism. Surprised we asked if this was common knowledge or only insider stories, and were told it was only the tip of the iceberg.

Finding the cold facts of violence, addiction, and hatred difficult to imagine in the bright sunlit park, particularly while standing among smiling neighbors and brightly laden buffets, we decided these were the tall tales of imaginative youngsters and quickly forgot about the disquieting information, continuing instead to enjoy our newfound paradise.

I remember the summer as a scented mass of wild flowers, spent reading books on the warm pasture while Motte fertilized the ground with horse manure, enjoying the unusual occupation and fresh air. We barbecued on the patio, and our city cats Minnie and Mickey finally became accustomed to the wide blue sky overhead, joining the wild cat gang and chasing mice and small vermin excitedly, whizzing through our legs with proudly raised, burr-covered tails. On our extensive hikes through the countryside we discovered a long-haired herd of French cattle grazing. Their owner, a heavy, jovial farmer, told us of the special care he took in keeping them well-fed and healthy; introducing us in detail to the other animals and telling us about the different stages of manure. Wide-ranging conversations about art with Antje, drinking heavy red wine and arguing for hours about whether art should be a mirror or an example for others was a favorite evening occupation. During the day we frolicked with the neighborhood children at fairs and festivities. Returning to Berlin, sunburned and relaxed on Monday mornings, we could hardly wait to drive back the next weekend.

Fall arrived quickly, an explosion of colors, with bright red leaves, orange pumpkins, green apples, and delicious ham everywhere. Antje's fireplace was lit constantly, with all of us cooking large meals together, knitting, chatting, and trying to think up events we could do in the area in order to earn money.

To keep from going broke in spite of our distance to the city, Motte and I worked steadily in the large studio space, writing music, painting large installation pieces, and preparing theater sets for international commissions. Somehow days seemed to go by slower in the country than in the city, and we would nonetheless be able to take the time to walk to the chapel, smell the last flowers, and discover the other villages nearby, standing in awe in front of the descendant of the famous pear tree in Ribbeck, described in Theodor Fontane's poem "Herr von Ribbeck auf Ribbeck im Havelland."

After it turned cold we were presented with beautiful snow-covered landscapes, frosted trees, and bushes with red berries, and spent our time breathlessly building snowmen, taking long walks through the icy forests, and sleigh rides down the small village hill, scraping ice from the car window in the morning, falling into a snowy dune on the way to the postbox, and looking up into the sky through the small window in the roof, watching the stars through a large telescope and discerning astrological alignments. Visually winter has always been my favorite season and experiencing the snow-covered landscapes in its most charming form was enthralling.

Our bliss was tarnished first by a sinister, chemical cloud of smoke curling over our roof from the fireplace of our neighbor, busy burning old plastic containers, which were cheaper than firewood, and covering our farmyard in a black, poisonous nightmare. Innocently Motte decided to go and offer him some of our firewood, mentioning that chemical fire was terribly bad for nature and that it was against the law. To his surprise he was received by an extremely aggressive response of being thrown out of the man's home and threatened with more in case we ever complained again.

The black fog grew worse, engulfing the village in a murky smell of rot and slime until our art community decided to call the Environmental Senate, not feeling comfortable with "squealing" on somebody but not knowing how else to deal with our uncompromising adversary. Confronted with "officials," the former underdogs of communism suddenly became compliant and immediately changed their habits, confronting us with a subservient attitude we had never before experienced in the demonstration-riddled Berlin, making it obvious that we had entered a sphere of unfamiliar rules.

In spite of this odd confrontation, we were annoyed but not alarmed, still too preoccupied with driving back and forth from Berlin, our sojourns in the country becoming longer and longer, inviting friends over for weekends to show off our new paradise. The space Motte had rented was a large studio apartment under the roof of one of the former barn buildings. We had filled it with books, comfortable armchairs, a new easel so I could paint, hammocks, and Indonesian art from a holiday in Bali, with a clothing line going along the back wall to hang wet laundry in the perfume of fresh country air. Because of the slanted roof and huge windows the studio was very bright, perfect for drawing or painting. I eagerly took the chance to start working on my own art again and after Motte had set up his studio, we spent weeks diligently immersed in our projects, time stretching immeasurably in the quiet countryside. I was surprised at how passionately I had fallen in love with the earthy nature of the Havelland, feeling as if its soil were part of my body and regularly taking a break from the strong linseed perfume of oil paints, which had been unthinkable before, brewing a coffee and wandering out into the late afternoon meadows, speaking to a cow grazing, waiting for frogs to appear in the glistening pond, popping up through the water and blinking at me with glistening, bulging eyes, or having a chat with the other inhabitants of Antje's residency.

I loved the golden haystacks in fall, offsetting the black contours of trees, spiky after having lost their leaves, and the long procession of storks arriving in spring, nesting on a deserted chimney nearby, throwing out their young to teach them how to fly. The fragrance from the lavender growing under our windows in summer wafted in gently while I pondered a bread recipe, and the heavy storms and thunderclaps, much closer than in the city, made me feel alive in a different, more alert manner than before. I started dreaming of giving up city life completely.

Seeing everything from a new perspective affected all areas in my life, so after directing Das Institut for one year as promised, I told Dimitri that working as a curator had been enjoyable, particularly discovering that it was something I was good at doing, but that my soul had not caught fire. The experiment had merely confirmed what I had suspected from the start: my priority lay in being an artist. Although Dimitri was disappointed he accepted my decision and we concluded the experiment, both turning to new projects but keeping track of each other over the following years. To use the knowledge I had acquired I decided to curate one big exhibition or event each year so I could present artists I considered outstanding, but my main goal now was to work on my own art again.

THE CASTLE

One memorable evening, while sitting around a fire and contentedly grilling lamb chops together with Joseas and his wife, artists who lived on the farmyard together with us, they mentioned speaking to the village mayor and asking if organizing an exhibition in the empty rooms of the castle would be possible. The beautiful architecture had started deteriorating and was obviously neglected, with smashed windows and crumbling walls. The mayor had reacted enthusiastically saying that a building needs life to maintain its atmosphere and invited us to write a proposal. Not realizing what implications our enthusiasm would have later on we started writing drafts of which artists we would ask and what type of event would make sense. After having finished a rough sketch of our ideas we made an appointment with the mayor to see how she would react.

After reading the concept and speaking about the history and mentality of Senzke, she offered to give us a tour of the castle. Repeatedly exclaiming that it would be marvelous for it to be used as a cultural venue and to transform its many large rooms into studios, harboring a youth center, kindergarten, small café, and internet chat rooms as we had suggested in our proposal, she agreed to rent it to us for free in the first year. The necessary renovation of painting hundreds of walls, repairing broken windowpanes, rebuilding torn stairways, drying out the moldy basement, and replacing the defective heating system would then be our responsibility if we decided to stay longer. Walking carefully through the creaky hallways, their worn, wooden floors moaning with every step, I was charmed by the "sleeping beauty," untouched by the sanitizing hand of renovation, a mysterious world with ghosts peeping through slivers of forgotten school wardrobes, mingling with the current moment, giving past and present once more the rare opportunity of meeting each other head on. The building was a physical manifestation of T. S. Eliot's poem "The Hollow Men":

Between the idea and the reality
Between the motion and the act
Falls the Shadow

...

Between the desire and the spasm
Between the potency and the existence
Between the essence and the descent
Falls the Shadow

Time here was tangible, emanating from every object in the frozen house. As I explored the spacious, silent classrooms with dirty windows overlooking the weed-corrupted grounds, my soul sank into the old-fashioned metal tables covered with ink stains, and I traced the scrawled hearts and signatures with my finger, wondering about the forgotten stories they signified. The still life of russet-colored, dented chairs lying on their side, roughly printed, dog-eared GDR schoolbooks carelessly lining the windowsills, a soiled chemistry lab yawning from behind a door, with frayed coloring pencils thrown into bleak boxes and teachers' alcoves harboring lumpy, beige-colored sofas were pieces from the past, never to be resurrected.

Our intimate tourist group was immersed inside a treasure chest filled with turn-of-the-century remnants enhanced with communist memorabilia and renovated East German post-Wall handicrafts. We ascended myriad narrow stairways to the decapitated tower and its legendary trapdoor, where the blocked passage behind supposedly ended at the frog pond in front of the chapel. It sent excited shivers up our spine, as we imagined nightly excursions and adventurous escapades, enjoying the possibility of spirits and H.P. Lovecraftian creatures hovering close by. After peering through the milky window panes at the dusty Havelland and the horizon, with modern wind turbines waving from afar, the musty, airless attic was our next destination, home to hundreds of pigeons and perfect for storage, the wood beams intact and dry, covered with industrial wool, not as decrepit as we had expected. Such a space raised the value of the building immediately. After inspecting multiple bathrooms with corroded showers, empty storage spaces, and a miniature elevator we were taken down to the ground floor and the impressive ballroom, which opened out onto an elegant, spacious terrace, which in turn led us to the park down generous, graceful stairs.

Standing at the marble banister, overlooking former gardens, past the alley of oak trees, into a green sea of forest slightly veiled by a haze of fog, we were thrown into a state of blissful prophecy. Motte loudly exclaimed that magnificent raves could be held in the park, Joseas imagined foreign student residencies and computer art workshops, leading him to immediately ask about electrical sockets, something always absent from East German habitats. I was trying to decide which classroom I would prefer as a space for making paintings. After that the mayor led us through the basement, a clutter of dark, dusty closets with uneven rooms circling an immense, ancient kitchen bursting with out-of-date wood stoves, refrigerators, a mammoth table, countless chairs, plates, cutlery, pots and pans, but by that point we had already reached our decision. We would rent the castle for one year and try to turn it into a thriving cultural center. If the probation period was a success, we would buy the estate for one Deutschmark and finance the renovation. The result would not only enable us to survive and work on the outskirts of Berlin but also contribute to the development of East Germany by creating jobs, a kindergarten, and a youth club, renting the old liquor factory across the street to turn it into a hotel and café for visitors. We hoped to build a self-sufficient universe in which exhibitions, events, workshops, conferences, and residencies, could be arranged and established for all.

We were not the only ones discovering the outskirts of our city and planning this kind of center. Around 1996 and 1997 was a time in which many Berliners woke up to their new surroundings, now having the incentive to explore the as yet unknown country of the suburbs, after having spent years rediscovering their altered city. Long forgotten farmyards, charming cottages, deserted churches, and small castles in the Havelland, Uckermark, and Potsdam were rented or bought, conveniently located close enough to Berlin so one could drive back and forth from "Mitte" regularly, and continue working in the city. Taking time to renovate these properties extensively, enthusiastically discovering country life, club owners began expanding their nightlife into daytime gardening, record label directors discovered the romance of owning horses, DJs were married in small castles on the edge of unknown lakes, and artists organized exhibitions in stables, pastures, and farmers' markets instead of industrial ruins, and collectives initiated theater or dance centers in rural Brandenburg. Berlin, a city known for its restlessness, was an exuberant but draining place to live, and its adjacent surroundings offered repose and relaxation. We were all eager to discover this curious new playground lying on the outskirts of the city.

The rural inhabitants regarded the new arrivals with misgivings; feeling ignored and irrelevant, unsure how to react or feel about the change. They responded differently, some aggressively protecting their boundaries, others welcoming the oncoming wave of enthusiasts.

She had invited a few girlfriends to come for the weekend, offering them luxurious rooms in which they could write, paint, or meditate, describing in detail her new, beloved "secret garden" with its qualities of peace, silence, clean air, dewdrops on grass in the morning, vegetable gardens ready to be harvested so they could make a fresh salad for dinner, lonely haystacks black against stunning sunsets, the lowing of cattle herds, and a shining pond. It was the first time she was organizing such an outing. The idea of using the castle as a residency had been spoken about often but the others had been too busy to realize the idea, working in the artists' community behind the safety of walls of stone.

Gloriously happy she packed her necessities, preparing a canvas for a triptych that would be two and a half by ten meters long, too large for her city studio, planning a cover-version of Otto Dix's famous nightlife painting Metropolis *with DJs depicted instead of jazz musicians and techno dancers replacing the 1920s cabaret dancers. She had noticed that many details of the original setting were identical to the clubs and crowds she saw in Berlin's nightlife today and was curious to find further similarities. The car trip went by quickly, eased by cheerful, nonstop conversation—four girls munching on cheese sandwiches, giggling helplessly to hilarious gossip, drinking cold Earl Gray tea sweetened with honey, exclaiming about the forlorn Russian military quarters they passed, elaborating about the work they planned on doing, buying chocolate at a small gas station and saying over and over again how happy they were to discover something new. By late afternoon they had arrived at the village of Senzke, and an expectant hush fell upon the party. Guiding the vehicle up the pebbled lane she parked her car in front of the main entrance, careful not to crush the freshly mown grass.*

They stood quietly, admiring the spaciousness and peace, deeply inhaling the wonderful air and then set about unpacking paintbrushes, books, rolls of canvas, sleeping bags, food supplies, and hiking shoes from her VW.

As they labored, a growing number of spectators ambled by, obviously taking note of their every move and pointedly ignoring their shy hellos. Taken aback by the unfriendliness, her girlfriends asked if they were breaking a regulation by entering the castle, accustomed to city life in which the goings on of neighbors are usually ignored.

Reassuring them, she explained that it was not easy for inhabitants of the former East to watch supposedly "rich" Westerners come to their village, and that they would get used to the change once they finally understood that they

were merely artists. Also, as she was one of the official tenants of the castle,
they had every right to enter the premises.
Reassured, the girls continued unpacking the car.
After living in the village for some time, the artists' community had become
dangerously oblivious to the barely veiled hostility outside of their property,
believing that "action speaks louder than words," staying friendly and polite
in spite of the increasingly dark glances, and worked on renovating the castle
as quickly as possible to encourage creative interaction for all.
As daylight receded her small group concentrated on dinner preparations, the
large kitchen growing steamier with each pot placed on the stove, telling jokes,
peeling potatoes, drinking coffee, smoking cigarettes, drinking wine late into
the night and then dropping into their sleeping bags happily.
She was awakened by a crashing noise. "What on earth ... ?"
Trying to find some socks in her suitcase, she was shocked by exploding glass
falling down on her pillow in small splinters. Running to the window she
looked out to see a small gang of children, ranging from four to twelve years of
age, looking up at her with sticks and stones in their hands.
The lock was easy to open.
"Hey! What do you think you're doing?"
"Go fuck yourself you stupid cunt!"
She stared down at them speechlessly.
"Who do you think you are anyway, you ugly bitch, get the fuck out otherwise
we will make you."
The twelve-year-old girl and leader of the gang was blond, dressed in tight,
cheaply glittering jeans, a light blue, torn T-shirt, and sneakers. The others,
red-cheeked and snot-nosed, gazed back at her puzzled face, holding their
sticks in front of their bodies so as not to poke each other.
"What's wrong with you? Why don't we have breakfast together and I can tell
you when the kindergarten will be reopened and we can decide together how
to design the teenager's clubroom. It's too early in the morning to fight—come
on, let's be friends."
Another stone flew in her direction, narrowly missing the next window.
"Shut up bitch, one more word and I'm coming to beat you up."
"That's ridiculous, if you want to come inside to have breakfast you're wel-
come, if you break another window I'm going to tell your parents."
As she closed the window the yells and curses continued but no more stones
were thrown.
Annoyed she went downstairs, meeting the other girls who had similar stories.
Deciding to work in a way that could not be perceived from outside they closed
the shutters and kept far away from the main room with its large terrace.

Trying to make themselves invisible they stayed within the castle's vicinity throughout their designated holiday, giving up the idea of long walks in the forest, quietly drinking tea instead, working on their projects without accompanying music.

Nonetheless the entire weekend they were the target of assaults. Regardless of what room the girls worked in, crude, muffled insults could be heard through windows and doors, the poisonous barbs rattling their souls, transforming their happiness into stubborn resistance, not bowing to or acknowledging the crude battering, until repacking the car with the fruits of their work Sunday afternoon and driving out of the small village, exhaling in relief, warily watching the village disappear in the rearview mirror, beautiful in the sunset, with golden rooftops and grazing horses, the perfect illustration of a Grimm's fairy tale.

"Kunst Oder König"

Inspite of right-wing hostility in the Havelland, living on Antje's farm continued to be an inspiration. I scarcely missed anything about the city: the cultural interaction within the art community was playful, with plenty of working space and more time than I'd had before. Thanks to friendly neighbors offering advice on how to fertilize the ground, grow tastier carrots or discern bad eggs from good, we acquired knowledge about agriculture and animals, and learned old-fashioned apple pie recipes and how to effectively get rid of insects in the summer.

The only missing factor was a regular income. We had managed to rent the castle but the huge enterprise of founding a cultural center was still a dream with nothing but our own meager finances to cover expenses. There was no use in waiting for anybody to step in and help, so we decided to initiate exhibitions in the castle to attract the attention of regional cultural centers and get the Brandenburg Senate interested in subsidizing the white spaces on their map. If we could generate an awareness of our endeavors, we might then receive money to make the project space we had envisioned possible.

The first exhibition organized was called "Havellandschaften." We invited friends to come and create installations of the Havel landscape presenting the area we were now living in to create a perception of its individuality and make it stick out from the other countless villages in the surrounding. Deciding to work with textures typical of Senzke, I collected earth, twigs, and wood, creating a sensual atmosphere with small candles and projections highlighting a woman's figure formed out of clay rising from the soil-covered floor. Interestingly the other artists worked with similar natural elements, using water, wind, and air as well, fascinated by the rural ingredients the city could not offer.

The exhibition was modest and low key. We mainly invited artists and others in the neighborhood to see how an event on this scale would work out. The result was surprisingly good, with everybody enthusiastic about the space and the work, the simple cafeteria filled with homemade cookies and coffee attracting visitors to hang out and relax. Relieved, we hoped our neighbors understood that we were not a menace and took their positive reactions as incentive to continue.

In 1999 I invited nineteen artists and musicians to decorate the rooms with club art installations, offering them the possibility of living in the castle rooms before preparing the installations. Jim Avignon, Cornelius Perino, Kiddy Citny, DAG, Mediamorph, Betty Stürmer, Skudi Optixs and many more underground icons confirmed their participation, eager to discover new realms of interaction.

This time Joseas had applied to the Cultural Senate of the Havelland for a grant, showing them the small catalogue we had made for the former exhibition, and had received enough money to feed all participants for a week. We started organizing the transportation and lodging for the volunteers who would help prepare the elaborate dinners made up of local vegetables, sponsored by neighboring farmyards. The weeks sped by, everybody busy with their area of preparation, and when the artists arrived the castle was ready, waiting for them to paint, hammer, set up sound systems, rearrange rooms, and move furniture.

The bustle was watched silently by the Senzkians who were not sure what to make of the unaccustomed activity.

Besides organizing the event, speaking with and helping the artists, shopping for food and organizing cooking shifts, I decided to install my newly finished oil triptych, surrounding it with golden hay, dancing scarecrows, film loops of dancing women and club drawings, merging the contrast of rural and urban rituals and traditions, curious to find similarities and discrepancies.

During our preparation the difference between working in the country and the city revealed itself in many ways, the most obvious in the form of mosquitoes and flies swarming in as soon as food was served on the terrace, our warm water turning ice cold after the first shower, and hay fever or other plant-induced allergies suddenly rearing their ugly heads, leaving participants sneezing, teary-eyed, and red-nosed. The positive aspects were good air, huge amounts of space in which to work and exhibit, homegrown food, and no distractions. The general atmosphere became very relaxed in spite of the bustle, with introverted artists opening up and telling each other stories, alternatively sitting in the sun, painting, napping, or drinking coffee in small groups, energetically discussing different philosophies, giving each other advice, asking questions, and wandering from room to room, enthusiastically inspecting the growing installations.

By the time Skudi Optix arrived to decorate the outside of the castle the interior was almost completed. Placing his huge projectors around the castle's exterior he created a crisscross of colorful flowers and oriental patterns, turning trees, bushes, and brown walls into bubbles of light and color, glowing far into the night. The castle had become a piece of art in itself.

On the morning of the event we arranged sleeping quarters and buffets for the audience, with Gordon W., a Canadian chef, driving in from Prenzlauer Berg and setting up a large tandoori oven to make naan bread, peppery salmon dishes, chai, and Indian pizza. Small tents were distributed and laboriously set up in the park for bands in case of rain, the main hall became a stir of people running back and forth, carrying bags of food, instruments, the PA and umbrellas, carefully avoiding CU Huth who was still hanging his large paper drawings onto the high walls and technicians installing a video installation by Mediamorph in the foyer, our symbolic welcome for the guests entering the transformed castle. I had always envisioned working in an artists' community similar to the legendary communes of the 1920s, in which artists spent time together during summer residencies, creating celebrated objects of art, discussing form and space, sharing enthusiasm and ideals. The collaboration in Senzke came very close to realizing this dream and the curiosity raised by our efforts had spread to neighboring art farms, Berlin's underground, and the offices of well-meaning politicians, making it possible to imaging a successful opening that would intertwine East and West in a glow of unity amid art and music.

There is a law in life that wherever a strong light appears the shadows around it seem to grow darker, and as moths to light, great enthusiasm attracts great powers of destruction.

I suppose it is the yin and yang of positive and negative forces that keeps our world in motion.

On the last evening of preparation, while our group was touring the finished rooms, admiring each other's settings and constructions dealing with city and country atmospheres, we abruptly realized that guests had arrived. A group of young, muscular men with close-shaved hair, heavy boots, and black wind jackets had walked into the foyer carrying one of the event's advertisements. They stood there silently holding the poster up for all to see.

Carefully greeting them as the organizer of the event, using my position of being a woman to thwart macho power battling, I asked if we could be of any help and was told that they had noticed outlandish names on the poster and were wondering if there would be any foreigners attending the event. I replied saying that I myself was a foreigner and that yes, we had tried making the lineup as international as possible, inviting different artists who resided in Berlin, a group that included Italian, Venezuelan, American, Portuguese, and African DJs or musicians.

I was told that they could not tolerate this kind of racial "dirt" in their neighborhood and that they had driven in from different towns in the vicinity to let us know that in case we actually went through with the event they would visit us with friends and would "take care" of everything. Speaking evenly, I asked them to leave, telling them that we would not let ourselves be intimidated by racist threats and that we would call the police if any of them tried menacing any of our artists or guests. To be well-prepared we decided to call a couple of our experienced bouncer friends in Berlin, who were well accustomed to such threatening posturing, and asked them if they would be willing to protect us for a small fee. Fortunately they immediately agreed to come, happy to guard us from any possible assault, considering it a matter of pride.

After we had polished every nook and corner of the castle so it would shine in the sun, with flowers from the garden casting their perfume along the long hallways, placing toilet paper in all bathrooms, preparing soup and baking bread, the first guests arrived, parking in designated areas and shyly walking towards the colorfully arranged castle. The crowd grew quickly with neighboring families bashfully huddling together and drinking coffee, appreciatively tasting local apple pie and watching the colorful Berlin residents arrive with their patchwork families and dogs. People got to know each other while standing in line for Gordon's naan bread, and the elegantly dressed senate officials, disheveled musicians, and colorful artists, as well as curious visitors, relaxed and mingled. Guests inspected the catalogues and information sheets, slowly promenading through the diverse installations; our audience was obviously enjoying themselves. When the first DJs started spinning records and bands began performing in their tents, attracting the younger generation, Gordon W. announced his next dish, making a performance out of his admirable cooking skills, managing to enrapture and seduce the local housewives with hilarious inside information on Indian spices and garlic substitutes and the event was universally declared a success with the six hundred guests laughing, chatting and cheering, any animosity forgotten.

Jubilantly meeting in the hallway, Motte, Joseas, and I danced a little jig, hugging and congratulating each other on the effort we had gone through for months, relieved all had gone well and believing that the huge amount of work had been worth it, when one of the bouncers came up and quietly said that a problem had arisen. Looking out of the front entrance, a threatening line of about ninety silent men became apparent, wearing heavy boots and carrying sticks, slowly circling the castle. We immediately closed the front entrance and called the police, Joseas telling our audience that a performance was taking place on the second floor in the beautiful smaller ballroom, herding the innocent visitors away from the threatening wolves. Within fifteen minutes the police arrived and unlike their previous passive reactions to threatening situations, this time, when faced with the many cars parked in front of the castle, they immediately made it clear that if the gang didn't disperse at once arrests would be made.

Furious, the skinheads consented, roaring their engines loudly and forming a convoy, shouting distinct threats about what they would do next time while threading out of the village toward their various meeting places in Brandenburg.

The strength of denial has always fascinated me. By living in Senzke I experienced firsthand how forcefully trying to concentrate on the positive side of a situation and hoping for the best, combined with repetitive shocking occurrences that are not immediately solved, enables one to accept things that would have been unacceptable in the first instance. It is comparable to being in an abusive relationship, when beaten for the first time the victim is overcome by disbelief, telling themselves that it must have been a mistake, and when the second time occurs, which it always does, the acceptance has already set in. It is very difficult to reestablish one's original boundaries after they have been lowered, for the aggressor as well as the victim.

Because of being an artist and dealing with themes and philosophies that necessitate open-mindedness and tolerance without set rules, I was confronted with this dilemma repeatedly, enduring unfair studio situations, abusive relationships, overbearing assistants, and disastrous situations because of not having stated and defended my borders from the start.

For Antje living within her secluded walls, natural borders that were visible and respected by all, Senzke remained for the most part a peaceful village, everybody minding their own business with the usual neighborly quarrels about garbage, fences, and noise. For the other artists who had entered an area of unclear boundaries, outside of the wall, in the middle of the village, different problems became manifest. Envisioning an environment of interaction and renewal, interested in change and development, we were very naïve at the outset, expecting everybody to be as enthusiastic as we were, not realizing that our life and taste in comparison to that of the original inhabitants of East Germany was so different that it seemed threatening and incomprehensible, causing them to react as if menaced. Sadly nobody knew how to solve the "misunderstanding," hoping that by ignoring the conflict it would disappear. But instead, the situation became worse, as is always the case with denial, and rather than the castle being converted into an international artists' resort with cultural benefits for all, instead it turned into a cancerous focal point of turmoil and conflict.

Outwardly the first "Kunst oder König" (Art or King) event was a success, TV and newspaper reviews enthusiastically describing the new interaction between East and West, enabling confused adolescents on the outskirts of Berlin to obtain an impression of what could be done in their deserted industrial sites or rural buildings, hopefully inspiring them to initiate parties and raves as well. Creating events appeared to offer the possibility of earning money, and we were approached by numerous cultural centers in neighboring towns enthusiastically asking us to organize similar events in their districts. Officials realized that the playful approach of our artistic happening could inspire adolescents without being condescending, as was the case with many government-sponsored projects. The artists of "Kunst oder König" were invited to DJ, project videos, and perform in various clubs and small venues all over Brandenburg.

The techno-oriented events in general were the most successful, with Motte reigning as a smiling guru for peace and tolerance, encouraging countless other techno DJs to travel through the former GDR, helping to initiate a fresh way of interaction.

But the atmosphere around the castle stayed somber and aggressive, with every attempt to work on developing its activities thwarted by insults and attacks. The numerous invisible aggressors would watch us from the shadows of cars, attacking quickly and then disappearing immediately, turning radios on full blast at night, smearing the entrance with dog shit or throwing rocks through the windowpanes. Disillusioned by the constant barricades I began staying overnight in Berlin more frequently, reconnecting with the friends and acquaintances I had neglected during my discovery of nature, speaking to them about my experiences and trying to find a solution to our dilemma.

Giò di Sera, an Italian artist residing in Kreuzberg who had participated in "Kunst oder König," was dealing with similar issues among the Turkish youth in his vicinity. Unhappy and lost in the culturally and religious foreign community their parents had forced them into, they regularly resorted to aggression and violence as well, not knowing how to make themselves heard otherwise. After watching the rising crime on the streets Giò had become socially very active, generating a creative surrounding for gang kids in Berlin, teaching them to turn to graffiti instead of fist fights, actively working together with the Naunynritze cultural center in which break dance, rap, and flamenco workshops were offered. We met frequently, speaking about different methods on how to approach antagonism, appreciating each other's art and adventurousness until we had become good friends and decided to organize an event outside of Germany, curious to see how it would be to present our art in Naples, Giò's hometown. I was happy to deal with another culture for the time being, hoping that might shed light on our conflict in Senzke. I was curious to observe another way of life, in which differences were not as submerged as those of the East and West, but rather were out in the open.

We decided to bring twenty visual artists, musicians, DJs, and bands from Berlin to mount an installation on the beach, and ask twenty artists from Naples to participate. The Italian city was know for its explosive, aggressive nature, being as chaotic and creative as Berlin but with a higher level of crime, poverty, corruption, and good weather. I had never been there in spite of my Italian forefathers and looked forward to experiencing the volcanic landscape, and was assigned to organize an exhibition in the beautiful, elaborate showrooms of the Goethe Institute. Collecting and choosing the artworks by Betty Stürmer, Cornelius Perino, Gio, Saba Laudanna, and local Italian artists, I made lists of transportation costs, packing the art in bubble wrap, preparing press info, collecting photos from all, and keeping up a constant interaction with the Goethe Institute and Giò, who was in charge of the other venues, musicians, and DJs. We invited a Turkish rap band, Dr. Motte, a Jamaican DJ, and a couple of Berlin instrumentalists to participate in the venture, adding a musical component to the already existing art event, which illuminated how these two art forms intermingle within Berlin's cultural scene.

Driving down in endorsed VW buses, we excitedly watched landscapes turn from gray German cities to dangerously steep mountain gorges, quaint Renaissance villages, and luscious Italian landscapes speckled with cypress trees until we finally saw the infamous Mount Vesuvius appearing on the horizon, proudly heralding the approach of Naples.

After arriving and swarming into the white marble hotel that had been reserved by the local organizer, which was beautifully set on the edge of the white, warm beach, where one could watch gorgeous sunsets over the sea, we were invited to a luxurious dinner on the beach, with plates of pasta, vegetables, and "dolci," patiently served by friendly waiters, who merely smiled when the uncultured Germans ordered cappuccinos after the heavy meal, telling us much later that an Italian would never consider doing this, knowing that the milk would curdle in their stomach.

I set out to meet the Goethe director in the city's center, a tall, handsome, white-haired, gentle man, who received me with trembling hands and worried eyes, saying, "Naples is worse than Lebanon during the Civil War. To get stuck in a traffic jam as a pedestrian at 2 a.m. is nothing special, but if a bomb does not go off every other day it is."

I set about inspecting the exhibition space, unpacking art, hanging the work, and in spite of having many helpers and assistants I was soon to realize that the man had not exaggerated. The city was the most violent place I had ever been; in comparison New York was peaceful and quiet. Traffic was congested at all times of the day, with hundreds of cars stuck in the tunnels leading in and out of town and staying jammed within the tiny passageways, obstructing the narrow streets and pathways with honking motorcycles, bicycles, lumpy cars, and swaying buses, people singing, shouting, laughing, and fighting constantly, their intense, fiery eyes accentuated by heavy eyebrows distorted into expressive masks of emotion, with the smell of dust and heat permeating every thread of clothing. The omnipresent threat of being robbed, pushed, raped, or bombed was comparable to news reports of war and threw us into a state of heightened awareness. This was not the dreamy Hollywood version of Italy being sold in travel agencies. It was the unbarred reality spilling from the obvious Mafia, terrorism, mountains of garbage swallowing national monuments, greed, and crime. The country's wildest elements infiltrated the city's impressive beauty and everything was conspicuously out in the open.

I loved it.

Busy helping Giò organize the events on his tiny moped, the two of us raced through congested streets, taking sidewalks if necessary, doing interviews, picking up hammers and nails, reassuring crying artists, many not able to take the pressure, going to the police on a daily basis. Our buses were robbed one by one in the monitored garages of our hotel. We tried to placate the Turkish hip-hop band who, after their arrival, checked in only to find that their entire car had been stolen when they came back out to get their luggage. We tried to keep violent affairs at bay, and soothe people who complained about the reggae DJ's snoring. The city was alive in a way only a volcano can inspire and I immediately felt comfortable, realizing once again that I preferred being in an openly controversial, maybe even dangerous situation rather than one in which ambition, aggression, and grudges are hidden behind polite, civilized masks.

Living in Senzke had been beautiful because of the peace and loveliness of nature, but we had encountered such a high level of unexpressed resentment, stubborn resistance to interaction, and aggression towards development that it was proving to be almost insurmountable in spite of our continuous efforts, the conflict too hidden to solve without knowledgeable mediators, sadly making our venture seem impossible.

I realized, standing in the Italian market full of explosive emotions, that I was becoming tired of undercover attacks.

I do not like converting or persuading and have always had bad experiences in trying to convince people about the worthiness of projects for too long, believing that an instinctive, basic understanding needs to be present to be able to create magic, something impartial to social standing, cultural heritage, or language, and became conscious of the fact that I had stopped believing in a positive outcome.

After completing the exhibitions in Naples successfully, making friends, and driving back home, the situation greeting us confirmed my suspicions. The muttered threats had become louder. We decided to give it one more try and organized a small Christmas exhibition, sending out invitations for friends and neighbors to come and partake in a large meal in the basement kitchen. As we stood in the warm, foggy room with children playing, potatoes boiling, cookies and cake baking in the oven, Christmas tree lights on in all the hallways and staircases, enveloping the visitors in a warm, golden hue of festivity, the windows suddenly crashed apart and large cracks of fire bolts entered the kitchen. We were being attacked with firecrackers. The men in the room ran out to stop the attack but they were awaited by pickaxes, sticks, and stones, the provokers viciously catching them unawares as they ran out of the main door. I called the police, who came quickly but couldn't help, since the antagonists disappeared before they had arrived. Horrified we quickly took down the exhibition and drove back to Berlin in a convoy.

I had had enough of feeling alienated, and the continuous attacks directed toward us could no longer be ignored. After Joseas told us that he had actually been shot at from behind after picking up his young daughter in the local transitional kindergarten group, and was planning to move, I packed my belongings into boxes, stowing them into Antje's garage and returned to my studio in Berlin for good.

THE TRANSITION

Back in Berlin it was obvious that my studio quarters were too small to continue living in so I decided to rent an apartment, my first since the fire. Luckily, a cheap one around the corner was available, in Tieckstrasse, and with three spacious rooms, warm water, a bathtub, beautifully stuccoed ceilings, and wooden floors— it was the most luxurious I had ever lived in.

My landlord was the BEWOGE (Berliner Wohn- und Geschäftshaus GmbH), an institution instructed to sublet ownerless Berlin apartments for minimal prices until the real estate had been reorganized, and the large space only cost 350 Deutschmarks, equal to about a 150 dollars. I happily signed the lease and began renovating the space when we were told that our bureau building had been sold and we would have to vacate within three months. While I began packing boxes Johannes and Blixa set about finding new rooms. The building in Chausseestrasse had always been very low key, with computers crashing regularly thanks to streetcars passing and the electricity of the East still being somewhat shaky. They decided to look for something in former West Berlin. After inspecting a few uninspiring buildings, they found an amazingly lavish building on Potsdamer Strasse, the former red-light district of West Berlin, the development of which had been neglected up to then, enabling a building with marble stairs, red walls, and ceilings with intricate frescos depicting hunting scenes to be affordable. Blixa was enchanted by the spacious residence and convinced Johannes that it would be perfect for all of us. I had my doubts about what to do, because I mainly needed a studio, but both Johannes and Blixa pleaded for me to stay and keep up our small community, so I decided to take the smallest room and use it as an office space to work on organizing my larger events.

Buying a small black desk, hanging photos of my work on the walls, installing a printer and my computer next to a large phone, my first office quickly became a professional working space filling up with newspaper articles, catalogues, and fax messages.

As things go, Fiona Bennet suddenly called and asked if I would be interested in taking over her studio, a huge 300 square meter flat within an industrial site occupied by artists' studios, clubs, and offices and only costing an incredibly cheap rent of 300 Deutschmarks. She had decided to open a boutique and go more public with her designs. The atelier space had been my favorite place for a long time and I immediately accepted the offer.

Within a short span of time a new office, apartment, and studio had appeared in my life out of nowhere and although it took some time to get used to being in the city again, especially since the noise, traffic, competition, renovation, and rebuilding of the city had increased enormously, it was very comforting that everything had worked out so well. I bought a large, gold metal bed frame, new bookshelves, bathroom accessories and a baroque mirror for my apartment, creating a comfortable mix of red velvet curtains and rugs, antique wooden chairs and a snug kitchen to sit and have breakfast in the morning. In the studio, Fiona had left behind countless chairs, sofas, rugs, fabric, pots, and pans so the rooms were perfectly equipped and with two long units of vast, sunlit windows I could immediately set about stretching canvases, arranging my colors and paintbrushes to start working in large formats: ten by five meters, something I had only been able to do in Senzke's castle before.

Everything had fallen into place perfectly and I felt the gods approved my decision to leave Senzke. Maybe we had been too impatient, but by leaving a seemingly impossible situation and taking another direction everything suddenly made sense again. My days would now start with a short stop at the new French café across the street, buying a croissant, *croque monsieur,* or grilled toast sandwich, slowly ambling past the beige, sandy buildings of the yet undiscovered Torstrasse, one of Mitte's invisible boundaries between yuppie territory and the workers' area, checking the vegetables in the one small grocery store on Tucholskystrasse hidden among galleries and fashion designers, walk by the Beate Uhse on Rosenthaler Platz, the largest sex shop in the area, and then enter the rusty, squeaking gate of Brunnenstrasse 102.

The estate consisted of two large buildings built diametrically opposite each other, the front entrance lined with weeds, industrial garbage, and large pieces of wood for the carpenter's studio on the ground floor. The tarnished stairs led upward crookedly, the pathway to architectural, design, and furniture studios where the screech of metal drills, sawing wood, and hammering filled the hallways. To enter the second building one had to pass through the first via a small external hallway, walk along a small stretch of weeds, and then enter a larger, even darker portal to a sweep of broken stairs leading to the Boudoir, Lena Braun's lesbian underground club, and then onwards to my heavenly new studio. The hallway was always a mass of garbage, dirt, and leftover furniture, but the studio was sunlit even during the freezing winter months when I would cover the windows with sheets of plastic to keep the wind from blowing in through the rickety window frames. Standing next to the gas canister heating which Fiona had left behind as a welcome gift, inhaling the unhealthy fumes and painting with gloves during December, drawing in a bikini in the summer, the blasting sun heating the rug to a toasty temperature, the studio felt like a dream come true nonetheless, making long hours of concentrated creativity finally possible. My body of art grew noticeably fast, at last I was able to experiment with countless techniques, having space and peace, and I delved into graphic experimentation inspired by South Pacific cultures, tattoos, symbolism, and Zen literature. This was long before tattooing became a mainstream trend and it was still considered a proletarian stigma. My in-depth research in these cultures led me to a group of people who were master connoisseurs of "Tiki Art" and who quickly became our friends. Their space was formerly located in the front area of our driveway where they set up one of the most legendary installations during 1993 and 1995 in Berlin, entitled *The Glowing Pickle.*

LAURA KIKAUKA

Laura Kikauka was born in Hamilton, Canada, the daughter of Lithuanian immigrants. In 1981 after studying at the Ontario College of Art, she turned to new technology, electronics, and performances, becoming a pro at developing mechanical objects. Interested in collectibles she started accumulating cheap, unusual objects found in dollar stores or thrift shops at a very early stage in life, developing the first "Funny Farm" on her parents' homestead in Ontario. Filling each room with objects of varying colors, shapes, and texture, she was fascinated with the notion of system within chaos, rhythm among matter, and putting together unusual components to create innovative perception. Arranging the rooms in hues, she delved into color experimentation; beginning with beige, adding turquoise and then pink, discovering that when these ugly colors were put together in an appropriate form they became beautiful. Animating the forgotten objects electronically by adding motors and blinking lights to the castoffs, she created glowing objects of desire which curious visitors could bring to life by passing hidden sound or light triggers, resulting in an interaction between stuffed animals, kitsch paintings, plastic hula dancers, children's record players, and plastic bats arranged in the rooms and causing live performances and hilarious reactions.

In 1992 she came to Berlin, Germany, together with her boyfriend Gordon Monahan, invited by the DAAD (German Academic Exchange Service) and they became a conspicuous artist couple, quickly known for their madcap, fun-loving experiments in their self-declared universe of Irritainment. *The Glowing Pickle* (1992), their first installation in the Brunnenstrasse garage, became legendary, with Laura and Bastian Maaris, a pyromaniac artist, presenting electrical waste, serving green vodka, and outdoing each other with unusual presentations. The electric setting immediately attracted attention and the regular evenings were packed with fans, eager to participate in necktie shredding sessions with Laura's "necktie shredding machine," looking at hundreds of objects found and collected, some of them altered, many of them left in their original shape, many from the former GDR.

I remember my first visit clearly, submerged in the surreal atmosphere of narrow, flickering corridors of electronic gadgets, filled with crouching, standing, sitting, talking, and laughing visitors holding small, green, fluorescent drinks in the badly lit garage and wondering what they were drinking. Laura could be seen flitting back and forth, arranging a slipped contraption, electrocuting a pickle, giggling with a friend or speaking to a collector, a ray of smiling light dressed in outrageous costumes of sequined diver's suits with pink, fluffy house shoes or knitted flower miniskirts with furry painted boots and braids, visible from afar and surrounded by an admiring group of onlookers chuckling at her anecdotes and hilarious actions, gluing, painting, stapling knick-knacks or DJ-ing her favorite Heino records, a constant flow of interaction and creation.

In 1995 after her "electronic installation" had been a success, the Volksbühne, a renowned radical theater in Berlin, commissioned her to decorate their glass pavilion.

Cheerfully consenting she created the *Spätkauf* (Late Buy), selling nylon stockings, sausage lamps, DIY kits, macramé bags, and displaying hundreds of Heino record covers on the walls. A tiny stage in the miniscule pavilion was built on which bands could play late into the night with Alexander Hacke crooning country ballads, Tex Morton playing guitar solos, or Gordon Monahan swinging away on his Hammond organ. Once more this installation was such a success that the Volksbühne was summoned by the police, noise complaints rose with hundreds of people wanting to partake in the fun and stay late into the morning hours, laughing, cheering, and singing.

The Volksbühne had a couple of alternativ venues and Laura was offered a space at the Prater, the oldest and largest beer garden in Berlin, whose vicinity also held a club, a restaurant, a theater, and various bars. Here she created the *Schmalzwald*, an installation which was to become the icon of Berlin Tiki culture, easy-listening music, and avant-garde Dadaistic creation, attracting hundreds of fans and admirers over the years, the fascinated audience sitting on skirt-wearing stools, at tables with telephones bearing large plastic ears, listening to Gordon's new band Fuzzy Love, a performance that invited everybody to be a star for ten minutes by coming up to sing along, no matter how badly, similar to an underground version of karaoke with live musicians.

I went to the *Schmalzwald* regularly, enjoying the guaranteed, incomparable amusement and fun on offer, with lines of wannabe singers waiting to perform, sweating and singing badly on stage, giggling hysterically with embarrassed hip moves while being booed off or grandiosely ignoring Gordon's laughing critique and starting a new song immediately, hogging the stage in front of the raucous crowd of 1970s-influenced dressers, copying Laura's outrageous mix of accessories and admiring her every move behind the DJ pulpit where she would pull out amazing rarities from her enormous record collection during the band's intermission.

The favorite, recurring singers usually distinguished themselves by bad hairstyles, looking like Clark Kent and singing with thin, squeaky voices, creating crooked, unrecognizable harmonies, but they were always dressed in wonderfully flared belly pant suits, embroidered with gold thread, and accessorized with white gloves, elegant, shiny leather boots, flowery capes, and scapegoat hats. My favorite was the mermaid who wore a costume with a fish fin and had to be carried onto the stage and held upright. In comparison to most of the competitors she had an amazing voice, but could only sing while wearing the costume, being too shy to perform otherwise.

Laura would watch attentively, chatting with friends and swaying to the wrong tunes in a fireman's suit or bikini, smiling her bright smiles onto the audience, winking to Gordon on stage, and enjoying the amusement, a natural born entertainer and philanthropist.

Museums had started taking note of her installations, inviting her to mount well-deserved exhibitions in Europe and Canada, where she filled their halls with her intricate concepts and beautifully absurd combinations. Her "bastelings" and "Ersatzgesamtkunstwerke" were shown in the Haus der Kulturen der Welt in Berlin, the Power Plant in Toronto, the MAK in Vienna, The Lima Art Museum and the Contemporary Art Center Vilnius, catapulting her into the international art market. As the basics of her work consisted in continuously raiding cheap secondhand stores or markets and her sense of humor and cynicism kept her from becoming too enamored of success, she remained as friendly and fun-loving as before, sustaining the difficult stunt of creating artwork that was serious and outrageously funny at the same time and juggling the underground and the high-brow academic worlds within her life, both appreciating her deeply.

One of my favorite memories of that time was experiencing *The Exotic Trilogy*, by the KBZ 2000, an event inspired by Eric Satie's 1893 quote that he would "refuse to enter any room that does not offer music as furniture." Approximately fifty years after Satie's piece had been presented, the concept of "furniture music" had been co-opted by the Muzak Corporation and used as background shopping music in the USA, filling shopping malls with background or elevator music, a general term indicating music that was played in rooms where many people came together with no intention whatsoever to listen to music. The specific sound usually involved themes of "soft" popular music or "light" classical and were generally worked over by slow strings. This shopping music in turn was taken by Laura and Gordon in 1991 and put to use in a eighteen-hour performance of "ersatz exotica," "exotic vexations," and "Irritainment." Initially celebrated at the Funny Farm, this event was performed in New York in 1992. The local artists and musicians they met there were invited to merge and mingle with the musicians in Berlin in 1993, creating a tight-knit group of friends who continued staging international acts for years to come. Gordon W. Gordon Monahan, Laura Kikauka, Alexander Hacke, Roland Wolf, Michael Evens, Lary 7, Jen Ken, Maria Zastrow, Lars Rudolf, Bastiaan Maris, Sir Spinner, Stiletto, and Fabio Roberti were the core of the group. The theme of the show was to play three songs repetitively throughout the duration of the event: "Quiet Village," "Caravan," and "Taboo." They were played in different versions, with varying instrumentations and musicians creating a hypnotic endless loop of recurring melodies, catapulting the hypnotized audience into a slowly squirming earworm. The happening in Berlin, supported by "Freunde Guter Musik E.V.," an Institute that had featured innovative music since 1983, took place at the Eimer, a former squat in East Berlin founded by the bands Freygang and Die Firma, which had an interesting history of organizing avant-garde music parties during the GDR regime. After the Wall fell, Hemingway, an American expat, discovered the space and began organizing experimental electronic music concerts as well, attracting a new, intellectual lineup of good music. The building held three floors with a large hole in the middle, making the stage on the second floor visible from all levels and giving the audience the possibility of looking down or up at the stage.

The KBZ 2000 began on the afternoon of 12th of June with a slightly awry parade, representing the members' appreciation of failure and celebrating it as art. This stance had developed over the years, inspired by the generally growing pressure of commercial success preached by industries, making financial gain the only accepted validation of talent, and "talent agents" the supposedly justified officiators. Controversially undermining the philosophy of "the winner takes it all" this group celebrated failure with enthusiastic cheers, proudly telling each other stories of terrible mishaps they had experienced on stage and off.

Cheerfully chatting, the participants strolled from the Eimer to Rosenthaler Platz and back in about three minutes, carrying Tiki objects that had been meant to spew fire from their eyes but failed to do so, the sudden, heavy rain quenching everything except the participants' thirst for fun.

Back in the Eimer a huge volcano wok had been set up on the ground floor and looking like a surreal Venetian gondolier, Gordon W. stood stirring vegetables with a huge wooden oar, filling the venue with clouds of piquant Indian spices and onions throughout the night. A small collection of Super-8 projectors had been set up on the second floor with Lary 7 showing Hawaiian monster movies from the 1950s, accompanied by a DJ playing different versions of the three songs and a slide show depicting their record covers. I remember the evening as a blur of Tiki statues, candles, black-and-white monsters attacking papier-mâché buildings, musicians adorned with plastic flower wreaths smiling wildly, drinking exotic cocktails, girls in straw hula skirts swaying to the never-ending music, falling into a hypnotic trance, and Gordon W., endlessly stirring food in the wok, as a black silhouette shimmering within pink smoke.

Encouraged by their success, Laura and the Gordons organized another KBZ 2000 in Munich at the Marstall Theater, the riding school of the former royal family, now the official Bavarian State Theater, directed by Elisabeth Schwäger, know as the "general" because of being the "general manager." With their enthusiastic international friends trailing along to create havoc and chaos, they generated another exhilarating event in the small nouveau-riche capital, with the inhabitants telling each other stories for years about the inexhaustible party.

Due to their success they were then invited to bring their show to Brighton, England. This would finally produce a perfectly executed piece of "Failed Art" with only two guests appearing. They also fell asleep during the show. Undaunted and inspired, the artists erased a 0 from the title and KBZ 2000 disappeared into oblivion as a wonderful memory of indestructible creativity, with KBZ 200 re-emerging as the new name.

In 1999 Fuzzy Love was invited to perform in Hong Kong at the Festival of Vision with Laura creating an extraordinary fashion show of flashbulb dresses, fur wigs, lampshade hats, sequined toy handbags, and wispy glue gun sunglasses, mesmerizing an enthusiastic Chinese audience, the models happily moving to the music which now had an official singer, "JJ." This blond, longhaired, lean, and smiling man was the perfect personification of pop culture as art form, turning his shortcomings into charming habits and flirting with his enchanted spectators, the missing ingredient finally found that made the band perfect. This combination gave the band a huge input of energy and the group toured Europe effectively for a couple of years until JJ decided to try his luck in Nashville.

While Gordon continued working on his more serious, minimal music installations, Laura was called by Wally Potts, an American expat who had settled down to stay in Germany's trendy capital and had rented a tiny commercial space in the Haus Schwarzenberg Hinterhof, home of the Dead Chickens, an artist community. Wally had formerly studied painting but after arriving in Berlin had decided to open up a restaurant, turning a miniscule space into a mélange that included a kitchen, a couple of tables, and a huge drum set. His low-priced American menu, great sense of humor, and keen sense of controversy immediately attracted an artistic crowd, enabling him to move to a larger location around the corner to satisfy the hungry individuals standing in front of his door.

The new restaurant, a deserted GDR Chinese diner, situated on Torstrasse, down the street from my apartment, was a haven of red walls, mock Asian decoration, endless labyrinths, and countless rooms. Wally asked Laura to help with the decoration and with her hundreds of boxes stored in different basements all over the city, filled with "stuff" she had collected, she transformed the vicinity into a sideshow of sausage lamps, blinking lights, strange stuffed animal mutations, dolls arms, chicken feet chandeliers, LED kitsch paintings with glowing eyes and tattooed signs telling the guests where to go, what to drink, and what not to think.

The finished bar/restaurant was an Ali Baba's cave of treasures, a glowing Christmas tree of outrageousness, an instant icon attracting international celebrities such as Mick Jagger, Marilyn Manson, Slayer, or Lemmy from Motörhead who dropped by to enjoy the "Marquis de Fuck" burgers or "Fuck You Fries," listening to an eclectic mix of provocative music. I was asked to organize events and exhibitions in the many rooms, so together with Wally, Alexander Hacke, Wolfgang Sinhardt, Trinity Serrat, Luscious Lloyd, and countless assistants we initiated burlesque fashion shows, transsexual karaoke shows, lesbian stripper performances, experimental acoustic concerts, Mexican Day of the Dead installations, a small KBZ 200 Tiki celebration, record release parties with Peaches DJ-ing, Electrocute singing and Trinity from Sin City Circus Ladies serving drinks to the heavily tattooed, bewigged, and exquisitely dressed up crowd. With regular exhibitions showing work by local photographers, artists, and drag queens, the large space was so tightly packed on every day of the week that the bouncers acquired celebrity status with people trying to blackmail their way into its heavenly vicinity, offering sex, drugs, blow jobs, money, and other handy occupations, desperate to be part of the crowd.

Every so often a club, bar, or restaurant pops up at the right time and place to become a legendary inspiration for the arts: Studio 54 in NYC in the 1970s, La Rotonde in Montparnasse, Paris in the 1920s, and the Hacienda in Manchester are but a few that have inspired fashion, music, and design trends for years to come. The White Trash heralded the era of an electroclash, avant-garde, tattooed rockabilly, retro 1980s look, and Lowbrow art admiration that snatched the reins away from the 1990s techno crowd, creating new heroes, legends, scandals, and excitement. I had always wondered what new philosophies the generation of 2000 would bring after experiencing the beginning of punk/Geniale Diletantten and techno in the years before but by 2000 technology and media had become so fast, so varied, so multifaceted that it turned out to be impossible to create a new trend as all-encompassing as techno had been. The new generation was too busy watching TV, dreaming of stardom in reality shows, writing SMS messages, or admiring Hollywood celebrities. Founding an underground movement not based on money or fame seemed pointless to most so the electroclash scene stayed relatively small, only one of many different fashion trends, quickly marketed by rockabilly stores and tattoo parlors. I enjoyed the energy and exhilaration of the intense crowd while it lasted, glad to have an entertaining living room around the corner where I was always sure to find friends, fun, and food while taking a break from my studio but continued following my usual path of sticking to my art. Obviously Laura was not an interior designer for clubs, her incentive for installing spaces was the controversy expressed in turning a room into something unexpected, mocking standard criteria about what was cool or embarrassing, sentimental, or considered valuable, turning cartwheels with a tongue-in-cheek attitude and creating comfort within the blatant irony of her many objects.

In 2005 Haus Schwarzenberg, one of the most important cultural centers in Berlin, had won a real estate auction and become legal. Laura and Gordon, longtime residents of the artists' quarters, had been spreading out into the corridors over the years, with Laura's boxes turning into mountains of "stuff" until they were told that the floor would be divided into smaller rooms and they would have to clean up the space. Gordon, who had been restless to return back to Canada, took this as a chance to start thinking about going home.

While contemplating what to do with her boxes Laura was contacted by the owner of the Prater in which the *Schmalzwald* had formerly taken place, inviting her to install her work in the Hechtclub, a club in the back of his beer garden, which had never become popular in spite of its beautiful 1950s décor and odd architectural structure. Thomas invited Laura to turn the building into an art space and use it as a showroom for her work, asking only a minimal fee for rent. A dream come true.

Impressed by the mountain of belongings Laura would be transporting I followed her for weeks with my camera, filming Gordon and a group of happily chattering friends carrying out one carton after another and placing them into rented trucks to be unpacked in the Prater. It took about half a year to pack, transport and again unpack everything but the result was a Funny Farm East, a surreal space with hundreds of costumes, a 1970s leopard couch, countless Tiki objects mixed with kitsch wallpaper, sausage lamps and record covers, once more offering a wonderful space for imaginative fun.

Laura could now settle down to being in Berlin for spring and fall to do exhibitions in Europe, and in Canada for the summer and winter, working on her farm, spending time with her family.

The older an artist becomes, the more their future becomes insecure. Not having a stable income on top of not receiving a pension and, as is true for most, not having earned millions, makes it necessary at one point to start thinking about how to survive after sixty. Our society hypes young artists, advertising their work in magazines, organizing competitions, grants, or residencies, knowingly supporting an group of whom two-thirds will have given up art a couple of years later, usually choosing a reliable designer or internet communications job after starting a family. By concentrating on young artists the industry always has a new generation to sell and advertise, making a profit by the high fluctuation. Polls have certified that within Germany about one percent of all artists and musicians can easily live off of their art, five percent can survive by doing jobs on the side and barely scrape by, and all the rest have regular employment and do their art on the side.

Not only is it difficult to convince banks and insurance companies to give an elderly artist credit, many of the grants and subsidies have an age deadline, so after turning forty, a period by which one is expected to have achieved success and financial freedom, the artist is left completely to his or her own devices. The few that have received enough financial gain to rely on their bank accounts are lucky but most, even if they have become reasonably successful, cannot count on such an income.

Living on the "idealist's razors' edge," not compromising in spite of hardships, lacking recognition, and patiently persevering on work that may never be discovered—these are stories that make great bestseller biographies after one's death, but during life this situation forces one to find a solution as to how to survive.

In spite of their international success Laura and Gordon wisely considered these issues and decided to turn their farm in Canada into an artists' residency, with workshops and conferences to generate money, founding a music festival, "The Electric Eclectics Festival for Music and Irritainment," to support themselves and support other artists as well.

In 2006 the first festival took place, with many international artists participating, flying in from New York, Los Angeles, Japan, and Germany. I had been invited to perform with Alexander Hacke and excitedly booked my flight not knowing what to expect. After a long journey and subsequent car ride we arrived in an unparalleled, glorious fantasy universe far beyond my wildest dreams. The nearest village was Meaford, a small, picturesque, Canadian habitat, hovering on the edge of the Georgian Bay with friendly inhabitants mowing their lawns or fishing. The Funny Farm was a fifteen-minute drive by car, situated on a small hill overlooking the neighboring fields and farms, with a slanted view of the lake. Watching Laura cast a line, swim, run with the dogs, light fires with leftover boxes, drive a trailer onto its designated position on the farm, blow up the large swimming pool, chase away raccoons, mow the lawn, and feed the cats suddenly made apparent what a nature girl she actually was. Something not necessarily apparent in the plastic *Ville* of her kitsch installations.

I spent the days helping to prepare the festival and watching her relaxed indifference towards the hounds of greed and achievement, ignoring emails or phone calls about jobs, preferring to relax and work in peace, reminding me of Beth Love, another nature girl/talented artist who's strength lay in drawing "ersatz" realties. I remembered my stay in Senzke and how city life became more mannerist when viewed from a distance, comparable to a gaudy tinsel rolling forward and backward, ceaselessly in motion, hypnotizing the onlooker with its sparkling artificiality.

I became reminiscent of my youth in Washington DC when I was twelve years old, a short year of being surrounded by quiet fields, beautiful forests with birds singing and leaves rustling, myself sitting on the grass for hours looking at a tree or a blade of grass with my red retriever sitting next to me watching my fingers move lazily. Kneeling on the Canadian festival stage, whitewashing the rough boards and watching the memorable sunsets, I remembered my favorite poem as a child, "Leisure," by William Henry Davies: "What is this life, if full of care. We have no time to stand and stare?" I had forgotten the close proximity of nature and wild animals in North America, Berlin being a metropolis with very little wildlife to speak of, and enjoyed watching the many wild animals flashing by or eating calmly in the distance. Deer, wild turkey, rabbits, fox, the phoebe, even a stray coyote could be heard at night, crying and giggling insanely. Watching a wild animal is very different from going to a zoo and I contemplated the concept of freedom and constraint, a theme often questioned by art.

Most of the artists performing in the festival were in their mid-thirties and forties, all of them icons of the international underground, seriously concentrating and cheerfully preparing their outsider art, a stubborn group of untamed, independent characters dedicated to content, provocation, and depth, and during the festival's progress I wandered through the fluorescent petals of the huge flower and herb garden in the evenings, smelling the light breath of their perfume, and contemplated how my life had developed during the years in Berlin, with further memories of my youth emerging. I was surprised by this nostalgia, especially as I had never had a specific hometown, traveling from one army base to the next, remembering the unhappiness of being a weird, teenage alien in Midwestern schools, but the feeling persisted, with a small voice saying, "I want to go home," ignoring that I had been gone for a long time, had lost my roots, my father was dead, his house gone, my friends flown off.

Unexpectedly, I had entered what was probably the most difficult phase an expat can enter, of being torn between the new and old, but in comparison to most who had homes, parents, apartments, friends, or even jobs they could visit or return to, I had nothing left except memories. Berlin was the only home I had.

THE GOETHE INSTITUTE

After leaving Senzke and moving back to Berlin fulltime in 1998, I set about showing my work as much as possible in order to attract collectors, mainly using my studio as an exhibition space. Although I had decided to stop working as a curator I continued believing in artists supporting each other, as good art managers or galleries were still rare, especially for non-academics, and due to my curatorial experience, artists and musicians frequently asked me to include them in my projects. So I decided to create hype for us all and once more initiated Christmas art fairs, sales parties, group exhibitions, and club installations. The combination of my large studio and the publicity resulted in my art becoming better known, our artists group becoming popular, and appreciative collectors crowded my studio. Then one day, one of the major cultural foundations of Germany came knocking at my door. The Goethe Institute was organizing a colossal event, the "Festival of Vision" in Hong Kong, and asked me to curate a weekend of young art in the large pavilion. After meeting with representatives and speaking about the lineup we reached an agreement and I was booked a flight to Asia.

With this invitation to a foreign country, the stationary phase of my life, which had lasted over a decade and immersed me in local events, now come to an end. The capital was no longer an enclosed island, cut off from the rest of the world, secretly living a secluded life. The doors had been opened, the curtain lowered, and the world was curious to experience Berlin's underground firsthand. Thus the Goethe Institute was asking me, to my great surprise, to represent Berlin.

Together with Goethe Institute employees I was flown over twice to help organize the event with Chinese curators.

My first impression of the metropolis was a huge harbor of metal storage crates standing next to the airport, with transportation vehicles moving busily back and forth. Sitting in the train riding into Hong Kong I felt a rush of excitement, watching the faraway skyline of skyscrapers coming closer and realizing how different the architecture, language, food, smell, size, and noise of the city were from Berlin. After checking into my hotel room on the twenty-third floor and taking a walk through the pungent market around the corner where booths sold odd-looking fish, unfamiliar vegetables, and beautiful fabrics, I was ecstatic, happy to be experiencing something completely new once again. After meeting the director and his assistants and realizing that organizing has the same structure everywhere, no matter if one is planning a concert for five hundred people or twenty, I comfortably dealt with the preparations, taking time to wander out into the old city quarters to visit fascinating night markets or have foot massages. The second time I returned, the artists I had chosen came along and I wandered through Hong Kong's exotic maze of small streets with Fetish, Chaos, Jim Avignon, Tulip Enterprise, and Skudi Optics. Hanging our artwork in the large bamboo pavilion and speaking to countless visitors was perfect. In this way I was surrounded by my beloved Berlin, traveling the world, showing my art, and earning money simultaneously.

One of the issues I was spoken to about frequently during the preparation for our event was the fact that the Hong Kong committee was especially interested in the artists I was representing because of their "Do it Yourself Attitude," hoping to inspire their placid youth. Due to the tough pressure of the economic world Hong Kong was said to have an alarmingly high rate of depressed, overwhelmed youth who felt helpless and insignificant in face of the competition. The Berlin way of creating our own universes creatively was viewed with high interest, hoping it could offer a playful way of confronting obstacles. This would become a theme of my future international collaborations. In general, whether in an economically strong or weak country, the cultural institutions were always looking for examples of how to motivate and enthuse a youth that was depressed by the continuous pressure of surviving in our world of commerce; their lives reduced to purely achieving this one goal.

Rome and Milan were next. How difficult it was, officials said, to carry the burden of an incredibly impressive history of culture and design, and told stories of youth being overpowered by the beauty surrounding them, feeling helpless and intimidated by the dominant world of wealth and corruption. Obviously I often felt intimidated by the assignment, and spoke about how the Love Parade had started, explaining the way we organized underground exhibitions or concerts in unusual spots, presenting TV interviews and hundreds of flyers, invitations, and newspaper reviews I had collected over the years. This was a seemingly successful way of demonstrating how initiative is as important as money, creativity more fulfilling than passive consumption, and that there are always tools to insure an inventive solution. In all the cities where we appeared, our parties, workshops, and lectures initiated lively discussions, valuable interaction, and lasting collaborations. I realized that with my miscellaneous artists, coming from different scenes and styles of music, representing techno, hip-hop, and easy listening, with clashing tastes in art and media, we attracted a large number of diverse guests, everybody finding something to identify with, on top of experiencing new and inspiring forms of art. The fact that none of us were trying to convert or pressure anybody, merely demonstrating how we had survived similar problems, created an atmosphere of being together in the same boat. I was surprised how interconnected I felt so far away from home.

After touring Italy I was contacted by a cultural center in Brandenburg, a city situated within former East Germany. The social workers there had been in a constant battle with local right-wing youth organizations and succeeded in clearing them out of the city. After experiencing my "Kunst oder König" event in Senzke they asked me to organize a similar event in Brandenburg, proposing to do an exhibition that would encompass the whole city, projecting colorful slides onto the ancient monastery, performing a concert in the church, mounting an installation in the wooden interior of the town hall, a sound installation in the Bauhaus swimming pool, creating a historic promenade to experience Brandenburg from a different angle, introducing the city and its inhabitants in a colorful and artistic fashion by mingling local and Berlin art. I was intrigued by the proposition and, hoping to establish a more positive interaction there than I had achieved in Senzke, consented to curate the event.

The "Jugend Kultur Fabrik Brandenburg" began applying for financial support and thanks to their excellent work managed to receive enough money to finance the ambitious event.

Thrilled by the large-scale endeavor, I invited Alexander Hacke and Andrew Unruh from Einstürzende Neubauten, Dr. Motte, Jim Avignon, DAG, Tulip Enterprise, Moritz Wolpert, Daniel Ginelli, and Radio Berlin to participate. Joseas, who had moved to Brandenburg after leaving Senzke, invited local artists such as Nora Schlecht, Peter Blau, Gabriel Kaluza, and Thomas Bartel. After we had all met in Thomas Bartel's studio in Brandenburg we went on a tour, inspecting the city and assigning the different locations to the most enthusiastic artists. Motte decided to do a sound and color installation in the lookout tower of the city, arranging light and tonality to the rhythm of a human spinal cord, to create a luminous lighthouse that would glow over the sleeping town at night.

Andrew Unruh set up a sound installation of door and bicycle bells and car horns in the ancient, geometrical Bauhaus swimming pool inside of which DAG painted a ten-meter-long paper strip within the basin on the weekend of the event, in front of a fascinated audience of children, teenagers, and parents, the abstract forms precisely placed to the rhythmical patterns of Andrew's sound.

A few streets further down, after crossing a bridge and heading toward the main square, Moritz Wolpert, the former drummer of Jever Mountain Boys, had set up his studio in the town hall, decorating the rooms with intricate, large woodprints, creating a cozy performance living room in which small, jazz-like, impromptu live performances were initiated by friends and visitors. The setting was reminiscent of the 1920s with dark-suited, cigar-smoking musicians quietly drinking beer, speaking about Dada art and music, comfortably inviting the passersby to sit down and participate in the anarchic gathering.

A similar live interaction was presented by Jim Avignon and his cheap art following, in the workshops of one of the oldest cottages in town, decorating the ancient wooden beams with colorful drawings hung onto clotheslines, creating a web of art within the rooms, and forcing the visitor to bow down low or step up in order to avoid tearing the paper. A large amount of coloring pencils were distributed, inviting not only children but also adults to sit down and participate in the fun, selling fruit juice and homemade cookies on the side.

In the evening Jim Avignon unpacked a keyboard and performed his live show, accompanying himself with masks he had designed and "cardboard stage sets" especially made for the different songs, and the crowd danced for hours, enthusiastically buying cheap art and mingling within the humid air, creating drops of residue on the gilded windowpanes, stripes of fun coursing down through the dust of neglect. The Dutch duo Tulip Enterprise had decided to install their work in the small Gothic chapel on the town's edge, with flowery techno projections transforming the walls into surreal patterns, moving to the DJ's electronic mix and making it the most popular hangout for the club-oriented youth in Brandenburg.

In the small river club where I had installed my paintings and projections, with Alexander Hacke and Jochen Arbeit composing live soundscapes to the pictures, we attracted an older audience who was interested in experimental electronic music with the buzz of interaction spilling throughout the night, beautifully complementing the sparkling, moonlit Havel river flowing past and giving the former East German countryside a peaceful, Mediterranean atmosphere.

Our goal of creating something that attracted all ages and tastes had been achieved and walking down the streets to the different venues one could meet groups of visitors excitedly chattering about what they had just seen, describing the glowing monastery where Thomas Bartel had projected his work and whispering in awe at the impressive video installation within.

The collaboration was inspiring, with friendships formed among former West and East German inhabitants, hotel rooms booked out, and plenty of positive feedback, so we decided to plan a similar event for the next year, hoping consistency would break down the last barriers and encourage more residents to participate in the future.

Organizing an event of this scale usually takes about a year of preparation, the "Haus der Offiziere" youth center contacts different cultural institutions like the Brandenburg Theater, the Senate, and a couple of commercial companies to apply for money, convincing investors that the proposition would add cultural value and commercial interest to their town. After receiving commitments of financial support the economic aspect was secured and it was my turn to start, writing a concept, thinking up collaborations that would be artistically interesting, contacting artists, musicians, and DJs in Brandenburg and convincing those in Berlin to make the effort of coming to the nearby city a couple of days ahead of time to prepare their installations for very little pay.

Thankfully many of the artists were interested in engendering communication through art and usually quickly confirmed their participation. I had started concentrating on this type of character back at the Institut gallery, realizing quickly that by being an artist myself, working on doing more than merely exhibiting my own art, I could only stay happy by representing those with similar views, not having the time or strength to carry around passive individuals.

We decided to initiate the event in the Offiziers Club, a large old villa with many rooms and corridors, perfect for presenting artists in different rooms with a large basement for live music. To interweave the event with the rest of the town we included the former toy factory around the corner, a huge industrial space, deserted and dusty, perfect for techno raves and large, projected room installations. After working for months, the preparation was done and the event was emminent. On Friday afternoon everything had been set up and when the official opening time came, the buildings gleamed like jewels in twilight, with sparkling colors pouring out of the windows and mingling with Scoody projections, turning the street into a nirvana of warmth and movement. The lineup of concerts and performances started with Jim Avignon and Fuzzy Love doing small concerts every twenty minutes and Alexander Hacke performing at 10 p.m., Jochen Arbeit accompanying him on the guitar, the heavy industrial sounds mixing effortlessly with the neighboring melodies and singing. Video installations by Peter Blau and Thomas Bartel could be visited in small groups, shining beautifully in the high attic of the factory and after Gordon W. had erected his huge tandoori oven on the terrace of the Offiziers building, the entire district was enveloped in a delicious smell of fish and spices, attracting a growing line of hungry artists. The atmosphere among them was friendly and good-natured, welcoming the families curiously inspecting the transformed building and although antagonism could still be felt, with local newspaper clippings maliciously claiming that the local artists had outshone the Berlin ones, and that the event attracted less spectators than the rock concert around the corner, everything had gone as planned and no troubling occurrences had happened, so we were satisfied.

Back in my studio, unpacking the pictures I had exhibited, I was suddenly hit by the realization that during the year's extensive preparation I had once more neglected my own work. In spite of my endeavor to balance my practice with the extensive work needed to represent artists professionally, I was still spending more time curating than working in my studio and the urge to express myself had become a silent, red light in my head, blinking STOP continuously. I tried to understand how I could have fooled myself into ignoring what I had decided to pursue after coming back from Senzke, not understanding if it was the true necessity of earning money or a running away from the scary situation of relying solely on my art work that consistently brought me back to putting more effort into promoting other people's development rather than my own, and decided to ruthlessly stop making excuses and either get down to working in my studio or stop complaining and give up on the idea altogether.

2000–2010

The long-distance connection made the voice sound tiny and lost.
"I can't go on, I'm going to kill myself."
Her heart fell, panic gripping her throat in a wave of pure, black fear.
"Don't ever think that."
"I've lost everything, my profession, my family, my health, my faith, there is nothing for me to live for, I don't have the strength, all I want to do is die."
Standing in the dark hallway, listening to the ghostly voice, she realized that if A. were to give up, everything she had believed in would be gone with one blow. With a blinding flash of clarity she realized that this long-time friend was the manifestation of everything she had ever loved and believed in and with him as a fallen victim it would be impossible and senseless to go on.
"Listen to me, don't hang up, listen, please."
"I can't, I think I'm going mad, nothing makes sense anymore, my brain won't stop working."
"Listen to me, I will do anything it takes, just give me the time to get back, I'll be back in two days, give L. a call in the meantime, she can help you and then when I'm back I promise things will get better, please, please promise you will wait."
The silence seemed endless, with hell's black, cold abyss opening slowly beneath her feet, disclosing a black pit of endless despair and misery. Finally the sad voice said quietly, "Ok, I'll wait for you to return."
And the phone went dead.

THE LIFE OF AN ARTIST

One of the main distinguishing features of working as a musician or a painter is the level of interaction with others. I am not one who can easily paint or draw in a crowded room and to have somebody look at an unfinished picture is painful, so I usually hide everything I am working on when I have guests.

I seldom listen to music, loud background noise disturbs me due to a sensitivity to sound acquired after Roland's death, so I usually work silently, whistling occasionally when preparing an exhibition. This can go on for weeks, even months, and usually means being alone, not seeing a soul for days, working in total concentration until the smell of turpentine makes me so dizzy it forces me out the door and into fresh air. The technical aspect of what I work on usually has the same archetype and consists in having an idea, putting it on paper carefully, sketching and erasing it countless times, attaining moments of deep satisfaction or terrifying unhappiness with nothing but a vision to follow. If it is meant to be an oil painting, the work continues after the drawing is done and I have decided on size, colors, and style, transferring the work onto freshly stretched canvas, adapting to the different technique, despairing, correcting, recorrecting, despairing again and so on until it is finally done. This can go very quickly or painfully slowly and it is always good to take a short break when desperation takes over, otherwise the temptation to destroy the canvas becomes dangerously close.

The front of my new studio on Brunnenstrasse was a commercial street, so usually after working for hours I would reach a point where I would either throw everything out of the window into the ravaged birch trees, forgotten garbage, and backyards of Ackerstrasse, or wander out into the bustling world of "Mitte," the Mecca of tourist entertainment and sunglass vendors, distracting myself from my despair by the new cafés lining the street, offering previously unobtainable luxuries of bagels, donuts, lattes, smoothies, and sushi to go. It was an odd experience to be sitting in small, stylish eateries, the waiters wearing "Ben and Jerry" T-shirts or serving lox with cream cheese. I would sit sipping a vanilla soy chai while looking through the windows into the squats across the street, dressed in paint-splattered overalls and feeling like a silly cliché with tourists looking at me and whispering to each other. "Look, that must be a real Berlin artist." For dinner I would usually go to the small, greasy Thai diner across the street, the side that had not been renovated, preferring the down-to-earth bustle of pots and pans clinking and clanking and watching the multiple family members taking orders quickly, enveloped in a buzz of noise unbroken by stylish tunes. I would eat their chop suey slowly, enjoying the spicy sauces, and sweet and sour combinations while thinking about how the city had changed since I saw the film *Wings of Desire* in

Cologne. It wasn't the fact of change that disturbed me, it was the urge to make my beloved city "fit in" with prefabricated mass production, considered more precious than handmade objects or self-realized ideas.

Because Berlin was bankrupt and could not afford the extensive overhaul it was going through, financiers coming in from the outside had decided what the capital should look like, and, using its artistic reputation, created by countless unsubsidized, non-academic artists, they decided it could be turned into a reputable moneymaker, offering sightseers a decent level of comfort combined with the possibility of seeing "wild" artists, historic sites, or experiencing adventure in underground clubs. I felt we had become an urban safari tour advertised by travel agencies, exploited by restaurant chains, real estate, beer labels, cigarette brands, or advertising companies.

Before 1999, art had mainly been supported by the Cultural Senate in Berlin. Germany did not want to place the responsibility of giving money into the hands of people who were merely rich and so, during the Cold War, extensive grants had been given out, fertilizing the city's creative soil continuously. But these grants had become rare in the face of the new political situation and for artists this meant higher living costs, less income, and no support. Although the city was being glorified as the most creative in Europe, photographed for magazines, art books, and schools, survival became increasingly difficult with everybody scrambling to maintain their former standard of living.

After working in the Brunnenstrasse for about a year I was informed that the building had been sold and the ateliers would need to be vacated within a couple of months. Most of the empty buildings in central Berlin had been renovated, making it difficult to find an affordable to space to work in, so I convinced a couple of my creative associates to join forces with me to try and find a solution.

During our appointment with the Kultur Amt Mitte (Cultural Bureau for Central Berlin), we asked them to find a new building for our studios, bearing in mind that we had been working in the city since the early 1980s, building its reputation, had been sent out as its "ambassadors" and represented a cultural aspect that was now generating a lot of money for everyone except us.

We were told point blank that of course they knew all of us very well, and yes, Berlin's reputation was in part due to our uninterrupted dedication, but that if every single artist and musician in Berlin would stop working immediately, the city could still continue making money off of their work for at least ten years, and as they were not dependent on our input they felt no need to invest money or time into helping us out of our difficult circumstances. After one of the artists threw a chair through the room we were politely led out.

Ironically, a film company asked me if my studio could be filmed for a movie about the Love Parade shortly before we had to move, and I received an unexpected, satisfying sum of money, making the move to a new studio possible and presenting me with support from a new area. Instead of confronting the bankrupt cultural institutions, we now accosted the new rulers, the industry, for backing. The only hurdle was how to keep an artistic project from turning into a McDonalds, Philip Morris, or Levi's commercial in the process. This was difficult. Looking around to see how other artists were managing I perceived that "product placement" had become popular since 1995, with a wave of commercially financed events or projects sweeping through the city. Artists had been appointed "Ministers" of Marlboro or Philip Morris and soon I was also being asked to act as a "trend scout," to voice my opinion on the latest developments in underground fashion, art and music at conferences, internet portals, or fairs. Hesitantly I observed a large group of hungry artists paint cars, airplanes, coffee mugs, or walls, design shoes, bags, TV ads or T-shirts in our "typical" anarchic Berlin style, trying to use the new capitalism to finance their art instead of letting it be taken for free. But this experiment only lasted for a short time, and by 2000 most of the sponsors had discovered that the Berliner taste was too individual to be hyped to the masses and lost interest, turning to professional graphic designers with a clean-cut, illustrative look. After barely surviving for a couple of months, worriedly scanning my surroundings for ideas I began investigating the conventional art market, something I had never thought of doing in my pursuit of independence.

I had not studied at a German art university, so many of the unspoken rules were unknown to me and it took some time and questioning until I realized that although I had been painting successfully for years, with a growing group of private buyers and admirers, a professional collector would not purchase my work unless I was represented by an acknowledged agent or gallery. These in turn would mainly be interested in artists who had studied with a known professor. Aside from the fact that I had not gone through this initiation, I was a female interdisciplinary artist, not only painting but also making music and films, who had been working independently for many years, with my art work influenced by pop culture, surrealism, and old-fashioned illustration, which was still considered decorative and commercial in Germany. My situation was not easy.

After saying goodbye to my studio at Brunnenstrasse, I moved my working materials into a large industrial loft around the corner of Friedrichstrasse, situated over a car-repair garage. To be able to enter the abode I had to walk through tightly parked, broken-down cars, be whistled at by repair men dressed in spotty overalls, walk up two flights of greasy, dusty stairs, past the garage's small, stinking toilet and unlock a heavy metal door securely protected by three metal bars. The space itself was large with no windows or heating, the icy cement walls resisted nails and screws, making it difficult to hang canvases high enough to work on, but with enough space to store my many canvases and oil paintings easily.

It was October of the year 2000 and Berlin had entered its period of gray, depressing skies. To be able to see colors in their natural hue I painted in the hallway, in front of the only window, trying to catch dim rays of sunlight so I could see my drawings and keep warm. Soon it turned cold and winter set in with sludgy snow and icicles. After trying to work in mittens, covering myself with fur coats, wool shawls, and mountains of blankets I gave up, buying a small wood stove to warm up the hundred-square-foot tomb. Chopping the wood into small pieces turned out to be hard work and quite superfluous, since the small, glowing, virtually exploding cube emitted warmth for about two feet, beyond that, at its invisible border, the cold set in at once, with me either burning or freezing in an effort to work. To keep from catching endless colds I took frequent breaks, jumping, skipping, or running down to the new Canadian deli, warming up for as long as possible, munching on a goat cheese baguette and working on small sketches. After my blood had recommenced flowing I would then usually stroll down to the waterside and fret about my future. Renovation had arrived hesitantly in this area and the street was still quiet, with deserted window fronts and torn sidewalks decorating the view. Strolling down Schiffbauerdamm, across the bridge, over the Spree, towards the large train station Friedrichstrasse, I could see countless distinctive chimneys puffing away, the familiar coal fumes tickling my nostrils and I stood, dreamily watching boats float by, sounding their horns, arranging pictures, melodies, and lyrics in my head before going back.

In spite of my many exhibitions, finances had come to an end quickly after I had stopped curating, and for the first time the rent was not paid. I had always considered myself lucky and safe, due to the fact that many of my friends were wealthy, repeatedly telling me that someday they would buy one of my paintings. The long-standing ritual of artists supporting artists, one on which we had all relied on over the years, had simulated a slight feeling of security, on which I had relied blindly. But Germany now entered such a financial depression that by the time I was broke everybody was worried about their own survival, and after overcoming my initial shyness, and calling people and asking them if they were now interested in some art, I was deeply shocked when all of them said yes but that they just couldn't afford it right now.

1999 was the year in which the German government had finally finished moving from Bonn to Berlin, inhabiting the renovated Reichstag. After the English architect Norman Foster had beautified the history-laden building, adding a glass dome, tourists came to climb up the spiraling stairs with a good view of the modernized horizon, walking about over the heads of the city's secretaries preparing new offices and conference rooms. In 2000 the Federal Chancellor moved into his only recently finished representative edifice built by Axel Schultes and in 2001 Berlin was upset by a severe bank scandal, resulting in Eberhard Diepgen, the city's mayor, resigning and Klaus Wowereit enthusiastically being elected new major of Berlin in spite of his admission to being gay. The economy in Germany had been heavily taxed after reunification and Berlin was beset by turmoil, change, and debt. Having been in financial mayhem for almost ten years, after being torn up, renovated, and rerouted, the city was left reeling in 2001 with a high number of unemployed inhabitants, many not sure that the change had been to their advantage. Although numerous companies and industries had moved to Berlin, many moved away again quickly, not finding the success they had expected, and countless newly erected architectural sites were left empty.

The launching of the euro in 2002 was one of the worst things that could have happened for many small companies and freelancers, the industry quickly raising prices by a hundred percent, without adapting salaries, resulting in the frightening situation of citizens having to pay twice as much for goods as they used to pay, but earning as little as before.

Artists never really have enough money, and are used to barely getting by and relying on small commissions and sales, but the fact that now seemingly nobody could afford to buy art suddenly hit all of us. After not having a single sale for months I became frantic, trying to think up workshops, portrait sessions, tourist guides, or pottery commissions, meeting with friends to share dinner, only going out to bars where acquaintances served free drinks, and walking instead of paying subway tickets.

But my situation became even worse and finally I just stayed at home, eating as little as possible, praying the phone would ring until one day it did.

A businesswoman from Hamburg who was putting together a commercial villa for economic conferences needed art to decorate the luxurious rooms and a friend had recommended that she look at my portfolio. Borrowing the money for a ticket I took a train to Hamburg and met the elegant, blond woman in her impressive mansion. After showing her my carefully packaged representation of work, we came to an agreement that I would create forty-five small paintings and drawings to be installed in three of the rooms and would sculpt six bronze statues for the second floor. Dumbfounded by the speed at which we reached an agreement, I sat in the train a couple of hours later, staring out blankly at the landscape, empty with relief, thinking of all the bills I could pay, hilariously happy to have such a large commission and thanking my guardian angel for the sudden change of fortune.

Back home I set about stretching canvases, building metal forms, buying new colors and paintbrushes, making sketches on rough paper, working on typography, rehearsing geometric patterns, and cleaning up my studio. I was incredibly proud of the trust in my abilities and felt that because of this commission I had finally been elevated to the realm of a serious artist. During the next few months

I finished pictures, met with foundry men, discussed themes and colors, worked on plaster models, read literature on architecture and poetry to inspire word compositions, and my employer became a friend, appreciating the resulting art works and asking me to paint three portraits of herself to display in her other home in Switzerland. Driving back and forth from Berlin to Hamburg, I met her employees and co-workers, all very supportive of my art, inviting me to exhibit in their large office space and helping me to make further sales.

The joy of being appreciated because of my creativity was indescribable, unlike any other success. Working on the different objects felt fulfilling in a way that not even the money I received could compete with, the payments functioning solely as a way to repay my debts and buy the materials I needed. I had never been very interested in buying luxury items, always confronted by the feeling that I should be making my own. After Dimitri's support I had now found a second important patron who considered my work important enough to be financed over the years and with my self-confidence strengthened and glowing, I now felt invincible.

I decided to start looking for an appropriate gallery, having accepted that I needed a representative. Looking around I found myself in the odd situation of not knowing where to look or whom to go to. In all my other areas of work I had a pretty good network of musicians, record labels, distribution labels, film companies, and managers. In the field of art I only knew artists and the Haus am Lützowplatz, the nonprofit gallery that had supported my Love Parade charity event years ago. So I decided to ask Karin Pott, the curator, for advice.

She said the best way would be to meet the art world personally, and invited me to present my work to her regular round table. She also introduced me to collectors and curators and exhibited my work in her small studio gallery. Through our combined efforts I was consequently noticed by an increasing number of people and participated in a growing number of international group shows over the next few years, experiencing their different methods of selling art with great interest, until I was contacted by an American gallery in 2006, the first to represent lowbrow and pop surrealist art in Berlin. I had been watching this art movement emerge in the United States for some time, even considering a move to Los Angeles because of its strong impact, and was delighted to discover that it had finally arrived in Europe. Although I was surprised at the large amount of artists the gallery was representing, I eventually realized that this was common in the States. In contrast to Germany, where most professional galleries focus on a small number of participants, standing by them for years and taking as much of a risk as the artists, many American galleries feature large group shows to see which artist will sell the most work. These monetarily driven results determine who will receive exclusive deals, be shown at fairs, and represented internationally. I was intrigued by this competitive stance and decided to try it out, wondering if it would accelerate my creativity. After a year of throwing out small, single pieces that were shown among forty to fifty other artists, based on the topics the gallery had proposed, I felt burned out and depressed, feeling like a commissioned illustrator who merely finished jobs instead of expressing feelings. After signing on with an illustration agent as well and experiencing similar unhappiness, illustrating mouse pads and T-shirts, I decided sadly that this approach was not for me and said goodbye to both. Looking around for a better fit I was approached by a small, up-and-coming gallery, Janine Bean, whose curator had been a fan of my work for some time and after seeing that she kept her group of artists small, decided to try this variation but quickly realized that she was the exact opposite of the previous gallery, putting her emphasis on her ideals and not necessarily selling work. I needed somebody older and more experienced. Bidding her farewell too, I decided to step back and let destiny have a go, tired of the effort I was making and the disappointing results. I had now been working solely as an artist for almost nine years, had proven to myself that I could survive, and was accumulating an ever-growing group of collectors. After giving up my curatorial work years before, I had also began working on film and music again, the additional amount of time allowing me to go into depth and develop these areas I had neglected. Being an interdisciplinary artist made survival a lot easier, and after more and more film work was commissioned, I was capable of switching back and forth, creating my own, specific way of presenting art, and decided to focus on this more and try to find new ways of getting my work noticed internationally without being dependent on merely hanging pictures in a gallery, hoping to find an agent along the way.

The breasts were huge. It was impossible to ignore or wish them away, there they sat directly in front of her, placed in a tight black bodice accentuating their unusual volume, swaying heavily to the rhythmically moving train. The breasts were paired with cold blue eyes closely scrutinizing their counterpart, obviously trying to figure out how to put their adversary to death.
"Woman who are over thirty years old should give up, who wants to be stuck with an old hag..."
The attack was aimed wildly, so it missed her heart.
"Don't you think that kind of philosophy will boomerang back to you at some point?" her opponent asked mildly, thinking of how the breasts had hysterically positioned themselves in front of the man the night before, and how she had noticed only after a while that his eyes were not on their titillating points but instead on the red lips of the girl he had been dreaming of, herself.
The breasts shook impatiently.
"No man can resist me and any woman who thinks she can keep me from what I want will have to deal with losing"
"Hmmm, you think it's only about sex and power?"
Shifting uncomfortably, the breasts hissed, "Who are you anyway, I haven't seen you around?"
"Guess I don't hang out in the same places you do. I'm an 'old' friend, in fact way over thirty."
The breasts stared at her silently, furtively checking out her clothes, shoes, nail polish, noting with satisfaction that they were chipped.
"You know, when we first met I thought we could be friends..."
Pure contempt in the form of loud, rude laughter violently erupted from the tight-lipped mouth, distorting the face into a mask of anger, to then suddenly, magically transform into an innocent smile of seduction as the door swung open and the object of desire entered the train compartment with six bottles of beer as promised.
Watching the breasts slink into an enticing position, arranging themselves within the low black neckline so that they could wink furtively, she thought of how this furious creature had hit her in the ribs with a pointed elbow, "accidentally" pushed her in the hallway, and spread mean gossip in an attempt start a general mobbing, making such an effort to hurt her when in fact she was only a small part of the ongoing warfare: men sticking their tongues into her mouth brutally, saying, she must be used to it as a groupie, slapping her behind as she walked by, the phone ringing in the middle of the night with

various voices whispering covert sexual invitations, hundreds of ex-affairs, girl-friends, and wives furiously declaring, "I am the number one in his life,"old friends suddenly calling out of the blue, not to chat but asking for favors to further their careers; being generally introduced as "the girlfriend of...," an array of eyes staring with undisguised envy and greed at every movement she made, considering her to be the main obstacle in their quest for fulfillment, pondering on how to get her out of the way. She wondered how it had come to be that she was in the strange and frightening position of being the girlfriend of a rock star.

ALEXANDER HACKE

Alexander Hacke was born in Neukölln, Berlin on the 11th of October 1965. As an only child of working parents he mainly grew up with his grandmother, a sturdy Prussian empress protecting him from harm or angry policemen.

Although he spent his younger years sketching and drawing, Alexander's main interest had always been music, he taught himself how to play the guitar and learned by heart the lyrics of the Ramones, his greatest heroes.

Being the skinny "kid with glasses," he quickly learned how to defend himself with humor, quick wit, and fists if necessary, building a reputation as the class clown, the teachers and pupils roaring with laughter at his outrageous jokes, though he still usually ended up in the detention room. After being kicked out of every school in Neukölln because of unruly behavior, his parents decided to enroll him in a music school for talented children, where he took the opportunity of quickly learning how to play drums before running away from home. Only thirteen years old, he had to be careful not be caught by the police, so after moving to Hamburg, the underage rebel covertly skirted around town, doing odd jobs, playing music, supported by well-meaning friends and his first girlfriend Christiane F., Germany's most renowned heroin addict.

After two years of hanging out in the red-light district he moved back to Berlin and joined the new band Einstürzende Neubauten, a combination of strong, independent characters well suited to his tastes. FM Einheit played drums, N.U. Unruh was on percussion, Mark Chung on bass, and Blixa Bargeld was the lead singer. Although this legendary posse would become his ersatz family over the next thirty years, Alexander continued cooperating with different musicians and music styles from the very start. His curiosity, paired with a stubborn streak and a desire for harmony, gave him the social skills needed to work with complicated and intricate characters, and he collaborated with the Australian band Crime and the City Solution, the French and German band Sprung aus den Wolken, and the Berlin-based Mona Mur, among others. In 1982 he released his first 12-inch EP, *Hiroshima*, which became an underground hit, making him a respected and admired figure not only within Berlin's walls but also among the international music scene, attracting countless fans and groupies. His hunger for adventure and new experiences was limitless, not only within the realm of music or art: after the end of his romance with Christiane F. he became a notorious heartbreaker, burning a trail through the 1980s music scene with countless entangled affairs and relationships.

We were introduced in 1987 while helping Roland transport some of his guitars, but we had seen each other before in various situations. I remember being especially impressed by his uncommon mode of listening, looking at the speaker intensely, not necessarily commenting on what had been said, instead looking at the speaker quizzically and waiting for the next sentence silently. This obviously made quite a few people uncomfortable, accustomed to the quick ping-pong of social conversation, wondering if they had said something stupid or thinking that he was arrogant. His incapacity for making small talk was outstanding, and he quickly became my personal model of integrity, individualism, and non-conformity. The fact that he was also genuinely nice and fun to be with was the cherry on top.

On the other hand his lifestyle, a high-speed timeline of mad, drunken escapades, and the fact that the tall, handsome man was forever accompanied by a vast group of admirers, breathlessly pushing him to take on any challenge or provocation, only to watch him land on his feet laughing uproariously and continue his breakneck journey, was too loud and group-oriented for my taste, so we kept a natural distance, watching each other go through different relationships and projects until Roland's death.

The demise of my fiancé and Alexander's closest friend locked us into an unspoken bond of loss. Having experienced each other's history for such a long time we instinctively reacted as a family, supporting each other wordlessly and sensing the other's mood, no matter how large the crowd, or drunk. In fact so strong was our connection, that even on stage, seeing me in the crowd, Alexander would sense if a song brought sad memories and would try comforting me through eye contact while playing the bass in front of thousands of people. In the following five years during which I moved to Senzke, emigrated back to Berlin, separated from Motte, had a destructive affair with a violent drummer, and worked with the Goethe Institute, Alexander had married, become the father of a second child, was bringing up his son from a previous relationship, and toured the world with Neubauten. We saw each other regularly at parties, dinners, and performances, encased by a group of friends, twinkling at each other from afar; always aware of how the other was doing. By 2000 it was apparent that something was going terribly wrong. In my case I had been beaten up so badly that my neck was permanently injured, causing pain for years to come, and in Alexander's case, his marriage had disintegrated violently into misery and public blowups, with the result that the couple split up in 2000 and divorced soon after.

Accordingly both of us were in a terrible state. I had problems sleeping or eating and Alexander's drinking habit had gotten so bad that the few performances he participated in were greeted with sadly shaken heads and comments on how he had once been so promising. Everybody thought the end of a brilliant career had arrived, and he would be just another man drowned in the ocean of whiskey. There is one saying, that "when the going gets tough the tough get going," and another claiming that "you grow through pain." I agree with the first but question the second.

When faced with the death of a dream, either because of an actual death or because of another form of final ending, the first response is to succumb either to bitterness, neurosis, sad distractions, or hate, frozen in the unexpected state of shock which such a transition brings. To find the strength or determination to tear oneself out of the abyss and decide to go on, to take the unbearable challenge of starting anew, not as a reaction to what happened but instead really starting over again is almost unfathomably difficult, mainly because pain weakens you. My experience is that a heart that has been torn apart can only grow as strong as it was before if it is cared for over a long time, and even so, the shadow of past pain will never completely disappear, the ghost of trouble is stamped onto one's memory forever. That is why it is so important to give children a happy childhood from the start, so they can have a strong heart without shadows to face reality with. How children growing up during a war ever recover is hard for me to imagine, they are so weakened that they don't even know what they should aspire to, never having experienced anything other than destruction. Consider the child of an alcoholic, who usually starts drinking later in life in spite of the memory of misery thrust upon him as a child; it is that which is most familiar that one instinctively trusts, instead of trying to pursue the more difficult path of finding an alternative.

Both of us had been raised in dysfunctional families and our development up to this point had followed similarly destructive paths that led us to the abyss we had landed in. So this time we both decided to find an alternative.

By 2001 we were simultaneously single, burdened by a mountain of bad habits, experiences, and pain, but with the unusual situation of having found somebody who had not only gone through similar pain but who had been in the other's life all along and to whom nothing had to be explained. We knew everything about each other in spite of having lived with different partners. This created an intimacy we each desperately needed. Being uncommitted we could spend endless time together and months went by when we just talked. In spite of our bad shape, it was a charmed period of endless conversations in dark hotel bars, bright sunlit park benches, cozy afternoon tea houses, cheap diners, expensive sushi bars, or train compartments, with a magical undercurrent flowing strongly in every encounter, hypnotizing us invisibly. Looking into Alexander's warm brown eyes, I felt I was speaking to somebody I had always known and for the first time in my life was relaxed, getting used to the situation that communication through my art was not necessary in this case. I found myself having fun with silly, small games and entertainment. Alex taught me how to play scopa, enjoy fantasy movies, presented his favorite comic books, tried to keep me from screaming in splatter movies and enticed me to hang out in cafés for hours instead of working. He told jokes and funny stories until I shook with laughter, taking me on excursions to fun fairs or amusement parks, in general teaching me how to lighten up and enjoy life.

The club's decor was elegant, consisting of many niches and platforms, black designer tables, leather chairs, stylish sofas, and a silver lacquered dance floor. The popular DJ spun top-of-the-pop-chart records in his transparent booth behind a large buffet of expensive cheeses, tiny finger food, and champagne. Actors, directors, and models mingled, opening oysters, nibbling nuts, or smoking large cigars between the high pillars, nonchalantly taking the admiring crowd for granted, grandly shaking hands as new acquaintances arrived.

Carefully she inched past the laughing guests, all dressed in expensive suits, low-cut dresses or miniskirts, many proudly bearing diamonds and sparkling rubies to enhance their best features. Most women were blond, heavily made up and very thin, their eyes darting back and forth, hoping the film moguls would notice and come over to speak to, discover, and seduce them, laughing in high, tinny voices, fluttering their long mascaraed lashes.

Feeling uncomfortable in her simple black dress she slipped past the bouncer quietly, showing him her VIP bracelet and climbed up the stairs to her seat. A. was speaking to a young actress who had starred in the movie, toasting her performance and congratulating her success.

Noticing D.'s arrival he turned, took her hand and pulled her down to him.

"What took you so long?"

"The line in the bathroom took forever."

"Probably all taking drugs, huh?"

"I guess so—most of the booths were filled with couples."

A producer came over, introducing himself to A., making a joke, ignoring her. Feeling awkward she reached over to the bottle of champagne on the table and poured herself a large glass.

"Would you like some ice?"

Turning, she was handed a bucket of ice by a thin brunette wearing heavy green eye shadow and a wraparound mini dress.

"I loved the movie, didn't you?" the brunette asked.

"Yes I did, I hope it is successful in the theaters."

"Oh, I'm sure it will be, her life was just so exciting, especially with all those rock musicians she was fucking."

"Well, I really liked the way she always did exactly what she thought best instead of following somebody else's rules."

"Yeah well... so did I. Oh look, isn't that B.? I saw him in his new movie last week, he is sooooooo cute...oh and there's C. She's gained so much weight lately I'm surprised she's still in business."

"Do you mind passing the champagne"? A. had stopped speaking to the producer and turned to look at her worriedly. "Are you ok? Not too bored?"

Her neighbor yelped excitedly. "Oh! Aren't you A.? I love your band, I've been a fan for years, can I have you autograph please?"

"Sure." Raising his eyebrows A. took a pen from his pocket and signed her leg as indicated.

R. the director came over, falling over a leg and landing on the sofa next to them. "Oops, sorry, having fun?"

"Yes, it's a great party! Congratulations again!" Smiling at her briefly, he spotted a well-known actor coming up the stairs and excused himself quickly, getting up from the sofa and hurrying away.

Tears burned under her eyelids for a moment, she had still not gotten used to the complete indifference.

Deciding to have fun anyway she turned, but her green-eyed neighbor had started speaking to a gray suit and was secretly taking a quick line of coke between his legs on the sofa.

Sighing, she inched back to the buffet, squeezing through the tightly packed crowd, but the food had been eaten, all that was left were a couple of drenched pretzels lying in puddles of water.

Back in her seat, she saw that A. was now speaking to an old acquaintance, a music producer who had supported his band many times, and she smiled politely, pretending to listen to the conversation, pouring another glass of champagne and wondering if she could ever get used to dealing with the world of fame.

LIVING IN THE SPOTLIGHT

In spite of the many unusual situations I had experienced in my life, I was not prepared for what was now to come and if I had known, I would probably not have believed it.

Innocently ignoring the fact that Alexander was an international underground icon, a rock star, a legend even, all I saw was the despondent and confused friend that Roland had always described as the most joyful man in the world, the only person he knew that could get up after a blow and chuckle, and who was now down on his knees struggling. How kindly he was helping me with my sadness in spite of his own despondency. It was the most important thing in the world for me that he continue laughing. No matter how drunk, depressed, or out of control he was, no matter from where he called, I would be there immediately, carrying him out of the bar, pushing him into a cab, leading him home, cleaning his wounds, cooking healthy food to balance the toxic intake, finding remedies for sudden allergies, and handing him aspirin to fight the effects of bad hangovers until he could start grinning, winking from beneath his light brown eyebrows. It was an odd situation to be in and difficult to understand but in supporting him I felt I was preserving the childhood heroes I had dreamed of as a lonely outcast in the US army barracks. Thus we continued strengthening each other, with deep mutual appreciation, until we suddenly realized that we had fallen in love. Although we had been attracted to each other for years we were caught by surprise, neither one of us having planned to enter another commitment so quickly, nor were we accustomed to such a peaceful romance, being used to chaos and desperation accompanying relationships. But this was to be different from anything we had experienced up to then and after realizing that being together felt completely natural, we decided to let fate decide if it was to be only a short-lived affair or something more serious.

Besides protecting each other emotionally we decided to collaborate professionally, both having been financially ruined by our previous relationships and in dire need of money. I had been working on my body of film loops more extensively and was frequently invited to set up installations in various clubs and theaters, the intricate universes I made having becoming popular among the many Berlin newcomers. So I included Alexander as the acoustic element, creating a dense world with flowing pictures enhanced by his droning Indian tabla machines, guitar, or throat singing. This way we were able to earn a little money besides Alexander's DJing and my random art sales, but were still barely able to pay our rents.

Our first real turn of luck was when Alexander received a large advance for a record in fall 2001. He had decided to work on a solo album to determine what direction he would take in the future and came up with the unusual idea of doing it in the form of a road record. Convincing BMG to finance the project so he could travel the world, he asked me to accompany him and document his travels with my camera. Thus we were suddenly touring the world together, working on an intricate project, moving from hotels to friends' apartments to other hotels, from Mexico City to Chicago, Los Angeles to New York, and so on for months, giving us the chance to explore our liaison while doing what we loved most, creating art and interacting with international colleagues.

The technical procedure of the project was that Alexander would record music with a colleague in one city and then move on, recording the next take with another associate in another town. After having recorded countless takes in different cities he would then mix the music and include overdubs with other participants. The ingenious aspect was that in this way it was very spontaneous, not at all preconceived, with unexpected suggestions and startling musical clashes happening constantly, something Alexander enjoyed immensely. At the same time it was a very personal, intimate experience. All of the participants were cherished friends who Alexander had collaborated with in the past, and in the end it was as if he had written a symphony in which all of the important voices in his life were singing in a choir, celebrating everything he had treasured over the years, generating energy and joy and, finally, reigniting his inner will to survive.

During this personal voyage it also became apparent that we got along remarkably well, despite exhausting travel, cramped living quarters, and a chaotic schedule. Alexander frequently commented that he had never felt such synchronicity. The fact that both of us enjoyed exploratory circumstances dealing with anti-establishment themes, Wild West atmospheres or carnival sideshows, catapulted us to very diverse settings. We enthusiastically visited Beth Love in Albuquerque, driving a shiny red 1950s mustang muscle car through Los Angeles, filming Hollywood cross-dressers dancing in water fountains, drunk mariachi players in Mexico City, discovering cartoon toys and collectibles in Brooklyn, admiring Indian reservations, broken pickup trucks, and wild cats in New Mexico, buying pointed cowboy boots in Chicago, eating delicious Indian food in Jackson Heights, Queens, in New York, investigated countless new books at City Lights, San Francisco's best bookstore, watching videos with David Yow and his wife in suburban Indiana, discovering Brujeria CDs at the largest flea market in Oaxaca, buying colorful devotional objects in downtown LA, recording friends rehearsing in Brooklyn, admiring Victorian mansions in Boston. When we finally landed at Tegel, Berlin's tiny airport, our four huge suitcases were filled to the brim with plastic skulls, Tiki mugs, rock T-shirts, a small vihuela, and countless hours of film and music material.

During the course of this journey our spirits finally lifted. The fact that we were far away from Berlin, traveling in a tight bubble of security since we exclusively dealt with a group of close artist-friends, who naturally treated both of us with respect, we had been able to heal.

Back home was another story.

When we left, both of us had been in such a mess that people backed off from us, worried about being entangled in a complicated net of separation, misery, and divorce. But as soon as we returned from our travels and were obviously a couple, stronger, happier, and healthier than before, there were many who wanted a piece of the cake.

In Alexander's case, as a celebrity, this meant almost everybody we met wanted him to show off to their friends, help their career, enhance their parties, brag about, have an affair with, or get money from, the usual things people want from stars.

As for me: they did not want me around.

Around celebrities, people in general will be louder, ruder, more aggressive, and amazingly ruthless. Normal polite behavior, such as maintaining a respectful distance, or observing the usual rules of privacy, is rare. When traveling internationally this aspect is not quite as blatant, since some degree of distance is insured by bouncers, managers, booking agents, or perhaps just by shyness. But in Berlin, where everybody had grown up together and had some story or anecdote about Alexander, he was considered a general possession. I was made to realize very quickly that as a rock star's girlfriend I was either a way in or an obstacle, depending on what the person in question wanted.

During the first couple of months I felt as if I had entered an upside-down world. People I had known and worked with for years suddenly did not recognize me when I entered a room with Alexander; they were too dazzled by being close to a legend, staring at him speechlessly.

I was puzzled, at first assuming it was a misunderstanding, but then, when only a very few of my female acquaintances refrained from trying to lure my boyfriend into bed—appearing naked in the morning, lolling seductively on our sofa, taking loud, impromptu showers at night after suddenly staying over, secretly calling him, sending emails, flirting heavily, antagonizing or ridiculing me in public, or just sitting and staring at him for hours, hoping to get a reaction; and other friends started calling out of the blue—inviting us to birthdays, private dinners, Christmas brunches, club openings or exhibitions, then spending all their time asking him for favors or showing him their work, forgetting that I was even in the room—I became depressed.

It was not only the feeling of abruptly having become transparent, turned into the invisible woman, it was also affecting my career with job offers deteriorating sharply. Suddenly I was being introduced as the "girlfriend of…" instead of as

"Danielle de Picciotto, the interdisciplinary artist." My long years of being hyped as one of Berlin's main underground artists seemed completely forgotten. The only interesting thing about me seemed to be that I had Alexander Hacke's private telephone number.

I do not believe that such responses to my person were intentionally dismissive or malicious, but the allure of celebrity, fame, and power is so strong that in its presence people are oblivious. When I asked the girlfriends of other well-known musicians for advice, most of them knew exactly what I was speaking about. They said that due to the greater support for males in general, it was very difficult to keep up recognition achieved if entering a relationship with a known artist, the female protagonist then usually perceived as a "hanger on," groupie, or just a protége, no matter what she had done before. They advised me to choose a handful of friends very carefully, and warned me that betrayal would always be close at hand. They told me to work on projects outside of his realm where nobody knew or could profit from his fame, and to mainly rely on family members for protection. Or to just to give up on my career altogether and have a baby.

I was shocked.

Taking their advice about filtering friends, I carefully selected a small but loyal army of companions, people I had always been able to rely upon, the most integral being one of my dearest friends, Stevie Burns, a talented designer who not only helped me design catalogues and my homepage but who also possessed the wonderful attribute of being completely unimpressed by fame, reacting to my boyfriend as I had thought most of my friends would, by appreciating Alex's humor and liking him as a person, but otherwise calling me up as usual and not changing anything in his attitude. Laura Kikauka was another, stoically remaining unimpressed by hype, always ready to have fun with both of us, laden with hilarious objects whenever we met and spreading a wonderful, laidback atmosphere of calm.

The word friendship took on new meaning and I now understood why my father had advised me to focus on a handful of true friends instead of cultivating many acquaintances. I had often responded by defiantly naming hundreds of loyal associations met over the years, calling him a recluse, not understanding his reservation, receiving the answer that there would come a time in my life in which I would need a true friend. His prophecy had been fulfilled. Considering the widespread use of MySpace, Facebook, and Twitter, I can only emphasize, especially to young, starstruck teenagers, how important true, real-life friends are in comparison to anonymous acquaintances or celebrities. I have met countless people who live in front of their computer and TV screens, replacing real life with a dream and ending up lonely and very depressed.

As for the recommendation that I concentrate on my own projects, neither Alexander nor I were willing to give up collaborating together, after having discovered how well we complemented each other. Finding a partner for long-term projects is difficult enough as it is: not only is it hard to find someone with similar vision, taste, work ethics, enthusiasm, character, and endurance, but one also has to like the other person enough to stand being together with them constantly. The idea of giving up on working with somebody who fulfilled all of these attributes, on top of being in love with that person, resulting in the ideal opportunity to live, travel, and work together, seemed silly. I decided to learn how to deal with the new situation and make the best of it, happily not knowing how many additional facets would soon be revealed. This eventual realization related to the final recommendation: family as such became a very confusing subject. I had become the stepmother of not only one, but two children by different mothers, and was to experience quickly that this was similar to being thrown into a lion's den, armed with only a paintbrush to defend myself.

BEING A STEPMOTHER

By 2001 the majority of the people I had met in Berlin were in their mid-thirties or early forties. Most of them worked as artists, musicians, journalists, actors, designers, club-owners and goers, DJs, or in other fields dealing with culture, most of them freelancers. In comparison to New York where having children is not an issue of huge concern, many couples realistically choosing not to have children because of high rents, limited space, surroundings that are inhospitable to children, or simply because of having no interest in becoming a parent, there had been a wave of early pregnancies in Berlin around 1986 and 1987, which I had barely perceived, the young mothers usually silently and quickly disappearing from the intense underground playground.

But the real tsunami started around 1999, when many of the women I knew were between thirty-five and thirty-nine years of age, and worried that it might soon be too late for them to have a biological child. Many had not been ready to take up traditional motherhood roles before spending significant time on their work, deciding to reach a certain level of recognition before focusing on a child, hoping that this way they would be able to satisfy both urges. Even so, the situation of being an artist with goals and dreams on top of being a mother turned out to be more difficult than expected.

Although most of the fathers were also freelancers, with flexible timetables and home studios, ready to break the rules of role allocation and willing to put time and effort into raising children (resulting in quaint scenarios of cowboy-hat-wearing musicians pushing strollers, tough, tattooed-covered performers organizing pink birthday parties for their tiny daughters, or leopard-skin-wearing artists trying to calm their hysterical sons screaming on the bus as bemused Turkish mothers looked on, offering chocolate or oranges to stop the terrible noise), a general pattern of divorce and separation became apparent after a couple of years. Artists' relationships are difficult to begin with, each one necessarily concentrating on their own form of expression, with a nonstop agenda of appointments, exhibitions, performances, tours, not to mention the ensuing exhaustion. With a child, either an elongated break has to be planned, or a very thorough timetable of babysitters organized. Unless both parents were willing to make huge compromises, problems arose very quickly. Besides the fact that artists are often vulnerable and extreme, and tend to be insecure and poor, it is also imperative for them to be curious and experimental, boycotting security. For art these are good attributes, but for relationships they are impractical and the speed with which couples produced babies and then split up was remarkable.

As an unsuspecting, childless, female artist used to interacting with most people on a creative level I was unprepared for the many emotional facets of this universe. After a difficult childhood I had long ago decided not to inflict a similar emotional nightmare on a child of my own, and as my life had always been a constant turmoil of low income, constant work, very little free time, and relationships with men in similar positions, I had instinctively come to the conclusion that I would not have children. I also do not consider it a necessity, not in our day and age in which women can find fulfillment in many different areas. There are many things one cannot do in a lifetime, the conviction that a person has to have or do everything is impossible to realize and once more simply a goal based on greed. I never really contemplated having kids or had the feeling of "missing out," dealing with children and teenagers frequently in workshops and installations, happy to communicate with them through art. The sudden reality of being a stepmother to two children caught me unawares. I had never expected or thought about what it meant to be going out with somebody who had children and watching it from afar was something very different from experiencing the real life I woke up to after falling in love with Alexander. Suddenly I was dealing with kindergarten adventures, teenage discussions, cough-ridden nights, heart-to-heart talks, quarrels, and shouting homework discussions, secret smoking, first loves, and combing lice out of dirty, knotted hair. These were things I had not expected to experience in my life but which fascinated me. I learned that as a stepmother there are many possibilities for how one can positively help kids with small things like providing them with good food, regular sleeping hours, reading books together instead of watching TV, spending hours figuring out complicated game rules, painting pictures, helping solve the math lessons I had never understood in school, practicing musical instruments, giving advice on how to deal with bullies and going to the zoo.

Being within an intimate family circle because of being married to the father, it was possible to deal with the children on a more personal level than I could have as a friend and also made me care much more deeply. Obviously, dealing with a teenage boy and girl is very different to interacting with galleries or venues, and learning how to understand child psychology is a rocky path of ups and downs. I had to face my own issues, fears, and childhood experiences, and spent countless nights musing over mistakes and worrying that I had caused more conflict, angered at my insecurities, cursing impatient comments until Alexander would comfort me saying that being a stepmother did not mean being a saint, and that dealing with children is always an up-and-down situation for everybody.

I have learned that as a stepmother one can love and care for a child. You see your partner in the features of the small faces of their offspring, and want them to prosper healthily. It is a very basic emotion of protection, which has nothing to do with ownership, and I was content and felt blessed to be able to experience interaction with children inspite of not having my own, hoping that what little I could offer would still be helpful.

Bada Bing!

After we had come back from our recording trip around the world, we now had to edit the material we had collected. In order to present the unusual settings in which Alexander had recorded his music, I had documented detailed scenes in New York, Chicago, Los Angeles, and New Mexico, besides doing detailed interviews with the musicians he had chosen. Most had been dealing with the music industry since the early 1980s and the stories I was told by Algis A. Kizys (Swans) James G. Thirlwell aka Foetus, Lary 7 (The Analog Society), Tim Farris of Celebrity Skin, and David Yow of Scratch Acid and The Jesus Lizard about their experiences in developing digital electronics, facing hierarchies within the system, living through international tours, and generating experimental projects similar to *Sanctuary* were comparable to our own experiences. To recognize the similarities and discrepancies between the American and the European experience (Neubauten were touring Europe since 1980...), was highly illuminating and exactly what Alexander had been looking for. He considered the creation of *Sanctuary* a learning process, a pursuit of new ways to mature musically, discovering original methods of recording, experimenting with different styles and instruments, brainstorming new ideas with old friends, and learning the latest computer programs for audio and video editing, photo processing, and animation.

I had been working on Super-8 film loops since early 1993, initially because of being bored with decorating clubs with slides or drawings. I had discovered the media when filming a model for one of my portraits, wanting to catch certain fluid movements or gestures and asking her to dance to some music. While looking at the loop later on I saw that the dancer always seemed to be dancing in rhythm no matter what music I was listening to. Fascinated I decided to film a row of dancers and present the loops on transparent gauzes in clubs to see what effect it would have on the audience. Filming friends instead of professional dancers in order to capture a certain shyness in their movements, I also asked them to decide what to wear, some choosing elaborate costumes, others masks, some in jeans. In this way the loops had a very natural, genuine feeling. A small photo store in Neukölln had been recommended to me as the only one dealing with Super-8 material in Berlin and I was thrilled to discover that they had a large collection of cheap, vintage Super-8 movie projectors, film, reels, and even guaranteed repair work. Accumulating about fifteen projectors I created club installations in which all of the walls were covered with iridescent dancers. The effect was mesmerizing. Not only did my projections dance in rhythm to any song that was playing, their intimacy was hypnotic, and people stood in front of them for hours, dancing closely to the soft apparitions in the glow of the projectors, fascinated at how the repetitive movements coincided so perfectly with different sounds and melodies.

I worked on these projections for years, exhibiting them in clubs and galleries until I discovered that I could conjure a more satisfying universe by placing them within surreal, constructed landscapes, turning dark, industrial Berlin dancehalls into flowery country landscapes, with enormous, fluorescent orange tulips gently swaying over veiled dancers performing intricate choreographies, and young gypsy girls silently swinging back and forth on wooden swings over graveyards. I was so preoccupied with puzzling together different slide and video projectors, as well as objects, and turning them into holistic installations, and enjoyed the process so much that it was years before I thought of filming an entire scene from start to finish.

While working on *Sanctuary* I discovered the medium of video. Although preferring the grainy, old-fashioned look of Super-8, it would have been too expensive to document months of work with that type of film. Just three minutes of footage cost twenty-three Deutschmarks, so I chose the less expensive option of video and was delighted by the added and unexpected luxury of immediate sound editing.

I have always enjoyed a natural progression, with one interest leading to the next, and have noticed that by being very open to new ideas this happens easily. After discovering how much fun filming with a mini DV Camcorder can be, Fred Alpi, a musician from Paris and fan of my film-loop installations, asked me to create a music video for his band. I had met Lillevän, a well-known Berlin video artist shortly before, during an event at which I had been invited to install my film loops. After speaking about visual art he recommended I learn Final Cut Pro, and even offered to teach me the new editing program. By accepting Alpi's financial offer I had the possibility of paying for Lillevän's lessons and by incorporating Japanese butoh dancers, circus sideshow atmospheres, and punk clubs to portray the songs lyrics I then realized that within film I could create not only wonderful fantasy worlds more easily than in cumbersome installations but could incorporate my drawings within the motion-picture landscapes. I decided to give *Sanctuary* this kind of look and began working on a short film for the CD. The combination of intricate, delicate art and color-processed film took quite some time to finish, but by the time Alexander's solo album was done, both of us had made enormous progress in all of our combined techniques.

During the months spent working in his small living room at Planufer, in Kreuzberg, both engrossed with our computers, cursing at an unexpected problem or losing hours of work because of forgetting to save the file, we continued recording and initiating live music sessions in order to be able to integrate Berlin musicians into the project, inviting various friends and colleagues to participate.

The *Purgatory* concerts were an eclectic mix of very different characters sharing the stage for two nights, mainly jamming, and we came up with various impressive, hilarious, or madcap results by working with Caspar Brötzman, Peaches, Jim Avignon, Zeitblom, and Nisse Wohlrabe, Alexander and myself recording everything.

Then I was contacted by Andreas Schwarz, the manager of the Big Eden, Berlins first discotheque in the 1970s, asking me if I were interested in organizing a regular event series. He had heard of the curative work I had done over the years and offered me a generous sum of money with which I could create any program I wanted, guaranteeing bands a small but definite fee to perform, an unusual offer for a Berlin club. Taking it as a the perfect way to create a new bubble bath of interaction, I offered Andreas the concept of organizing a monthly event in which different bands representing various styles would perform, making them clash and collide, comparable to the "Kunst oder König" events, except on a much smaller scale. To make the events visually exciting as well, I invited burlesque dancers, then unheard of in Berlin, to participate. They wore Mexican wrestling masks and performed between dancing among my visual projections and the huge wooden, tattooed sculptures with which I decorated the stage, swaying to the rhythm, and giving everything a multilayered impression of mad dreams. Alexander was to be master of ceremonies, wearing outrageous outfits, wigs, and platform boots, announcing the show, making quick music improvisations and inviting guest musicians on stage. Andreas loved the idea and straight away set a date for the first show. After deciding to call the evenings Bada Bing!, in tribute to our favorite TV series, *The Sopranos,* Alexander and I set about choosing bands.

After returning from our long journey we had noticed a new generation of musicians who had emerged in Berlin, with experienced old-timers meeting excited beginners. Boy From Brazil, Electrocute, Mignon, Sin City Circus Ladies, Cry Babies, or Fuzzy Love were but a few presenting electroclash, a combination of 1980s-influenced modern electronic digital music accompanied by live instruments, s/m influenced costumes and surreal stage sets. We decided to present this novelty together with classic rock bands, nose flute orchestras, French chansons, spoken-word sessions, Slayer cover bands, or gay drag shows, creating the most outrageous clashes we could think of to keep everybody amused.

Due to this event series we encountered a multitude of new musicians, artists, music styles, and creative influences enthusiastically participating in the madcap atmosphere. Alexander dressed up in enormous afro wigs, cowboy hats, and elegant white suits, growling his announcements through the microphone, jumping from the stage and mingling with the audience at lightening speed, screaming at the top of his voice or whispering seductively to the burlesque dancers, who were dressed in feathery costumes and seductive masks, and followed him in his excursions, helping the musicians set up flowery microphone stands, heavy amps, and tacky sofas on the smoke-filled stage, amid imitation tiger fur and red velvet drapes covered with my projections of looped dancers and psychedelic animals. A hype began to flourish that Berlin had been lacking for some time. Due to the growing commerciality of nightlife, it had been turned into a matter-of-fact, repetitive, moneymaking blandness.

Bada Bing! recalled Berlin's original madness, that upon which the city's legend is based, replete with secondhand 1970s flares, 1980s leggings, fake jewelry, striptease shows, and wild, uninhibited music styles. The clean-cut, minimal style of the late 1990s was now rudely corrupted by dirt, noise, and conscious mistakes, sex openly flaunted after years of asexuality, with audiences stripping wildly, queens, rock fans, or computer nerds screaming in sync and moving violently to audacious happenings on stage. Anarchy was back.

Overjoyed, other clubs and promoters began offering electroclash lineups, and newspapers were introduced to the new music style in hilarious press meetings that included frisky artists, goats, and other animals. Musicians made obscene comments, started drunken brawls, and hilariously acted as scandalously as possible, pleased to be caught up in a mad wave of eccentricity and initiating another hectic rush of international artists moving to Berlin, having heard tell of unusual happenings and eager to experience the thrill of controversy for themselves.

They were amazingly good looking.

Everywhere they went women fell for them, conquered by their good manners and impressive talent, inviting them to parties, concerts, small dinners, and intimate gatherings, holding their hands, smiling up into their faces, cuddling closely whenever possible.

Having decided to move to Berlin after an initial concert, delighted by the great appreciation and warm welcome, tired of being on tour constantly, they quickly became an attraction, three renegade outlaws, roaming the streets, drinking gallons of whiskey, filling the clubs with their sweltering charm, and seducing the city so effectively that it capitulated helplessly.

"We are drinking way too much," they would repeat, looking down at the redheads or blondes, wincing at the thought of the headache looming in their near future, and downing the first cocktail with regret.

"But then, why not have fun?" a gorgeous brunette with bright red lips would retort, ordering a beer with the next shot and the evening would begin.

"Be careful," friends would warn, "Berlin is a dangerous and moody mistress."

"Ah, don't worry, we've seen worse," they would retort waltzing off delightedly to the tunes of a Mexican ballad.

Deciding to celebrate the holidays appropriately they met in a small bar known for absinthe, inviting their girlfriends from home, who had flown in to see their dearly missed.

Dressed in elegant suits and white shirts their ties were soon to hang askew, the green, sticky liquid evoking grimaces on their faces.

"Hmmm, tastes sweet, that's dangerous," they decided.

"Let's have another."

Glasses were poured and downed. And more.

Berlin became a cotton-candy atmosphere of sticky kisses, mistaken hugs, mysteriously arriving women, and shocked reactions, with screams and threats, tears and regret, awkward explanations, and more absinthe. Lost in the dark abyss of excess, forgotten goodbyes were hurled and bodies stumbled home in a fog, not understanding what had happened.

The next morning no one could remember exactly who had participated but the harm had been done, innocence lost, feelings hurt, the magic spell broken, and girlfriends gone, dipping the adventurers into reality and sobriety.

The city looked down at them, smirking at the surprise marking their lined faces as they lay defeated in the gray afternoon smog.

She never had appreciated being underestimated.

The Melting Pot

Berlin has always had many international inhabitants, with Russian, English, and French areas stemming from the time of the Cold War, and Turkish, African, Korean, Italian, Polish, and Indian immigrants arriving more recently for economical or political reasons. Australians and Americans were attracted by the culture and individualism. Even though the diversity of the German capital's ethnic make-up paled in comparison to London, Istanbul, or Mexico City, the flow of enthusiasts moving to Berlin after 1990 grew steadily. As was true of New York, Berlin had always been a metropolis embracing foreigners within its creative scene. Meeting a native Berliner was rare even during the 1980s, like native New Yorkers, and both cities thrive on the electric melting pot of languages, traditions, tastes, and cultures, gaining the reputation of being super hip because of their throbbing diversity.

This Babylonian state of life seemed to foster a certain state of mind. In contrast to what advertising agencies or manipulative Freudian psychologists preach, the Berlin imperative was not about money, fame, or power, nor even necessarily the goal of finding personal happiness, instead, in many instances it was simply about breaking down boundaries, building new bridges, discovering something untouched, unnamed, unpredictable. Berlin's culture alternated between high activity or sleepy exhaustion, with a group of ever-changing, multilingual pioneers ensuring hibernation would never last long. Depending on the month or year, visitors could have entirely different impressions of the city, either leaving in disappointment, wondering what the hype was about, or deciding to stay forever after experiencing weeks of delirious interaction. But for a long time the people attracted to Berlin were ones that were interested in nonconformity.

In the the 1970s David Bowie and Iggy Pop, in the 1980s Nick Cave and Einstürzende Neubauten were the most legendary residents, in the 1990s countless techno experimentalists arrived from Detroit, mainly invited by Dimitri, such as Derrick May, Juan Atkins, or Blake Baxter, originally having come just to perform but often staying longer than they anticipated.

In 2003 while we were starting Bada Bing!, another younger wave of curious artists arrived and were happily invited to perform on our stage, including the Devastations from Melbourne, Michelle Carr from Los Angeles, BabaZula from Istanbul and Dahlia from New York each taking bows, delighted at the enthusiastic reception.

Alexander and I enjoyed the constant communication, riding on the electroclash wave and thinking up screwball enterprises with local promoters to keep the crowd on their toes, offering relentless entertainment and material for gossip.

Berlin experienced a long wave of bubbling creativity, roaring parties, music events, and ingenious interaction, the excitement spreading quickly. But the difference to Berlin in the 1980s or the young techno scene in the 1990s was that this gathering was much smaller than the one before. During the 1980s a general feeling of community existed, with everybody being proud of belonging to the infamous underground, mingling and going from one club to the next, working together, creating a tight network of interaction in spite of having different musical tastes. It was comparable to the feeling of belonging to a secret society, to which one's membership was understood simply via a code and nod of the head.

In the 1990s the techno crowd developed an intense "techno philosophy" adapting music, art, fashion, and even food into their electronic cyber universe, printing newspapers and magazines to hype their new lifestyle and proclaiming everything else old-fashioned or boring. Not everybody could afford the new and pricey "techno" standard of living or wanted to be part of such an all-encompassing philosophy and a gulf between the techno crowd and other music styles developed, resulting in two main crowds, those who loved techno and those who hated it. Nonetheless, creative Berlin's main occupation remained nightclubbing with hundreds of venues, bars, late-night galleries or illegal parties happening twenty-four hours a day, each day of the week, satisfying any underground taste.

The electrotrash" development, which popped up around 2002, was much smaller and more exclusive than the movements before, largely due to the fact that the renovated city had become more commercial and attracted a new type of person in general, the slick, career-oriented young modern, who got up early, shaved regularly, wore fashionable hairstyles, and designer glasses, concerned mainly with opening trendy businesses and being a fashionable individual, but not in subscribing to an outlaw or renegade lifestyle, considering hangovers, stubble. or self-dyed hair embarrassing, more interested in reading established interior design magazines, or going to spas and getting facials than browsing secondhand shops or flea markets.

Sleeping late, drinking heavily, spending time listening to music or hanging out in cafés had been replaced by surfing the internet, emailing, Googling, discovering MySpace and Facebook, substituting eye contact or shoulder rubbing with anonymous names. This stance began attracting a different set of tourists to Berlin, ones attracted to predictable amusement.

Young, up-and-coming musicians willing to go without a job, desperate artists, or middle-aged idealists still believing in the importance of underground music or art brut had begun to disappear, pushed towards the outskirts by a growing mainstream, but a small and uncontrollable group of rebels continued making a ruckus, attracting international attention and American, Italian, English, or Danish composers, filmmakers, writers, directors, and artists to travel to and stay in

Berlin in order to experience the radical art of Christoph Schlingensief, the new formation of Einstürzende Neubauten, the Dead Chickens, Jonathan Meese, and the electroclash movement.

Each of these different areas had their specific meeting points now, moving about in a world of their own, but once in a while their paths would still cross and Jonathan could be seen in the Big Eden, Christoph Schlingensief at the Dead Chickens, Neurotitan or Neubauten at the White Trash. This last period of a collective feeling in the underground, combined with wild interaction and exchange, lasted for about three years and then vanished on the city's horizon.

When the White Trash Fast Food restaurant and Tresor nightclub closed their doors in 2005 and 2006, although they relocated, an era came to an end.

The city now was made up of separate entities, each following their own personal pursuit of happiness and financial success, politely greeting each other but otherwise remaining aloof. Hundreds of clubs, bars, and restaurants continued opening and closing with friends interacting and pursuing their hedonistic goals, but they were places of recreation to go to after work, usually designed and installed by professional interior decorators. Art was only exhibited in professional galleries and museums, anything else was considered unprofessional.

Nightlife was now based on small talk.

Alexander and I stopped organizing Bada Bing! in 2004, incorporating the inspiration we'd received into our art. My video assignments were going well and after finishing the music video for Fred Alpi's song "La ballade de John Massis", I was commissioned by one of my favorite Berlin bands, Martin Dean, to direct a music video for their song "Roll On." Integrating White Trash characters into a madcap super-star competition for a storyboard, the film captures what the Berlin atmosphere was like in early 2000. When Electrocute's management in Los Angeles called, needing a music clip for their song "Kleiner Dicker Junge," I spent months looking for and building film sets, collecting props, and discussing costumes with the girls. Discovering the world through a camera lens became increasingly enticing, since the altered perception of a fisheye or zoom lens made it possible to feature fascinating details, and I was able to turn everyday scenarios into surreal Hieronymus Bosch environments, and combine my different medias-within this art form. It became my favorite occupation.

Luckily this new area of work was one in which I could actually earn some money, since bands and agents consider their videos necessary advertising.

After realizing that our relationship had become increasingly strong in spite of all its challenges, Alexander and I decided to move into a house together in 2003 and rented a "remise" in the northern, less commercial, and tougher area called Wedding. Berlin's architecture is known for the way courtyards are lined up behind one another. Some of these backyards end with small, detached houses, the former servants' quarters. Turned into family quarters, these offered the added luxury of a small garden, something I had missed since my sojourn in Senzke. We found one in Wedding, a neighborhood that satisfied our taste for unusual settings and diverse cultures, with its Turkish kebab delis, Indian spice shops, and Thai grocery stores scattered throughout the vicinity. Hipsters had not yet discovered Wedding, and the situation of living in an immense, centrally located house that was large enough to accommodate two studios, two children's rooms, and a luxurious backyard had an invigorating effect on all aspects of our life. Instead of going out to bars we could invite friends over for dinner, sit in the garden, and dream up collaborations while barbequing, have fun cheese fondue parties in the living room during winter months, work on different projects in our studios, running up and down the stairs to interact, host international guests in our many rooms, and cultivate a continuing buzz of underground creativity right in our backyard.

As nightlife was becoming increasingly boring to us, due to the lack of originality, we focused on discovering new areas. During long bike rides we discovered Berlin's many parks. Wedding has huge playgrounds and countless, beautiful lakes. We always knew about Berlin's thriving creative scene, but we now noticed that it offered much more than that, with many options for outdoor entertainment. During the long and cold winter it was difficult to have fun in the slush-filled streets, dripping with mud, the drab buildings sullenly echoing the gray sky, but as soon as spring approached Berlin became friendly and colorful, offering breakfast possibilities on various boats anchored in Kreuzberg, tea or coffee in the Tiergarten overlooking the flamingos in the vast Zoologischergarten, Berlin's zoo, and fake beaches lined along the banks of the Spree river, each precinct offering a certain style of music and food within the sand dunes, the Yaam had dub music and african food, Bar 25 featured romantic swings in swaying weeping willows and techno music, the Strandmarkt, another one of White Trash Wally's enterprises, had Wild West elements with beach chairs, spareribs, and T-bone steaks—it was where burlesque dancers and rock singers came to relax in the sun. Countless antique fairs, flea markets, food markets, and book stalls would line the many large boulevards, old-fashioned cafés opened their balconies to blue skies and sun, offering rich cream cakes, strawberry tarts, and Viennese coffee to tourists who watched the countless parades, marathons, demonstrations, political convoys, football celebrations, or colorful street parties pass by, demonstrating the unquenchable Berliner thirst for action.

Together with Alexander's children we would slowly pedal our bicycles from one attraction to the next, enjoying the sun and feeling like tourists in our own hometown, curiously discovering streets, bridges, and tunnels that had emerged during the years of renovation. Berlin had been in the process of being refurbished for over a decade, and now that the ugliest and worst stage was over, it slowly revealed picturesque corners and avant-garde architecture, surprising its original inhabitants with shopping malls, colorful children's museums, or playful shop installations.

In spite of these positive developments the majority of Berlin's population remained poor. Tourists and wealthy hipsters could afford the luxurious additions but the workers became more destitute and for an artist it continued being difficult to survive on the meager number of jobs available, with rent and food costs rising constantly. After going through BMG's advance to finance Alexander's solo project, our debts began accumulating despite my video commissions, and combined with an ineffective personal manager and high child support payments, our situation became precarious once more. After realizing that the only jobs we were actually being paid to do were the ones that I had organized, such as joint performances in theaters and clubs as a DJ/Visual team, or programming Bada Bing!, Alexander asked me to work as his manager/agent. Thanks to my long experience in representing artists I knew how to set up contracts, acquire new contacts, and deal with the music industry. Although again it would take time away from my creative work, we had to think economically. We would save money by not paying another expensive representative, and as Alexander could not represent himself without looking unprofessional, I had no choice but to set about trying to improve our financial situation. To reduce our vast amount of unpaid bills, I had to deal with tight-lipped businessmen, learn how to write bulletproof contracts, forcing companies to take Alexander seriously and fulfill conditions appropriate for a musician of his significance. I spent years despairing over the ruthlessness of managers, journalists, producers, and "old friends," crying in my husband's arms, not knowing how to maintain my idealism and trust in people. The only comfort came from a few rewarding experiences of uprightness and appreciation, working on my art, to which I could flee after spending hours on the phone or computer, and my love for Alexander.

It took approximately six years to pay back our debts and create a suitable situation and recognition of Alexander, building his reputation not only as a Neubauten member but also as a solo musician. The positive aspect of this experience was that I learned to comprehend the market and its psychology of pressure; it did not intimidate me anymore. I could now state very clearly what an idea or talent was worth and could recognize if somebody was trying to manipulate me or understand who was actually benefitting by a deal.

Picasso once said that a good painter needs three things to become successful: talent, charisma, and a good manager. I agree.

Although I consider my management duties to be the unpleasant day job that needs to be done in order to survive and am sure that there are many far more professional agents, I managed to increase Alexander's income a hundred percent, merely by focusing on his work, liberating him from having to deal with monetary issues and "selling" his efforts as professionally as possible. Although he is brilliantly talented and wonderfully charismatic, without this support he would not have been able to survive. I have seen many talented musicians trying to juggle three jobs even at fifty years of age, largely because they cannot afford or find good managers.

The difficult side to becoming Alexander's manager, besides being seen as the enemy, was that the more successful he became the less time I had for my own art, once more spending eight to ten hours a day writing emails, calling venues, managers, and musicians, writing concepts, contacting lawyers, and discussing job proposals, catapulting myself into the typical situation of a male/female artistic relationship in which the woman manages the man and neglects her own work which is already being neglected by the outside world because of her affiliation with the partner artist. During the first few years my priority was to eliminate the red numbers and get rid of our debts, positioning Alexander so that he could concentrate on interesting projects and have a healthier lifestyle, realizing that this was imperative for us to be happy and our relationship working out.

After this had been achieved, my ongoing conflict of promoting others instead of my art returned with a vengeance, resulting in my becoming a full-blown workaholic, chased by the hounds of stress, spending every spare minute drawing, composing, thinking up concepts, and writing notes, feeling mountains of ideas piling up behind me, clamoring for attention, their voices turning into a piercing choir of screams following me everywhere, pushing me into an unhealthy state of desperation and aggression, not knowing how to change my position without endangering our income and survival. Trying to placate my hysteria I told myself that things would change, that nothing in my life had ever developed quickly, and that with the wonderful luck of a good relationship to give me strength, I should uphold my belief in a positive outcome until a solution appeared.

Carrying her camera, the recorded DV tapes, and tripod she pushed through the crowd. Black-clad, longhaired, ghostly powdered fans stood in her way, increasingly immobile as she progressed. Pushing the bodies as hard as possible to get by, she lost hold of her tripod and, cursing the forest of legs, bent down to crawl and look for it.

Back on her feet she continued plowing through the resistant mass, nobody reacting, everyone focused on watching the backstage entrance where a tour manager flitted in and out, carrying instruments and flight cases.

Finally arriving she knocked loudly and quickly opened the door to squeeze in. As she disappeared a sound went through the crowd, anxious voices calling, bodies pushing hard against her back, trying to move forward with her, having seen a musician's silhouette.

Slamming the door shut she muttered, "The crowd is really obnoxious out there, better be careful boys, there are a lot of groupies ready to jump you."

The half-naked men, covered with bath towels and drying their hair, reacted slightly, nodding in acknowledgement, winking or brushing their teeth, busy changing out of their sweaty stage clothes into new garments.

Placing her equipment into the suitcase, she adjusted her lipstick and announced, "The supporters have already been brought to the lounge but you will have to go through the crowd in front to get there, this place is really built inconveniently, do you think you need more security?"

"Naw," "Maybe," "No way."

The different members looked at each other, "Ok, well maybe one or two."

The tour manager immediately left, organizing the bouncers and ten minutes later the band was ready to depart.

As soon as the door opened a groan went through the crowd "I love you," "I want to have your baby," "Could you please sign my autograph."

Girls and boys alike pushed and clawed to get closer to their idols, clinging to their legs, arms, and crotches. As the crowd started circling the polite men signing books, records, T-shirts, bags, arms, and legs, the tour manger shooed the clinging mass, barking at the most persistent, hastening the procession as much as possible.

Finally the lounge had been reached and the door shut, with a doorman positioned so that no one could enter without a backstage pass, and the supporters were introduced.

In contrast to the crowd, they were shy and intimidated, blushing or whispering their requests, offering homemade cake, presents, or CDs as offerings.

Sitting down on the various sofas the band members attracted small clusters around them, shaking hands, learning names, exchanging jokes or email addresses, drinking wine or beer while signing piles of records, nibbling on a chip or piece of chocolate every so often.

Watching the rapt, smiling faces memorizing the anecdotes they were being told, she spoke quietly with the crew members now arriving, asking them how the show had gone for them, how many CDs and merch had been sold and ate a piece of cheesecake one of the supporters had brought along.

After two hours the tour manager came into the room calling curfew, shooing the band members toward the back door, collecting their bags, suits, presents, shoes, and towels, saying goodbye to their visitors, arranging left-over fruit in a box for the bus, and the room emptied within fifteen minutes.

The men spoke easily to each other, as very old friends and companions do.

"Did you see that one tall girl in the crowd?"

"She was nuts, she wouldn't let go of my crotch while the other was wailing, 'I love you.'"

They entered the nightliner and grouped comfortably around the refrigerator, lighting cigarettes, opening wine bottles, discussing what DVD they could watch and what had gone wrong during the show.

"So did you have fun today?"

A. was quizzically looking at her tired face.

Hesitantly she looked into his kind brown eyes and smiled.

Einstürzende Neubauten

In my opinion every city, town, or village has its own character or personality. It can be male or female, melancholic, frivolous, aggressive, friendly, or haughty, and can develop over the years to become more mature, reserved, wise, or bitter, essentially growing up. Visualizing this helps me understand systems and social interaction better: some cities love fashion, some art, and others politics, music, agriculture, or science and so forth. Expecting success or recognition in a field that is not a city's forte can be difficult in comparison to doing the same thing in a place more conducive to fostering that field. If a personality, group, or project coincides perfectly with the development of a municipality, the magical result of becoming a human manifestation of a metropolis can happen, melting both into one essence, forever linked in history. This is one of those rare, enchanted coincidences that sends shivers of anticipation throughout a generation, realizing they are witnessing something special.

The first time I heard of the band was in 1982 in New York.

A friend of mine, Bob, the bouncer at Danceteria, an "it" club where I was a regular, had seen them play at the Palladium the night before. He enthusiastically described their terrifying screams, eccentric rubber clothing, strange, handmade instruments, odd sounds, and the fire they had set to the curtain that abruptly ended the performance, with the singer almost being cut in half by the iron curtain, security pulling him from stage. He mentioned that he had heard they were from Berlin, Germany and had an unpronounceable name. Since I understood German I remember the way he tried pronouncing "Einstürzende Neubauten (Collapsing New Buildings)," the wrong sound tickling my ears. Bob's excitement was unusual, being a laidback, experienced New York underground personality not easily surprised by anything. The manner in which he repeatedly mentioned what he had seen was so out of the ordinary that it remained fixed as a marker within my personal history, one of the signposts imperceptibly influencing my journey.

As my main concerns then were art and fashion I internalized the incident but didn't go out to buy a record or listen to the music. I was haunting secondhand stores, rummaging in Jewish fabric shops, or browsing the sales section in Pearl Paint on Canal street, or else was immersed in taking in one of the lectures or attending a workshop at F.I.T. and Parsons.

It was only when I had moved to Cologne and started working night shifts in bars that music reentered my life with a force, introducing me to numerous underground bands and musicians, rekindling my earlier passion for sound and lyrics, reawakening my interest in music as well as art. It was in the Rose Club that I met the first Neubauten fans, whispering about their music in awe, dressing and looking like the band members. I was taken aback by the extreme worship surrounding them, having never been comfortable among fanatics of any stripe, and although I liked the music when I finally heard it, I backed off, feeling like a groupie while listening to it. After moving to Berlin, the collective awareness of this band was palpable, everybody knew them and either loved or hated them. I couldn't understand the intense attention they received, having experienced groups of fans admiring Andy Warhol and fashion students adoring John Paul Gaultier in New York, but never a whole city being singularly focused on a small group of individuals. Although they were as poor as everyone else, living in the same cheap apartments, wearing secondhand clothes, working behind bars, and going to the parties, a wave of adrenaline would sweep the room if Andrew Unruh, Blixa Bargeld, Alexander Hacke, FM Einheit, or Mark Chung entered.

Working on costumes and drawings during my first years in Berlin I interacted with people who had little to do with the music world and experienced the intense Neubauten idolization only from the periphery, usually meeting them during day-to-day interactions with Roland, carrying his instruments in and out of our factory hall after a combined Nick Cave and Neubauten tour or performance. Their sociable attitude when introduced to me was very different from their alarming reputation of aggressive scandals, arrogance, and recklessness and I thought of them first and foremost as friendly people before seeing any of their shows.

Then Roland took me to my first Neubauten concert, and as we stood in the back of the hall quietly watching the band galvanize the crowd with their magnetism, presenting a scene of unconditional anarchy, with large shadows moving heavily, and a combination of music, fire, metal, electricity, guttural voices, heavy rhythms, and ferocious interaction between each other and the crowd, I finally understood how the sheer force of their performance could sweep people off their feet and believed they were a perfect embodiment of Berlin's anarchic state of mind in the 1980s. No wonder the whole city felt represented by this band. Backstage, after the show, I watched the musicians move about, mingling with friends, and perceived that even as individuals they personified the extreme character traits of the city: the perfectionist, intelligent mind of Blixa, never accepting a superficial answer, questioning everything over and over again, represented the city's intellectual side; Andrew's anarchic, inquisitive stance, permanently ready to destroy and rebuild objects into a fresh creation, was equivalent to Berlin's eternal creativity, a refusal to accept any concept as finished, instead always adding a personal touch, individualizing everything; Alexander's good-natured consumption of gallons of booze and multitudes of women, roaming restlessly, ever on the lookout for yet another dare, rocking the walls with his uncontrollable, uninhibited, boundless energy, jibed with Berlin's unrepentant, ungovernable spirit; FM Einheit, a force of nature, like Zeus shaking the steel foundations with his strength, a bastion of power, stubbornly ready to knock anybody over that underestimated his strength or endurance, reminded me of the city's historic foundation. And Mark Chung, with his quiet capacity for dealing with the world and finding unusual ways of organizing and profiting from chaos, represented the invincible side of Berlin, always winning in the end, in spite of the tumultuous events that had tried to overcome it. Together they became an entity as unconventional and overwhelming as Berlin. Their music was the city's voice.

Over the years the parallels between Berlin and Einstürzende Neubauten became my compass as to what direction the city was going in, even between 1994 and 2000, the years in which I felt most uncomfortable in Berlin because of the rising commercialism, the band mirrored the transformation and confusion of new structures. At that time they were trying out new melodies, styles, and musicians. FM Einheit and Mark Chung left and were replace by Jochen Arbeit and Rudi Moser. The band's restructuring was as dramatic as the city, less disobedient and loud, the rough edges smoothed away and refined. Rudolph Moser replaced FM Einheit's impressive force with a delicate, well-groomed stream of rhythms and Jochen Arbeit introduced ghostly, ethereal compositions more appropriate to Blixa's new poetic stance which he had adopted since abandoning his frenzied screaming of yore.

Never lacking elegance, unusual content, or intelligence in their music, Neubauten helped me accept the metamorphosis of Berlin. They saw change as something universally important, and all objects as subject to examination, before they changed once more. Their personal lives developed, their tastes became more refined, low-key, healthier, they started families, and though they matured they nonetheless remained unapologetic and uncompromising, maintaining a certain standard of quality and continuing to fascinate their original fans, their fan's children, and even their grandchildren over decades.

After a long international tour in 2000 they decided to take a break, not certain if they would continue working together as a band after twenty years, each member busy with solo projects until Erin Zhu, the future wife of Blixa Bargeld, proposed a venture so enticing that they immediately felt like trying it out.

For some time the international music industry had started to collapse due to music being available online. With cheap hardware, musicians could build their own studios and found record companies, managing, designing, and promoting themselves, the costs of releasing a record suddenly manageable. Downloading music became easy, and powerful labels were toppled, no longer able to decide who was "profitable," leaving investors horrified and unable to come up with any marketable ideas aside from ring tones.

Erin's idea was to package the whole procedure on the internet, offering Neubauten fans the chance to pre-order records, similar to a book club, instead of having a record company finance the product in advance. The bonus for the "supporters" would be that they could watch the band record the album in their studio via webcasts with small video surveillance cameras. This would take place every time the band met. On top of this, they would receive a finished record with bonus tracks only for supporters. In other words, by financing a Neubauten record in advance, paying thirty-five euros, they not only received a limited edition record but a year's worth of steady entertainment as well. The supporters were to be given an email address and had the possibility of chatting with each other and the band during the recording sessions, commenting on the developing music for all to hear, keeping interaction possible at all times. The prospect of being watched during the process of creation, a nightmare for most artists, was so outrageous that it tempted the unconventional band to prove that it was possible for them to write good music in spite of hundreds of people commenting on their progress, and the fact that they would be producing and releasing their own records, independent of any record company convinced them utterly. Einstürzende Neubauten had always been very slow in composing, taking up to four years to finish an album, with costs and tempers exploding, but by following this new strategy of meeting every second month for two years, arriving punctually to each session and steadily writing one song after another, knowing seven hundred to two thousand supporters were out there waiting for results in front of their computers, forced them to come up with good work. It was a courageous and very different way of going about being creative, one that could probably only have been thought up by a non-musician, who has not experienced the frightening pitfalls of creative blocks, insecurities, or complicated group dynamics, just seeing it as a business enterprise. For the band it was exactly the kind of challenge they appreciated, and they relisted the thought of defying the many prejudices that accompanied the project.

The subsequent "first phase" was an exciting adventure during which they realized that they could attract enough supporters to finance the remaining time needed to finish an album. The band was surprised that a large amount of the supporters were not rock "fans" or artists but instead people who mainly worked in areas dealing with computers, internet designers, software specialists, biology or chemistry researchers, journalists, and writers. Doing the first webcasts Blixa held small speeches, explaining what they were going to try and achieve during one day, and the band would then compose music in front of hundreds of invisible eyes, with chatrooms and blogs accompanying their every movement, a twist to Orwell's cyberspace vision of one watching many: in this case the many were watching one.

Not everybody was happy with the project. Many old fans complained the band was selling out and had destroyed their illusions, but Neubauten couldn't have cared less. They enjoyed the controversy and wrote more music than ever, releasing one album after another, with special supporter editions developing on top of their official albums.

Besides releasing official publications on their record label Potomak, they also composed a very experimental edition of *Musterhaus* series, and came up with *Jewels*, song ideas not completed for the albums but strong enough to be released, combining them with a beautiful book which sold out immediately, and short videos accompanying the music.

The experiment was incredibly successful and when Einstürzende Neubauten won the New Media Award of Germany given out by Forward 2 Business, a company that specializes in discovering new business modules. Alexander Hacke and Klaus Maeck, Neubauten's manager, held a speech in front of a sold-out tent of businessmen listening breathlessly to the simple but effective project, describing their success in comparison to the Armani suit-wearing tradesmen who could only complain of defeat.

With *Alles Wieder Offen*, their second album in 2008, Einstürzende Neubauten not only managed to release their record internationally but also sold more records than they had done before with the Mute label, their record sales going up by twenty percent in comparison to industry sales, which had sunk twenty percent.

The music industry watched the development silently, trying to find a similar niche into which they could squeeze.

Obviously the success was not only due to the well thought-out approach, it was the natural consequence of an attitude they had had for years that gave them the strength to pull off such a venture. In spite of being successful in the 1980s and considered German cultural icons, flattered and schmoozed by the industry, they had never bowed to the many propositions a band of such reputation receives, stubbornly insisting on progressing exactly as they chose, ignoring well-meant advice, PR proposals, profitable management offers, even quite a few very well-paid performances, moodily determined to forge their own path. They did not earn the amount of money they could have or reach the top of the charts, but instead, following what interested them most, breaking norms and finding ways of existing outside of the usual methods, they created their own universe in a decisive manner. To create something new one must be willing and courageous enough to destroy antiquated structures or thoughts and the strength of Einstürzende Neubauten was that they did not fear change or failure, knowing that both can produce a masterpiece.

After the album *Perpetuum Mobile* was finished in 2004 they decided to prepare an international tour. This had always been an immense problem because of their large setup, with truckloads of heavy instruments, metal pipes, plastic tubes, huge containers, merchandise, and about thirty-five people participating. In the general mood of reinventing new methods Erin came up with another in ingenious idea of how to be able to afford this next venture: she had discovered CD duplication towers and bought two in China. Each tower had the power of copying seven CDs simultaneously, two towers fourteen CDs within three minutes. A small recorder and a cheap photo-printing case was also acquired, with the plan that Boris Wilsdorf, the Neubauten front-of-house engineer would record each concert live while mixing the band in a simple, one-track recording. The concerts usually lasted three hours so after the first sixty minutes the CD would be changed and handed over to the crew in charge of the burners. They would start burning one hundred CDs, which would take about as long as the concert without the encores. Boris would record the second part of the concert and then hand it over for them to finish the live double album just in time for the concert to be over.

Elegant, white, gleaming covers were pre-manufactured and my job was to take a picture of the band during sound check, multiplying pictures with the small photo printer and gluing them into the covers by hand, giving each product a personal touch. The finished product was then handed over to the merchandise table and usually sold out immediately. The venture was so successful that we made up to 180 CDs a night and earned enough money for the tour to be a financial triumph. After a three-month journey through Europe the band announced its arrival in Washington DC. During the preparations, tour manager Ton Masson mentioned the CD towers, asking about electricity, not knowing the club was owned by Clear Channel, a large media conglomerate company in the US, the largest owner of full-power AM, FM, and shortwave radio stations. After hearing about the lucrative business plan the heads of office immediately registered the copyright and informed Ton that the band could do it if they paid Clear Channel percentages of the income. Outraged, Erin responded with a complaint, saying that the band had come up with the idea first, that this could be easily proven and that they were not willing to pay Clear Channel anything. After a suspenseful period Clear Channel conceded, saying that the band would only be expected to pay a symbolic fee of one dollar for the complete tour through the States and would be able to record all of their concerts this last time for free.

Years later this copyright was taken away from Clear Channel after countless bands sued, understandably complaining that nobody had the right to expect them to pay for recording and selling CDs of their own concert. The idea has become generally popular, with fans cherishing the souvenir and musicians happy to have an extra product to sell.

Besides taking pictures of the sound checks, Blixa also asked me to film each concert of the tour, to keep a visual record of the concerts that could be interesting for future products. So I organized three cameras and started contacting supporters via web chat, asking for help in filming different angles. During the organization and after receiving many enthusiastic offers of assistance, I came up with the idea of interviewing supporters in each city, relishing the idea of being able to document their opinions and getting to know the invisible faces of the allies who had made this project possible in the first place. Equipped with a list of volunteers, cameras, tripods, bags of mini DV material, and appointments with unknown interview partners, I set out on my first large-scale music tour, traveling together with Alexander and the band in a nightliner through Europe.

The tour was perfectly planned and I quickly experienced how tight a timetable has to be on such a large scale. We would usually start traveling around ten in the morning if the band had slept in a hotel, or on longer stretches, as in the United States, we would sleep on the nightliner throughout the night and morning. There were two buses, one for the crew and one for the musicians, and a large truck for the PA. The crew seldom slept in hotels, arriving early in the morning, around 10 a.m., and working all day, setting up the stage, moving instruments during the concert, and taking everything down late into the night. Most of them were friends who had accompanied Neubauten for years and the easy comradeship combined with the professional attitude of the band made work possible without too much chaos.

Our bus with the band would usually arrive around 4 p.m., in time for the sound check, during which I would take the picture, print it out manually 150 times and then glue it into the pre-prepared CD covers. After handing these to the merchandiser setting up his booth I would meet the supporters who had volunteered to help, explain the procedure of the filming, do the interviews, all of which usually took two hours, and then meet the band, who had just finished the sound check, for dinner. After the meal we would go check into the hotel, get showered, dressed, and prepared for the show. Sometimes there was only one shower for everybody, especially in the United States, so we would hang out together, chatting with bath towels around our necks, waiting for our turn, joking or reading to pass the time. Then I would rush back to the venue to set up my cameras. Assigning the supporters to their designated areas, giving them the mini DV tapes, answering questions and then going to my place, next to the engineer in front-of-house, and filming the frontal view was a fulltime preoccupation during which I saw nothing of the city or the surroundings in which I had arrived. During the show I would shoot footage, after the show collect the cameras, and put everything back into the bus and then go backstage again. The Neubauten. org project had announced that supporters would be able to meet the musicians after the show so after the concert the band would go backstage, quickly shower once more and then sign T-shirts, shake hands, and get to know the people with whom they had spoken to over the Web. Sometimes there were twenty supporters, and sometimes a hundred and fifty, depending on the city. A surprising feature was that they were very polite and reserved in comparison to regular fans and the groupies who would stand around trying to convince band members to work, drink, or have sex with them. The supporters seemed extremely sensitive to how the band felt after having experienced the making of the album so intimately and surprisingly the project had not resulted in them taking things for granted but in fact feeling responsible for the band. Nobody abused their insider status, but instead respected the band's privacy even more.

Originally I had been worried about going along, not knowing if I would enjoy being with the band members on such a day-to-day basis. Being part of somebody else's project instead of working on my own ideas seemed frightening and especially after having read *The Dirt*, a biography of Mötley Crüe, I was apprehensive about witnessing groupie sex orgies, drug-crazed hotel destruction, endless after-show parties with fans clustering for autographs, and imagined myself out of place and unhappy. As Alexander and I had agreed early on that in order to be able to maintain our relationship in spite of constant touring we would always accompany each other on trips, I decided to take the risk and discovered within a very short time that combined with the friendly professionalism of the band and the amount of time I could spend on my own work on the side, being on tour turned out to be a perfect setting. Traveling, sitting on the bus, watching the landscape changing slowly while drawing in my sketch book or filming the musicians, and reading, writing, or working on the next day's schedule together with Ton, stopping at gas stations in snow-covered mountains, sandy riversides, or dense forests, experiencing different climates at a quick pace, discovering cities I had wondered about, seeing Oslo, Athens, Istanbul, Copenhagen, and smelling the different, new fragrances like a pet released from its apartment and discovering the huge universe outside, I enjoyed having only a suitcase, packed with the most important things—my cameras, my drawing pads, a couple of art books, clothes, the photo printer, and a pair of Mexican trousers—and felt entirely content.

Traveling the world with the man I loved and the band which represented Berlin so well grew in meaning as the weeks progressed, leaving the impression that this was not merely a fun experience I was participating in but a very important and personal journey, answering questions and explaining occurrences that had been bothering me.

By listening to the daily concerts of my personal Berlin mouthpiece, taking note of the different answers the supporters gave during the interviews, about why they appreciated the band, the internet project, Blixa's lyrics and Neubauten's questioning of everything, the curtain suddenly dropped to disclose the reasons behind my shifting moods and strange restlessness. Ever since Berlin had started changing its façade, turning into a typical twentieth-century capital, meticulously erasing signs of history and putting commerce at its peak, I had felt increasingly forlorn and displaced, as if losing my valuable safe haven, becoming increasingly frantic, worried that if it disappeared completely I would be left outside the door once more, losing the only place I could feel happy in. Listening to Einstürzende Neubauten performing in Luxembourg, Los Angeles, Paris, and London, meeting people in these places who appreciated their stance and stubbornness, surprisingly feeling at home and comfortable everywhere, watching the band interact with the many different cultures in their typical Berlin manner, I finally understood my lesson, and realized that because of its unusual, shut-off situation in the 1980s, the city had been able to represent one specific character trait for many years, one of liberty of the mind, in spite or because of constricting surroundings, enticing me to love its ruins and gray façade. But it had not only been the actual buildings, streets, bars, clubs, or cafés I had fallen in love with, it had been the vast alliance of uncomfortable and obstinate viewpoints bowing to nothing, resisting the multifaceted seductions of trends, marketing strategies, VIP adulation, religion, cults, or luxury, the tools that our society uses to influence or engineer people's lives. I had been watching the surface of the city changing and not understood that the truth lies beyond the façade. As long as I stayed close to this character trait, maintaining my sense of integrity and inquisitiveness, the city I had known when I first arrived in the 1980s would continue existing as a metaphor, and I could find happiness anywhere. I finally understood that happiness did not require living in a certain city but having a certain state of mind.

The Transition

Arriving home after months of being on tour was odd. A typical effect of being together with the same group of people for a long time in an enclosed space is that they seem to become a part of yourself, shining brightly in a crowd, making everybody else seem vague and shadow-like. During concerts I could easily discern the crew or the band no matter where they were, in a huge venue, a marketplace or party, an invisible thread connected us, so we instinctively knew where everybody stood. Back home these new body parts went back to being separate individuals, returning to their normal routines, and life seemed emptier, more neutral and forlorn. It took a couple of weeks for old friends to become as "real" as the band had been, transforming from ghostly whispers to blood-and-flesh people. This state of mind is commonly described as post-tour depression. Alexander and I roamed galleries, museums, bars, clubs, and visited friends to get back into the general atmosphere and realized quickly that the uproarious electroclash movement had almost completely disappeared, Berlin having shifted its focus once again. In clubs or bars we hardly knew anybody in the crowd, many artists of my generation had disappeared, struggling to survive, moving away or staying at home to save costs. Survival was an issue we were facing ourselves, so we concentrated on finishing and releasing Alexander's solo album *Sanctuary* in 2005.

Alexander had contacted B. Gould, former bass player of Faith No More after meeting him years before on a Neubauten tour where Billy had been their driver, doing odd jobs aside from playing bass in his band, months before their album *The Real Thing* became a hit. Signing to a record company that belonged to a musician seemed to make sense and we flew out to meet Billy in San Francisco, setting up a contract and shaking hands on the deal.

After releasing the album in late spring we decided to organize a tour to promote it and asked Ash Wednesday to play keyboards, Sugar Pie Jones bass, and Gordon W. percussion. In spite of trying to organize everything as well as possible, hiring a professional booker, organizing sleeping places for everybody, and designing beautiful posters and T-shirts, the tour was a chaotic mix of badly booked shows, stolen instruments, burgled buses, complaining band members and canceled gigs; but while mixing visuals live to Alexander's singing it became apparent that we had found a remedy to all of our difficulties. A pattern of traveling was becoming stronger and stronger in our relationship and creative development, guaranteeing a regular income, interesting encounters, and new projects in which we both could be presented as artists.

As happened frequently in my life, after having understood how I could continue, a possibility quickly came my way. This time it came in the form of Markus Orschiedt, Big Eden's financial manager calling, and asking me if we would be interested in organizing a performance for the ten-year anniversary of the Arena, one of their affiliated clubs. He explained that Falk Walter, the owner of the Arena, had been so impressed by the quality of our Bada Bing! shows that he would give us complete freedom to invite anybody we would like to join in.

Although we had enjoyed the complex creativity and enthusiasm generated by our project series, we now had a different objective than we had had two years before and said that we would not be interested in merely organizing an event but would prefer creating a performance in which the elements of Bada Bing! were combined into having musicians and artists of very different styles perform a single story.

Alexander had always fantasized about working on H.P. Lovecraft material, loving the horror stories and their endless descriptions of unnamable events, while I envisioned sideshow and evil carnival characters, so when Markus asked us who we thought would be most fitting to invite to do such a performance we simultaneously said: the Tiger Lillies.

THE TIGER LILLIES

The first time I heard the Tiger Lillies it was as if I had found the perfect soundtrack to all of my favorite children's books. *Oliver Twist, Struwwelpeter, Grimm's Fairy Tales, Peter Pan, Mother Goose, Rip Van Winkle, The Magician's Nephew,* and the many Edward Gorey stories I had hovered over for years, relishing the dark and rainy atmospheres, suddenly came alive again and I was thrilled instantly, loving the carnival riotousness and madcap musical interaction among the musicians. Later I found out that they had actually interpreted many of these stories and I became a fan, eagerly collecting the albums and listening to them day and night. When finally seeing them perform live I felt as if I were in a dream, experiencing Martyn Jacques sing his operatic tenor, thickly made up in white makeup and heavy black eyeliner, a bloodcurdling goblin in a bowler hat and suit, grabbing the audience by their throats, pulling them close with a fierce look in his eyes, and whispering incredibly obscene or outrageous lyrics about murder, incest, and evil children while breathing into a glistening harmonica, or pounding his piano. Feeling like Alice after she had entered Wonderland I watched breathlessly as the band unfurled their universe, the other musicians as fantastic as their leader, with Adrian Stout, reminiscent of a melancholy Karl Valentin or Buster Keaton, beautifully stroking the singing saw, directing the theremin or jauntily plucking an upright bass, a pale face staring into the silent hall, presenting the perfect mirror to Adrian Huge, the embodiment of screwball humor, with his odd assortment of children's drums, plastic chickens, fur rats, bells, honks, and eccentric hats radiating into the night.

In comparison to most circus shows or cabaret performances, thriving on nostalgia and silly clowns, carnivals have always captured my interest by baring taboos, freaks, geeks, obesity, tattoos, and malformations, the buried, pushed-away secrets of our society, presented proudly in these extraordinary performances, demanding money from the fascinated crowd to be able to look at what they are scared of most. It is no coincidence that these shows have almost completely disappeared in our perfect world of Botox and glisteningly white teeth. To discover a band that enabled these ghosts to resurrect and show themselves in the twenty-first century was deeply satisfying, their international success even more so.

After seeing their performances, and their theater piece, *Shockheaded Peter,* in London, I was not only their admirer but had been inspired tremendously. The theater pieces that had impressed me most until then had been: *Krapp's Last Tape* by Beckett, in a remarkable minimal performance by an unknown actor in lower Manhattan, concentrating on the amazing text and keeping his own personality completely removed from the show, and *Strider,* the sad story of a horse, with the audience sitting on hard benches, watching talented protagonists wearing little else but straw horsetails, presenting the story very simply, forcing the audience's imagination to fill in the white spaces with amazing results. Although my parents had put great emphasis on taking their children to the theater regularly, my lasting impression of commercial Broadway shows, loud and screaming experimental performances, or amazingly boring stage direction was not very positive and I had refrained from repeating the experience for a long time after leaving home.

I had often wondered if it was possible to combine different clashing elements on stage to create a new style of theater but had been too busy experiencing the different fields within my own life. Seeing the Tiger Lillies finally awakened me to performance art, something that I had ignored ever since seeing bad body-painting shows, expressionist outbursts, or embarrassing monologues in the 1980s. The idea to take a piece of literature and interpret it through music and art, not as a musical or cabaret, instead more as an avant-garde performance, discussing language, highlighting taboo themes, and using dark humor instead of dry conceptualism inspired me deeply and I left the theater glowing, stimulated by what potential such a performance could hold for us if we intermingled modern music, video projections, classic literature, ancient philosophy, and pop culture, connecting the past with the present in one performance.

When Markus called it was a dream come true, we had met the Tiger Lillies in San Francisco and kept Adrian's phone number, spending an evening speaking to him in a red velvet cocktail lounge. After writing our concept for the show and Falk agreeing to the project we called Adrian and told him about our idea, asking if the band had time and interest to participate in an H. P. Lovecraft performance. Happily the Tiger Lillies confirmed quickly and having decided to interpret a couple of stories from the book *Mountains of Madness* we individually went about preparing our parts. Being a Neubauten member known for industrial experimentalism, Alexander decided that he would concentrate on electronic music soundscapes and speaking parts. In contrast to the Tiger Lillies' acoustic instruments and Martyn's high falsetto singing his extremely deep voice and 4.5 surround-music compositions would create a new, unexpected atmosphere for all.

I concentrated on drawings, an old-fashioned ink-and-pen style combined with modern monsters, horror, and iconic ideology, giving the pictures the look of innocent fairytale drawings with ferociously scary content. Up to then I had always worked with oil and acrylic, had not been very interested in drawing and was surprised that it turned out to be my forte.

I had always especially enjoyed doing detailed work but had found it difficult to create tiny lines with paintbrushes, no matter how thin. Now, during the continuing Neubauten tours in fall 2004 and spring 2005, I sat in the tour bus drawing countless images of "unspeakable, unnamable, unimaginable, monstrous" creatures, sunken cities, magical labyrinths, sea serpents, and lost souls, and engrossed myself in mountains of grapes, bones, natura morte corpses, and tattooed animals, delighted in having discovered a technique with which I was completely satisfied for the first time.

Besides hearing Alex experiment with different electronic sounds on his computer after Neubauten *Grundstück* sound checks, and in his bunk on the nightliner, I had no idea what he was preparing for the show, both of us too busy working on the necessities of tour life. The Tiger Lillies, who had been on the road for almost ten years, sent us random emails from the different cities they were performing in, only vaguely mentioning continuous progress on their songs, so none of us had a clue of what the others were preparing. This work style continued until July 2005, one month before the actual performance, when we decided it was time to meet and see if our different thoughts actually fit together, hopefully holding enough potential for a good show. Alexander and I arrived in London a couple of days after the terrible subway bombings on the 7th of July, catapulted into a vacant town, the shocked Londoners staying at home, subway stations closed, buses transferred to new routes, and cabs almost impossible to get, leaving us to wearily drag our computers and overweight monitors through the city in its oppressive heat, cursing suicide bombers and global terrorism. In Adrian's living room, we then nervously unpacked computers, keyboards, and instruments, everybody eyeing each other in anticipation, not knowing what to expect. After a little small talk, Martyn decided to initiate the start and began singing his lyrics to the rough piano and accordion melodies he had composed. Even in the small living room his voice was amazing in its strength and beauty, the pure volume naturally amplified, and looking out of the open window, I could see passersby stop and look up into the sky wondering where the piercing falsetto describing rats, butchers, and mountains of madness had suddenly emerged from.

After we had all set in it quickly became apparent that our prepared compositions fitted together wonderfully and we separated from one another relieved, knowing that the show was good enough to be presented without a qualm.

The weeks after were spent in promoting the event with Markus, building the stage with Andreas, and asking Lutz John and Boris Wilsdorf, the Neubauten sound and light technicians, to participate. Arena had insisted in having us perform twice and both evenings were sold out with cheering, clapping, and an audience screaming "encore." Later on, backstage, everybody admitted to having been terribly nervous, relieved that it had gone so well with only one rehearsal and a short sound check. When Falk, the owner of Arena, appeared, enthusiastically congratulating us all on the success and saying, "Now we get the show on the road," we agreed enthusiastically and ended up touring Europe for almost three years. During this phase I was to learn an important lesson.

I had decided not to be on stage, still battling stage fright, and preferring to stand next to the sound engineer and animating my drawings invisibly to the music. Not being visible turned out to be a mistake, as I realized only after we started touring. Visuals in a live show are mainly perceived as an accompaniment to the music and by standing next to the music engineer I was identified as a technician or crew member by venues and audience alike. I realized that the show was not being recognized for what it had been conceived to be: an audio and visual performance rather than a concert, with the goal of triggering different senses to create a new kind of performance. We tried announcing that I would be mixing the animations live during the performance, with the band loudly asking me to come on stage at the end of the show for applause, but nothing helped; due to my decision to remain out of sight the concept was not understood. Most people thought the drawings were decorative, fairytale illustrations from an old book. As the stage sets, tech riders, and lighting had been arranged early on with signed contracts, it was too complicated to change the positions in hindsight, so I remained standing next to the lighting designer during the shows and my participation would be for the most part ignored by the press throughout the tour. My work was not acknowledged and I came to the painful realization that in order for performing to become an alternative to exhibiting in galleries I would have to overcome my shyness and get up on stage.

This predicament is one that most visual artists encounter in the world of performance or theater. Not only do they earn less than musicians, actors, or DJs but they also receive less credit and are considered dispensable. The necessity of their work is clear after imagining how the shows would look without the visuals. A similar prejudice exists in the world of cinema, in which the composers of film scores are treated as if they were replaceable; their names seldom mentioned in press releases, their work regarded merely as an accessory. In both areas the quieter fields of work are as complex and significant to determining the final outcome. After my experience of being ignored, Alexander and I decided to emphasize this in all of our future shows, in an effort to popularize an underrated niche.

Besides touring with the show Alexander and I had decided to produce a video of the concert. After having done decades of events, projects, exhibitions, and concerts and having almost no documentation whatsoever of any of our works we had decided that in the future a product had to be financed for every important project that we conceived. Both of us realized that, as we would be artists for the rest of our lives and did not have any family inheritance or pension to rely on, we would have to create our own safety net. Neubauten's example of releasing records and disentangling themselves from cumbersome percentage deals was inspiring, and the idea of releasing CDs and DVDs ourselves and promoting them via homepages and Amazon was the most straightforward solution we could think of. The first self-released product was accompanied by a number of mistakes, paying exorbitant prices to create the package and ruling out any chance of profit, but we learned from our mistakes. We had discovered another way to survive in the long run.

Ich bin ein Berliner

Touring with *Mountains of Madness* from 2005 to 2008 marked the beginning of a completely new era in my life.

Realizing the possibilities touring offered in terms of presenting my art and music internationally, and of being able to earn a fee immediately at the end of the evening, I had discovered a new, flexible method of working perfectly suited to my personality. In the following years, Alexander and I created two more shows, *The History of Electricity,* a minimal electronic performance, and *The Ship Of Fools,* based on the medieval book by Sebastian Brandt. The idea of merging literature, unusual musical components, and visual aspects continues to be my favorite way of working, it is an ideal way of interacting with my husband and earning a living at the same time. My occupation with painting, drawing, film, and music continues to be a driving force in my life and after developing a tight network of loyal bookers, assistants, and managers to help us to survive, I have finally been able to stop curating and concentrate solely on my own art. Commissions coming in from cultural foundations have increased over the years; the German Goethe Institute and the Germany Foreign Ministry invite me to initiate projects focused especially on youth culture, an area I especially enjoy working in. I have learned to do this artistically instead of organizationally, creating personal projects in which I can integrate my own art with that of other participants.

In 2006, after Alexander appeared in Fatih Akin's internationally celebrated movie, *Crossing the Bridge—The Sound of Istanbul,* a film demonstrating how a country can be understood and seen in a different light purely because of its music, we discovered new ways in which artists can be communally active and responsible. Pinpointing positive cultural aspects, instead of focusing on difficult politics or religious disputes, initiating interaction and appreciation, cultivating friendship and enthusiasm that goes beyond contradictory tastes, beliefs, and morals, proves culture to be valuable in helping to solve global difficulties in unexpected ways.

Both Alexander and I have experienced how rewarding it is to work creatively with different cultures and countries and in spite of working on my art and not considering myself a social worker or therapist, I have found myself drawing with street kids from Lichtenberg, a Nazi-oriented area in Berlin; touring Bosnia with Alexander, performing and doing workshops amid destroyed towns riddled with bullet holes, speaking of how artists in Berlin created their own musical instruments out of leftover post-war rubble, exhibiting in deserted ruins and initiating the Love Parade without a cent; explaining to depressed rich kids in Hong Kong how we had decorated clubs in the Berlin underground not caring about stock markets or business models, working with students from Turin and teaching them how to start interesting exhibitions or events outside of expensive, trendy clubs or galleries, and doing video and slide performances in Japan, speaking about how to find and create "a room of your own" as a female artist.

Interaction is our favorite topic, and these experiences have always been a give-and-take, with all participants going home with new ideas and inspirations.

I have spent less time in Berlin with the result of being able to see it from a distant perspective, and am relieved to see that in spite of growing mass tourism and suffocating commercialism the original Berlin stance has not been quenched. Instead, the many artists I have worked with have adapted to modern times, using new technology to their advantage, launching independent companies and supporting music and art they consider relevant, instead of signing up to the many large industries moving into the city and letting themselves be manipulated. Looking around I am impressed by the productivity that has quietly formed and reinvented itself once more in the many different realms. Gudrun Gut and Ellen Alien are expanding their record labels, cooperating with international markets, and representing innovative music experimentation on top of working on their personal artistic development. Die Gestalten, the company that had helped me print my own flyers for events in the early 1990s, situated in a small backyard, is now an internationally renowned art publishing company, releasing countless art and design catalogues featuring the work of young, promising artists and designers every year. Tanja Ries, a chanson artist, who commissioned me to decorate her shows in the 1990s, is now organizing regular performances with homeless teenagers, showing them alternative ways of dealing with anger, and Motte is supporting initiatives to preserve cultural spaces in Berlin. Like Alexander and myself, many others move in international circles, representing and living Berlin's individuality. Christoph Dreher, a former Haut musician, teaches creative film in Stuttgart and directs documentaries about Berlin's cultural history, Blixa Bargeld travels to China and San Francisco, producing young industrial Chinese bands and doing art projects with students at Stanford University; Jim Avignon resettled in New York and is continuously surrounded by admirers, pursuing his concept of cheap art, teaching his audiences to see the value of inexpensive objects as well as the expensive ones, and Dimitri acquired a monastery close to Berlin and founded a Land Art initiative.

Realizing that the experimental research has not been stopped or corrupted by modern commerce, but instead is developing as effectively as before, and is as unconventional and stubborn, spreading its wings out into the world, removed my qualms and I accepted that both Berlin and I had matured and moved on. Berlin as always is smiling at my insecurities, knowing that her subversive roots are much stronger than any passing trend.

Kennedy's famous salute was to a German city that on the one hand carried a huge burden of united guilt, while on the other hand managed to prove that it is possible to break down restrictive systems without a single bomb. The city thwarted modern commercialism by staying proudly independent, creating an international "Luftbrücke" of creativity and offering true alternatives. His salute still rings true and whenever I am asked I am happy to say: "Yes, I am a Berliner," thankful for having had the luck to experience the beauty of transgression.

Epilogue

The crowd was hushed.

Standing on stage next to the politician she looked down at the many faces of club goers, musicians, acquaintances, artists, diplomats, society ladies, and dancers.

She could scarcely believe that they had all come to celebrate her work. Noticing the cameras and journalists in the first row she smiled, remembering not to look shy or hunched over.

While listening to the speech on her film, she contemplated the weeks she had spent drawing hundreds of pictures, editing the clips, speaking to the animation artist, the dancers, musicians, and assistants, going to the foreign ministry, meeting with translators, teaching herself to use an electronic drawing pad to speed things up, contacting sound engineers, renting studios, and how happy she had been the entire time.

Her dream of being acknowledged as an artist had finally come true, and she was being proudly presented by the highest cultural spokesperson of the country. While thanking the many assistants for their support, she silently included the guardian angels who led her through the many difficult phases in her life, helping her to survive in spite of obstacles and walk in beauty in spite of pain, making the present success possible.

"How lucky I have been," she mused as the hall darkened and the movie started, thinking of the friends who had stood by her side, comforting, appreciating, and supporting her in all the topsy-turvy situations.

Smiling blissfully, she stood looking up at the flickering images, when the film suddenly broke off with a bang.

In the shocked hush the engineer's voice could be heard cursing, pushing buttons, running back and forth from behind the mixing desk, trying to save the situation, but nothing could be done. The projector had collapsed because of the heat and two thousand guests had to leave without having seen the work she had produced.

Silently she stood amid her stunned friends, watching them move in slow motion, shouting, speaking, leaving, and realized that her long and winding road was not over by far, it would always stay bumpy, just like her horoscope had predicted. But later, sitting in the bar, surrounded by her worried husband, her friends, and the ambassadors—all of them trying to make her feel better by cheering and toasting her work which they had seen evolve during the months of editing, already now organizing its next screening—she looked into their supportive eyes and felt nothing but waves of gratitude within her heart.

Imprint

The Beauty of Transgression
A Berlin Memoir
Danielle de Picciotto

Cover photography by Sven Marquardt
Cover layout by Hendrik Hellige for Gestalten
Layout by Natalie Reed for Gestalten
Typeface: Bonesana PRO by Matthieu Cortat
Foundry: www.gestaltenfonts.com

Project management by Elisabeth Honerla for Gestalten
Production management by Janine Milstrey for Gestalten
Proofreading by Claire Barliant and Bettina Klein
Printed by Sing Cheong Printing Co. Ltd., Hong Kong
Published by Gestalten, Berlin 2011
ISBN 978-3-89955-328-4

For more information, please visit www.gestalten.com

Bibliographic information published by the Deutsche Nationalbibliothek.
The Deutsche Nationalbibliothek lists this publication in the Deutsche Nationalbibliografie; detailed bibliographic data is available online at http://dnb.d-nb.de.

This book has been printed on FSC® certified paper.

Gestalten is a climate-neutral company and so are our products. We collaborate with the non-profit carbon offset provider myclimate (www.myclimate.org) to neutralize the company's carbon footprint produced through our worldwide business activities by investing in projects that reduce CO_2 emissions (www.gestalten.com/myclimate).